André Theuriet

A Woodland Queen
(REINE DES BOIS)
By ANDRÉ THEURIET

Crowned by the French Academy

With a Preface by MELCHIOR DE
VOGUÉ, of the French Academy

WILDSIDE PRESS

ANDRÉ THEURIET

CLAUDE-ADHEMAR-ANDRÉ THEURIET was born at Marly-le-Roi (Seine et Oise), October 8, 1833. His ancestors came from Lorraine. He was educated at Bar-le-Duc and went to Paris in 1854 to study jurisprudence. After finishing his courses he entered the Department of the Treasury, and after an honorable career there, resigned as chef-de bureau. He is a poet, a dramatist, but, above all, a writer of great fiction.

As early as 1857 the poems of Theuriet were printed in the *Revue de Paris* and the *Revue des Deux Mondes*. His greatest novel. *Reine des Bois* (Woodland Queen), was crowned by the Académie Française in 1890. To the public in general he became first known in 1870 by his *Nouvelles Intimes*. Since that time he has published a great many volumes of poems, drama, and fiction. A great writer, he perhaps meets the wishes of that large class of readers who seek in literature agreeable rest and distraction, rather than excitement or æsthetic gratification. He is one of the greatest spirits that survived the bankruptcy of Romanticism. He excels in the description of country nooks and corners; of that polite rusticity which knows nothing of the delving laborers of *La*

[v]

Terre, but only of graceful and learned leisure, of solitude nursed in revery, and of passion that seems the springtide of germinating nature. He possesses great originality and the passionate spirit of a *paysagiste*: pictures of provincial life and family-interiors seem to appeal to his most pronounced sympathies. His taste is delicate, his style healthy and frank, and at the same time limpid and animated.

After receiving, in 1890, the Prix Vitet for the ensemble of his literary productions, he was elected to the Academy in 1896. To the stage Theuriet has given *Jean-Marie*, drama in verses (Odéon, February 11, 1871). It is yet kept on the repertoire together with his *Maison de deux Barbeaux* (1865), *Raymonde* (1887), and *Les Maugars* (1901).

His novels, tales, and poems comprise a long list. *Le Bleu et le Noir* (1873) was also crowned by the Academy. Then followed, at short intervals: *Mademoiselle Guignon* (1874); *Le Mariage de Gérard* (1875); *La Fortune d'Angèle* (1876); *Raymonde* (1877), a romance of modern life, vastly esteemed by the reading public; *Le Don Juan de Vireloup* (1877); *Sous Bois, Impressions d'un Forestier* (1878); *Le Filleul d'un Marquis* (1878); *Les Nids* (1879); *Le fils Maugars* (1879); *La Maison de deux Barbeaux* (1879); *Toute seule* (1880); *Sauvageonne* (1880), his most realistic work; *Les Enchantements de la Forêt* (1881); *Le Livre de la Payse* (poetry, 1882); *Madame Heurteloup* (1882); *Pêche de Jeunesse* (1883); *Le Journal de Tristan*, mostly autobiographical; *Bigarreau* (1885); *Eusèbe Lombard* (1885); *Les Œillets de Kerlatz* (1885); *Hélène* (1886); *Nos Oiseaux* (beauti-

PREFACE

ful verses, 1886); *La Vie Rustique* (1887); *Amour d'Automne* (1888); *Josette* (1888); *Deux Sœurs* (1889); *Contes pour les Soirs d'Hiver* (1890); *Charme Dangereux* (1891); *La Ronde des Saisons et des Mois* (1892); *La Charmeresse* (1893); *Fleur de Nice* (1896); *Bois Fleury* (1897); *Refuge* (1898); *Villa Tranquille* (1899); *Claudette* (1900); *La Petite Dernière* (1901); *Le Manuscrit du Chanoine* (1902), etc.

Besides this abundant production André Theuriet has also contributed to various journals and magazines: *Le Moniteur, Le Musée Universal, L'Illustration, Le Figaro, Le Gaulois, La République Française*, etc.; he has lectured in Belgium, Holland, and Switzerland, and has even found leisure to fill the post as Mayor of Bourg-la-Reine (Seine et Oise), perhaps no onerous office (1882–1900). He has also been an *Officier de la Légion d'Honneur* since 1895.

M⁰ de Vogüé

de l'Académie Française.

CONTENTS

CONTENTS

MLLE. DESROCHES

CONTENTS

CHAPTER XI

CHAPTER XII

CHAPTER XIII

CHAPTER XIV

CHAPTER XV

A WOODLAND QUEEN

CHAPTER I

THE UNFINISHED WILL

OWARD the middle of October, about the time of the beechnut harvest, M. Eustache Destourbet, Justice of the Peace of Auberive, accompanied by his clerk, Etienne Seurrot, left his home at Abbatiale, in order to repair to the Château of Vivey, where he was to take part in removing the seals on some property whose owner had deceased.

At that period, 1857, the canton of Auberive, which stretches its massive forests like a thick wall between the level plain of Langres and the ancient Châtillonais, had but one main road of communication: that from Langres to Bar-sur-Aube. The almost parallel adjacent route, from Auberive to Vivey, was not then in existence; and in order to reach this last commune, or hamlet, the traveller had to follow a narrow grass-bordered path, leading through the forest up the hill of Charbonnière, from the summit of which was seen that intermingling of narrow gorges and wooded heights which is so characteristic of this mountainous region. On all sides were indented horizons of trees, among which a few,

1   [1]

of more dominant height, projected their sharp outlines against the sky; in the distance were rocky steeps, with here and there a clump of brambles, down which trickled slender rivulets; still farther, like little islands, half submerged in a sea of foliage, were pastures of tender green dotted with juniper bushes, almost black in their density, and fields of rye struggling painfully through the stony soil—the entire scene presenting a picture of mingled wildness and cultivation, aridity and luxuriant freshness.

Justice Destourbet, having strong, wiry limbs, ascended cheerily the steep mountain-path. His tall, spare figure, always in advance of his companion, was visible through the tender green of the young oaks, clothed in a brown coat, a black cravat, and a very high hat, which the justice, who loved correctness in details, thought it his duty to don whenever called upon to perform his judicial functions. The clerk, Seurrot, more obese, and of maturer age, protuberant in front, and somewhat curved in the back, dragged heavily behind, perspiring and out of breath, trying to keep up with his patron, who, now and then seized with compassion, would come to a halt and wait for his subordinate.

"I trust," said Destourbet, after one of these intervals which enabled the clerk to walk by his side, "I trust we shall find Maître Arbillot down there; we shall have need of his services in looking over and filing the papers of the deceased."

"Yes, Monsieur," answered Seurrot, "the notary will meet us at the château; he went to Praslay to find out from his associates whether Monsieur de Buxières had not left a will in his keeping. . In my humble opinion, that is hardly likely; for the deceased had great confidence in Maître Arbillot, and it seems strange that he should choose to confide his testamentary intentions to a rival notary."

"Well," observed the justice, "perhaps when the seals are raised, we may discover an autograph will in some corner of a drawer."

"It is to be hoped so, Monsieur," replied Seurrot; "I wish it with all my heart, for the sake of Claudet Séjournant, for he is a good fellow, although on the sinister bar of the escutcheon, and a right jolly companion."

"Yes; and a marvellous good shot," interrupted the justice. "I recognize all that; but even if he had a hundred other good qualities, the *grand chasserot*, as they call him here, will be on the wrong side of the hedge if Monsieur de Buxières has unfortunately died intestate. In the eye of the law, as you are doubtless aware, a natural child, who has not been acknowledged, is looked upon as a stranger."

"Monsieur de Buxières always treated Claudet as his own son, and every one knew that he so considered him."

"Possibly, but if the law were to keep count of all such cases, there would be no end to their labors; especially in all questions of the *cujus*. Odouart de Buxières was a terribly wild fellow, and they say that these old beech-trees of Vivey forest could tell many a tale of his exploits."

[3]

"He, he!" assented the clerk, laughing slyly, and showing his toothless gums, "there is some truth in that. The deceased had the devil in his boots. He could see neither a deer nor a pretty girl without flying in pursuit. Ah, yes! Many a trick has he played them —talk of your miracles, forsooth!—well, Claudet was his favorite, and Monsieur de Buxières has told me, over and over again, that he would make him his heir, and I shall be very much astonished if we do not find a will."

"Seurrot, my friend," replied the justice, calmly, "you are too experienced not to know that our country folks dread nothing so much as testifying to their last wishes—to make a will, to them, is to put one foot into the grave. They will not call in the priest or the notary until the very last moment, and very often they delay until it is too late. Now, as the deceased was at heart a rustic, I fear greatly that he did not carry his intentions into execution."

"That would be a pity—for the château, the lands, and the entire fortune would go to an heir of whom Monsieur Odouart never had taken account—to one of the younger branch of Buxières, whom he had never seen, having quarrelled with the family."

"A cousin, I believe," said the justice.

"Yes, a Monsieur Julien de Buxières, who is employed by the Government at Nancy."

"In fact, then, and until we receive more ample information, he is, for us, the sole legitimate heir. Has he been notified?"

"Yes, Monsieur. He has even sent his power of attorney to Monsieur Arbillot's clerk."

A WOODLAND QUEEN

"So much the better," said M. Destourbet, "in that case, we can proceed regularly without delay."

While thus conversing, they had traversed the forest, and emerged on the hill overlooking Vivey. From the border line where they stood, they could discover, between the half-denuded branches of the line of aspens, the sinuous, deep-set gorge, in which the Aubette wound its tortuous way, at the extremity of which the village lay embanked against an almost upright wall of thicket and pointed rocks. On the west this narrow defile was closed by a mill, standing like a sentinel on guard, in its uniform of solid gray; on each side of the river a verdant line of meadow led the eye gradually toward the clump of ancient and lofty ash-trees, behind which rose the Buxières domicile. This magnificent grove of trees, and a monumental fence of cast-iron, were the only excuse for giving the title of château to a very commonplace structure, of which the main body presented bare, whitewashed walls, flanked by two small towers on turrets shaped like extinguishers, and otherwise resembling very ordinary pigeon-houses.

This château, or rather country squire's residence, had belonged to the Odouart de Buxières for more than two centuries. Before the Revolution, Christophe de Buxières, grandfather of the last proprietor, had owned a large portion of Vivey, besides several forges in operation on the Aube and Aubette rivers. He had had three children: one daughter, who had embraced religion as a vocation; Claude Antoine, the elder son, to whom he left his entire fortune, and Julien Abdon, the younger, officer in the regiment of Rohan Soubise, with whom he was not on good terms. After emigrating and serving in Condé's army, the younger Buxières had returned to France during the Restoration, had married, and been appointed special receiver in a small town in southern France. But since his return, he had not resumed relations with his elder brother, whom he accused of having defrauded him of his rights. The older one had married also, one of the Rochetaillée family; he had had but one son, Claude Odouart de Buxières, whose recent decease had brought about the visit of the Justice of Auberive and his clerk.

Claude de Buxières had lived all his life at Vivey. Inheriting from his father and grandfather flourishing health and a robust constitution, he had also from them strong love for his native territory, a passion for the chase, and a horror of the constraint and decorum exacted by worldly obligations. He was a spoiled child, brought up by a weak-minded mother and a preceptor without authority, who had succeeded in imparting to him only the most elementary amount of instruction, and he had, from a very early age, taken his own pleasure as his sole rule of life. He lived side by side with peasants and poachers, and had himself become a regular country yeoman, wearing a blouse, dining at the wineshop, and taking more pleasure in speaking the mountain *patois* than his own native French. The untimely death of his father, killed by an awkward huntsman while following the hounds, had emancipated him at the age of twenty years. From this period he lived his life freely, as he understood it; always in the open air, without hindrance of any sort, and entirely unrestrained.

A WOODLAND QUEEN

Nothing was exaggerated in the stories told concerning him. He was a handsome fellow, jovial and dashing in his ways, and lavish with his money, so he met with few rebuffs. Married women, maids, widows, any peasant girl of attractive form or feature, all had had to resist his advances, and with more than one the resistance had been very slight. It was no false report which affirmed that he had peopled the district with his illegitimate progeny. He was not hard to please, either; strawberry-pickers, shepherd-girls, wood-pilers, day-workers, all were equally charming in his sight; he sought only youth, health, and a kindly disposition.

Marriage would have been the only safeguard for him; but aside from the fact that his reputation of reckless huntsman and general scapegrace naturally kept aloof the daughters of the nobles, and even the Langarian middle classes, he dreaded more than anything else in the world the monotonous regularity of conjugal life. He did not care to be restricted always to the same dishes—preferring, as he said, his meat sometimes roast, sometimes boiled, or even fried, according to his humor and his appetite.

Nevertheless, about the time that Claude de Buxières attained his thirty-sixth year, it was noticed that he had a more settled air, and that his habits were becoming more sedentary. The chase was still his favorite pastime, but he frequented less places of questionable repute, seldom slept away from home, and seemed to take greater pleasure in remaining under his own roof. The cause of this change was ascribed by some to the advance of years creeping over him; others, more perspicacious, verified a curious coincidence between the entrance of a new servant in the château and the sudden good behavior of Claude.

This girl, a native of Aprey, named Manette Séjournant, was not, strictly speaking, a beauty, but she had magnificent blonde hair, gray, caressing eyes, and a silvery, musical voice. Well built, supple as an adder, modest and prudish in mien, she knew how to wait upon and cosset her master, accustoming him by imperceptible degrees to prefer the cuisine of the château to that of the wine-shops. After a while, by dint of making her merits appreciated, and her presence continually desired, she became the mistress of Odouart de Buxières, whom she managed to retain by proving herself immeasurably superior, both in culinary skill and in sentiment, to the class of females from whom he had hitherto been seeking his creature comforts.

Matters went on in this fashion for a year or so, until Manette went on a three months' vacation. When she reappeared at the château, she brought with her an infant, six weeks old, which she declared was the child of a sister, lately deceased, but which bore a strange likeness to Claude. However, nobody made remarks, especially as M. de Buxières, after he had been drinking a little, took no pains to hide his paternity. He himself held the little fellow at the baptismal font, and later, consigned him to the care of the Abbé Pernot, the curate of Vivey, who prepared the little Claudet for his first communion, at the same time that he instructed him in reading, writing, and the first four rules of arithmetic. As soon as the lad reached his fifteenth year,

A WOODLAND QUEEN

Claude put a gun into his hands, and took him hunting with him. Under the teaching of M. de Buxières, Claudet did honor to his master, and soon became such an expert that he could give points to all the huntsmen of the canton. None could equal him in tracing a dog; he knew all the passes, by-paths, and enclosures of the forest; swooped down upon the game with the keen scent and the velocity of a bird of prey, and never was known to miss his mark. Thus it was that the country people surnamed him the *grand chasserot*, the term which we here apply to the sparrow-hawk. Besides all these advantages, he was handsome, alert, straight, and well made, dark-haired and olive-skinned, like all the Buxières; he had his mother's caressing glance, but also the overhanging eyelids and somewhat stern expression of his father, from whom he inherited also a passionate temperament, and a spirit averse to all kinds of restraint. They were fond of him throughout the country, and M. de Buxières, who felt his youth renewed in him, was very proud of his adroitness and his good looks. He would invite him to his pleasure parties, and·make him sit at his own table, and confided unhesitatingly all his secrets to him. In short, Claudet, finding himself quite at home at the château, naturally considered himself as one of the family. There was but one formality wanting to that end: recognizance according to law. At certain favorable times, Manette Séjournant would gently urge M. de Buxiéres to have the situation legally authorized, to which he would invariably reply, from a natural dislike to taking legal advisers into his confidence:

"Don't worry about anything; I have no direct heir, and Claudet will have all my fortune; my will and testament will be worth more to him than a legal acknowledgment."

He would refer so often and so decidedly to his settled intention of making Claudet his sole heir, that Manette, who knew very little about what was required in such cases, considered the matter already secure. She continued in unsuspecting serenity until Claude de Buxières, in his sixty-second year, died suddenly from a stroke of apoplexy.

The will, which was to insure Claudet's future prospects, and to which the deceased had so often alluded, did it really exist? Neither Manette nor the *grand chasserot* had been able to obtain any certain knowledge in the matter, the hasty search for it after the decease having been suddenly interrupted by the arrival of the mayor of Vivey, and by the proceedings of the justice of the peace. The seals being once imposed, there was no means, in the absence of a verified will, of ascertaining on whom the inheritance devolved, until the opening of the inventory; and thus the Séjournants awaited with feverish anxiety the return of the justice of the peace and his bailiff.

M. Destourbet and Stephen Seurrot pushed open a small door to the right of the main gateway, passed rapidly under the arched canopy of beeches, the leaves of which, just touched by the first frost, were already falling from the branches, and, stamping their muddy feet on the outer steps, advanced into the vestibule. The wide corridor, flagged with black-and-white pave-

ment, presented a cheerless aspect of bare walls dis-
colored by damp, and adorned alternately by stags'
heads and family portraits in a crumbling state of
decay. The floor was thus divided: on the right, the
dining-room and the kitchen; on the left, drawing-room
and a billiard-hall. A stone staircase, built in one of
the turrets, led to the upper floors. Only one of these
rooms, the kitchen, which the justice and his bailiff
entered, was occupied by the household. A cold light,
equally diffused in all directions, and falling from a large
window, facing north across the gardens, allowed every
detail of the apartment to be seen clearly; opposite the
door of entrance, the tall chimney-place, with its deep
embrasure, gave ample shelter to the notary, who installed himself upon a stool and lighted his pipe at one
of the embers, while his principal clerk sat at the long
table, itemizing the objects contained in the inventory.

In the opposite angle of the chimney-place, a lad of
twenty-four years, no other than Claudet, called by the
friendly nickname of the *grand chasserot*, kept company
with the notary, while he toyed, in an absent fashion,
with the silky ears of a spaniel, whose fluffy little head
lay in his lap. Behind him, Manette Séjournant stood
putting away her shawl and prayerbook in a closet.
A mass had been said in the morning at the church,
for the repose of the soul of the late Claude de Buxières,
and mother and son had donned their Sunday garments
to assist at the ceremony.

Claudet appeared ill at ease in his black, tightly
buttoned suit, and kept his eyes with their heavy lids
steadily bent upon the head of the animal. To all

the notary's questions, he replied only by monosyllables, passing his fingers every now and then through his bushy brown locks, and twining them in his forked beard, a sure indication with him of preoccupation and bad humor.

Manette had acquired with years an amount of *embonpoint* which detracted materially from the supple and undulating beauty which had so captivated Claude de Buxières. The imprisonment of a tight corset caused undue development of the bust at the expense of her neck and throat, which seemed disproportionately short and thick. Her cheeks had lost their gracious curves and her double chin was more pronounced. All that remained of her former attractions were the caressing glance of her eye, tresses still golden and abundant, especially as seen under the close cap of black net, white teeth, and a voice that had lost nothing of its insinuating sweetness.

As the justice and his bailiff entered, Maître Arbillot, and a petulant little man with squirrel-like eyes and a small moustache, arose quickly.

"Good-morning, gentlemen," he cried. "I was anxiously expecting you—if you are willing, we will begin our work at once, for at this season night comes on quickly."

"At your orders, Maître Arbillot," replied the justice, laying his hat down carefully on the window-sill; "we shall draw out the formula for raising the seals. By the way, has no will yet been found?"

"None to my knowledge. It is quite clear to me that the deceased made no testament, none at least before a notary."

A WOODLAND QUEEN

"But," objected M. Destourbet, "he may have executed a holograph testament."

"It is certain, gentlemen," interrupted Manette, with her soft, plaintive voice, "that our dear gentleman did not go without putting his affairs in order. 'Manette,' said he, not more than two weeks ago; 'I do not intend you shall be worried, neither you nor Claudet, when I am no longer here. All shall be arranged to your satisfaction.' Oh! he certainly must have put down his last wishes on paper. Look well around, gentlemen; you will find a will in some drawer or other."

While she applied her handkerchief ostentatiously to her nose and wiped her eyes, the justice exchanged glances with the notary.

"Maître Arbillot, you think doubtless with me, that we ought to begin operations by examining the furniture of the bedroom?"

The notary inclined his head, and notified his chief clerk to remove his papers to the first floor.

"Show us the way, Madame," said the justice to the housekeeper; and the quartet of men of the law followed Manette, carrying with them a huge bunch of keys.

Claudet had risen from his seat when the justice arrived. As the party moved onward, he followed hesitatingly, and then halted, uncertain how to decide between the desire to assist in the search and the fear of intruding. The notary, noticing his hesitation, called to him:

"Come, you also, Claudet, are not you one of the guardians of the seals?"

And they wended their silent way up the winding

staircase of the turret. The high, dark silhouette of Manette headed the procession; then followed the justice, carefully choosing his foothold on the well-worn stairs, the asthmatic old bailiff, breathing short and hard, the notary, beating his foot impatiently every time that Seurrot stopped to take breath, and finally the principal clerk and Claudet.

Manette, opening noiselessly the door of the deceased's room, entered, as if it were a church, the somewhat stifling apartment. Then she threw open the shutters, and the afternoon sun revealed an interior decorated and furnished in the style of the close of the eighteenth century. An inlaid secretary, with white marble top and copper fittings, stood near the bed, of which the coverings had been removed, showing the mattresses piled up under a down bed covered with blue-and-white check.

As soon as the door was closed, the clerk settled himself at the table with his packet of stamped paper, and began to run over, in a low, rapid voice, the preliminaries of the inventory. In this confused murmuring some fragments of phrases would occasionally strike the ear: "Château of Vivey—deceased the eighth of October last—at the requisition of Marie-Julien de Buxières, comptroller of direct contributions at Nancy—styling himself heir to Claude Odouart de ·Buxières, his cousin-german by blood——"

This last phrase elicited from Claudet a sudden movement of surprise. ·

"The inventory," explained Maître Arbillot, "is drawn up at the requisition of the only heir named, to whom we must make application, if necessary, for the property left by the deceased."

There was a moment of silence, interrupted by a plaintive sigh from Manette Séjournant and afterward by the tearing sound of the sealed bands across the bureau, the drawers and pigeonholes of which were promptly ransacked by the justice and his assistant.

Odouart de Buxières had not been much of a scribe. A double Liége almanac, a memorandum-book, in which he had entered the money received from the sale of his wood and the dates of the payments made by his farmers; a day-book, in which he had made careful note of the number of head of game killed each day—that was all the bureau contained.

"Let us examine another piece of furniture," murmured the justice.

Manette and Claudet remained unmoved. They apparently knew the reason why none but insignificant papers had been found in the drawers, for their features expressed neither surprise nor disappointment.

Another search through a high chest of drawers with large copper handles was equally unprofitable. Then they attacked the secretary, and after the key had been turned twice in the noisy lock, the lid went slowly down. The countenances of both mother and son, hitherto so unconcerned, underwent a slight but anxious change. The bailiff continued his scrupulous search of each drawer under the watchful eye of the justice, finding nothing but documents of mediocre importance; old titles to property, bundles of letters, tradesmen's bills, etc. Suddenly, at the opening of the last drawer, a significant "Ah!" from Stephen Seurrot drew round him the heads of the justice and the notary, and made Manette and Claudet, standing at the foot of the bed, start with expectation. On the dark ground of a rose-wood box lay a sheet of white paper, on which was written:

"This is my testament."

With the compression of lip and significant shake of the head of a physician about to take in hand a hopeless case of illness, the justice made known to his two neighbors the text of the sheet of paper, on which Claude Odouart de Buxières had written, in his coarse, ill-regulated hand, the following lines:

"Not knowing my collateral heirs, and caring nothing about them, I give and bequeath all my goods and chattels——"

The testator had stopped there, either because he thought it better, before going any further, to consult some legal authority more experienced than himself, or because he had been interrupted in his labor and had deferred completing this testifying of his last will until some future opportunity.

M. Destourbet, after once more reading aloud this unfinished sentence, exclaimed:

"Monsieur de Buxières did not finish—it is much to be regretted!"

"My God! is it possible?" interrupted the house-keeper; "you think, then, Monsieur Justice, that Claudet does not inherit anything?"

"According to my idea," replied he, "we have here only a scrap of unimportant paper; the name of the legatee is not indicated, and even were it indicated, the testament would still be without force, being neither dated nor signed."

"But perhaps Monsieur de Buxiéres made another?"

"I think not; I am more inclined to suppose that he did not have time to complete the arrangements that he wished to make, and the proof lies in the very existence of this incomplete document in the only piece of furniture in which he kept his papers." Then, turning toward the notary and the bailiff: "You are doubtless, gentlemen, of the same opinion as myself; it will be wise, therefore, to defer raising the remainder of the seals until the arrival of the legal heir. Maître Arbillot, Monsieur Julien de Buxières must be notified, and asked to be here in Vivey as soon as possible."

"I will write this evening," said the notary; "in the meanwhile, the keeping of the seals will be continued by Claudet Séjournant."

The justice inclined his head to Manette, who was standing, pale and motionless, at the foot of the bed; stunned by the unexpected announcement; the bailiff and the chief clerk, after gathering up their papers, shook hands sympathizingly with Claudet.

"I am grieved to the heart, my dear fellow," said the notary, in his turn, "at what has happened! It is hard to swallow, but you will always keep a courageous heart, and be able to rise to the top; besides, even if, legally, you own nothing here, this unfinished testament of Monsieur de Buxières will constitute a moral title in your favor, and I trust that the heir will have enough justice and right feeling to treat you properly."

ANDRÉ THEURIET

"I want nothing from him!" muttered Claudet, between his teeth; then, leaving his mother to attend to the rest of the legal fraternity, he went hastily to his room, next that of the deceased, tore off his dress-coat, slipped on a hunting-coat, put on his gaiters, donned his old felt hat, and descended to the kitchen, where Manette was sitting, huddled up in front of the embers, weeping and bewailing her fate.

Since she had become housekeeper and mistress of the Buxières household, she had adopted a more polished speech and a more purely French mode of expression, but in this moment of discouragement and despair the rude dialect of her native country rose to her lips, and in her own *patois* she inveighed against the deceased:

"Ah! the bad man, the mean man! Didn't I tell him, time and again, that he would leave us in trouble! Where can we seek our bread this late in the day? We shall have to beg in the streets!"

"Hush! hush! mother," interrupted Claudet, sternly, placing his hand on her shoulder, "it does not mend matters to give way like that. Calm thyself—so long as I have hands on the ends of my arms, we never shall be beggars. But I must go out—I need air."

And crossing the gardens rapidly, he soon reached the outskirts of the brambly thicket.

This landscape, both rugged and smiling in its wildness, hardly conveyed the idea of silence, but rather of profound meditation, absolute calm; the calmness of solitude, the religious meditation induced by spacious forest depths. The woods seemed asleep, and the low

murmurings, which from time to time escaped from
their recesses, seemed like the unconscious sighs exhaled by a dreamer. The very odor peculiar to trees in
autumn, the penetrating and spicy odor of the dying
leaves, had a delicate and subtle aroma harmonizing
with this quietude of fairyland.

Now and then, through the vaporous golden atmosphere of the late autumn sunset, through the pensive
stillness of the hushed woods, the distant sound of feminine voices, calling to one another, echoed from the
hills, and beyond the hedges was heard the crackling of
branches, snapped by invisible hands, and the rattle of
nuts dropping on the earth. It was the noise made by
the gatherers of beechnuts, for in the years when the
beech produces abundantly, this harvest, under the
sanction of the guardians of the forest, draws together
the whole population of women and children, who
collect these triangular nuts, from which an excellent
species of oil is procured.

Wending his way along the copse, Claudet suddenly
perceived, through an opening in the trees, several large
white sheets spread under the beeches, and covered
with brown heaps of the fallen fruit. One or two familiar voices hailed him as he passed, but he was not disposed to gossip, for the moment, and turned abruptly
into the bushwood, so as to avoid any encounter. The
unexpected event which had just taken place, and
which was to change his present mode of life, as well as
his plans for the future, was of too recent occurrence for
him to view it with any degree of calmness.

He was like a man who has received a violent blow

[19]

on the head, and is for the moment stunned by it. He suffered vaguely, without seeking to know from what cause; he had not been able as yet to realize the extent of his misfortune; and every now and then a vague hope came over him that all would come right.

So on he went, straight ahead, his eyes on the ground, and his hands in his pockets, until he emerged upon one of the old forest roads where the grass had begun to burst through the stony interstices; and there, in the distance, under the light tracery of weaving branches, a delicate female silhouette was outlined on the dark background. A young woman, dressed in a petticoat of gray woolen material, and a jacket of the same, close-fitting at the waist, her arms bare to the elbows and supporting on her head a bag of nuts enveloped in a white sheet, advanced toward him with a quick and rhythmical step. The manner in which she carried her burden showed the elegance of her form, the perfect grace of her chest and throat. She was not very tall, but finely proportioned. As she approached, the slanting rays of the setting sun shone on her heavy brown hair, twisted into a thick coil at the back of her head, and revealed the amber paleness of her clear skin, the long oval of her eyes, the firm outline of her chin and somewhat full lips; and Claudet, roused from his lethargic reverie by the sound of her rapid footsteps, raised his eyes, and recognized the daughter of Père Vincart, the proprietor of La Thuilière.

At the same moment, the young girl, doubtless fatigued with the weight of her bundle, had laid it down by the roadside while she recovered her breath. In a few seconds Claudet was by her side.

"Good-evening, Reine," said he, in a voice singularly softened in tone, "shall I give you a lift with that?"

"Good-evening, Claudet," replied she; "truly, now, that is not an offer to be refused. The weight is greater than I thought."

"Have you come far thus laden?"

"No; our people are nutting in the Bois des Ronces; I came on before, because I don't like to leave father alone for long at a time and, as I was coming, I wished to bring my share with me."

"No one can reproach you with shirking work, Reine, nor of being afraid to take hold of things. To see you all day trotting about the farm, no one would think you had been to school in the city, like a young lady."

And Claudet's countenance became irradiated with a glow of innocent and tender admiration. It was evident that his eyes looked with delight into the dark limpid orbs of Reine, on her pure and rosy lips, and on her partly uncovered neck, the whiteness of which two little brown moles only served to enhance.

"How can it be helped?" replied she, smiling, "it must be done; when there is no man in the house to give orders, the women must take a hand themselves. My father was not very strong when my mother died, and since he had that attack he has become quite helpless, and I have had to take his place."

While she spoke, Claudet took hold of the bundle, and, lifting it as if it had been a feather, threw it over his shoulder. They walked on, side by side, in the direction of La Thuilière; the sun had set, and a penetrating moisture, arising from the damp soil of the adjacent pasture lands, encircled them in a bluish fog.

"So he is worse, your father, is he?" said Claudet, after a moment's silence.

"He can not move from his armchair, his mental faculties are weakening, and I am obliged to amuse him like a child.   But how is it with yourself, Claudet?" she asked, turning her frank, cordial gaze upon him. "You have had your share of trouble since we last met, and great events have happened.   Poor Monsieur de Buxières was taken away very suddenly!"

The close relationship that united Claudet with the deceased was a secret to no one; Reine, as well as all the country people, knew and admitted the fact, however irregular, as one sanctioned by time and continuity. Therefore, in speaking to the young man, her voice had that tone of affectionate interest usual in conversing with a bereaved friend on a death that concerns him.

The countenance of the *grand chasserot*, which had cleared for a time under her influence, became again clouded.

"Yes;" sighed he, "he was taken too soon!"

"And now, Claudet, you are sole master at the château?"

"Neither—master—nor even valet!" he returned, with such bitterness that the young girl stood still with surprise.

"What do you mean?" she exclaimed, "was it not agreed with Monsieur de Buxières that you should inherit all his property?"

"Such was his intention, but he did not have time to put it in execution; he died without leaving any will, and, as I am nothing in the eye of the law, the patrimony will go to a distant relative, a de Buxières whom Monsieur Odouart did not even know."

Reine's dark eyes filled with tears.

"What a misfortune!" she exclaimed, "and who could have expected such a thing? Oh! my poor Claudet!"

She was so moved, and spoke with such sincere compassion, that Claudet was perhaps misled, and thought he read in her glistening eyes a tenderer sentiment than pity; he trembled, took her hand, and held it long in his.

"Thank you, Reine! Yes," he added, after a pause, "it is a rude shock to wake up one morning without hearth or home, when one has been in the habit of living on one's income."

"What do you intend to do?" inquired Reine, gravely.

Claudet shrugged his shoulders.

"To work for my bread—or, if I can find no suitable trade, enlist in a regiment. I think I should not make a bad soldier. Everything is going round and round in my head like a mill-wheel. The first thing to do is to see about my mother, who is lamenting down there at the house—I must find her a comfortable place to live."

The young girl had become very thoughtful.

"Claudet," replied she, "I know you are very proud, very sensitive, and could not wish to hurt your feelings. Therefore, I pray you not to take in ill part that which

I am going to say—in short, if you should get into any trouble, you will, I hope, remember that you have friends at La Thuilière, and that you will come to seek us."

The *grand chasserot* reddened.

"I shall never take amiss what you may say to me, Reine!" faltered he; "for I can not doubt your good heart—I have known it since the time when we played together in the curé's garden, while waiting for the time to repeat the catechism. But there is no hurry as yet; the heir will not arrive for several weeks, and by that time, I trust, we shall have had a chance to turn round."

They had reached the boundary of the forest where the fields of La Thuilière begin.

By the last fading light of day they could distinguish the black outline of the ancient forge, now become a grange, and a light was twinkling in one of the low windows of the farm.

"Here you are at home," continued Claudet, laying the bundle of nuts on the flat stone wall which surrounded the farm buildings; "I wish you good-night."

"Will you not come in and get warm?"

"No; I must go back," replied he.

"Good-night, then, Claudet; *au revoir* and good courage!"

He gazed at her for a moment in the deepening twilight, then, abruptly pressing her hands:

"Thank you, Reine," murmured he in a choking voice, "you are a good girl, and I love you very much!"

He left the young mistress of the farm precipitately, and plunged again into the woods.

CHAPTER II

WHILE these events were happening at Vivey, the person whose name excited the curiosity and the conversational powers of the villagers—Marie-Julien de Buxières—ensconced in his unpretentious apartment in the Rue Stanislaus, Nancy, still pondered over the astonishing news contained in the Auberive notary's first letter. The announcement of his inheritance, dropping from the skies, as it were, had found him quite unprepared, and, at first, somewhat sceptical. He remembered, it is true, hearing his father once speak of a cousin who had remained a bachelor and who owned a fine piece of property in some corner of the Haute Marne; but, as all intercourse had long been broken off between the two families, M. de Buxières the elder had mentioned the subject only in relation to barely possible hopes which had very little chance of being realized. Julien had never placed any reliance on this chimerical inheritance, and he received almost with indifference the official announcement of the death of Claude Odouart de Buxières.

By direct line from his late father, he became in fact the only legitimate heir of the château and lands of

Vivey; still, there was a strong probability that Claude de Buxières had made a will in favor of some one more within his own circle. The second missive from Arbillot the notary, announcing that the deceased had died intestate, and requesting the legal heir to come to Vivey as soon as possible, put a sudden end to the young man's doubts, which merged into a complex feeling, less of joy than of stupefaction.

Up to the present time, Julien de Buxières had not been spoiled by Fortune's gifts. His parents, who had died prematurely, had left him nothing. He lived in a very mediocre style on his slender salary as comptroller of direct contributions, and, although twenty-seven years old, was housed like a supernumerary in a small furnished room on the second floor above the ground. At this time his physique was that of a young man of medium height, slight, pale, and nervous, sensitive in disposition, reserved and introspective in habit. His delicate features, his intelligent forehead surmounted by soft chestnut hair, his pathetic blue eyes, his curved, dissatisfied mouth, shaded by a slight, dark moustache, indicated a melancholy, unquiet temperament and precocious moral fatigue.

There are some men who never have had any childhood, or rather, whose childhood never has had its happy time of laughter. Julien was one of these. That which imparts to childhood its charm and enjoyment is the warm and tender atmosphere of the home; the constant and continued caressing of a mother; the gentle and intimate creations of one's native country where, by degrees, the senses awaken to the marvellous sights of the outer world; where the alternating seasons in their course first arouse the student's ambition and cause the heart of the adolescent youth to thrill with emotion; where every street corner, every tree, every turn of the soil, has some history to relate. Julien had had no experiences of this peaceful family life, during which are stored up such treasures of childhood's recollections. He was the son of a government official, who had been trotted over all France at the caprice of the administration, and he had never known, so to speak, any associations of the land in which he was born, or the hearth on which he was raised. Chance had located his birth in a small town among the Pyrenees, and when he was two years old he had been transplanted to one of the industrial cities of Artois. At the end of two years more came another removal to one of the midland towns, and thus his tender childhood had been buffeted about, from east to west, from north to south, taking root nowhere. All he could remember of these early years was an unpleasant impression of hasty packing and removal, of long journeys by diligence, and of uncomfortable resettling. His mother had died just as he was entering upon his eighth year; his father, absorbed in official work, and not caring to leave the child· to the management of servants, had placed him at that early age in a college directed by priests. Julien thus passed his second term of childhood, and his boyhood was spent behind these stern, gloomy walls, bending resignedly under a discipline which, though gentle, was narrow and suspicious, and allowed little scope for personal development. He obtained only occasional

ANDRÉ THEURIET

glimpses of nature during the monotonous daily walks across a flat, meaningless country. At very rare intervals, one of his father's colleagues would take him visiting; but these stiff and ceremonious calls only left a wearisome sensation of restraint and dull fatigue. During the long vacation he used to rejoin his father, whom he almost always found in a new residence. The poor man had alighted there for a time, like a bird on a tree; and among these continually shifting scenes, the lad had felt himself more than ever a stranger among strangers; so that he experienced always a secret though joyless satisfaction in returning to the cloisters of the St. Hilaire college and submitting himself to the yoke of the paternal but inflexible discipline of the Church.

He was naturally inclined, by the tenderness of his nature, toward a devotional life, and accepted with blind confidence the religious and moral teaching of the reverend fathers. A doctrine which preached separation from profane things; the attractions of a meditative and pious life, and mistrust of the world and its perilous pleasures, harmonized with the shy and melancholy timidity of his nature. Human beings, especially women, inspired him with secret aversion, which was increased by consciousness of his awkwardness and remissness whenever he found himself in the society of women or young girls.

The beauties of nature did not affect him; the flowers in the springtime, the glories of the summer sun, the rich coloring of autumn skies, having no connection in his mind with any joyous recollection, left him cold and unmoved; he even professed an almost hostile indifference

[28]

to such purely material sights as disturbing and dangerous to the inner life. He lived within himself and could not see beyond.

His mind, imbued with a mystic idealism, delighted itself in solitary reading or in meditations in the house of prayer. The only emotion he ever betrayed was caused by the organ music accompanying the hymnal plain-song, and by the pomp of religious ceremony.

At the age of eighteen, he left the St. Hilaire college in order to prepare his baccalaureate, and his father, becoming alarmed at his increasing moodiness and mysticism, endeavored to infuse into him the tastes and habits of a man of the world by introducing him into the society of his equals in the town where he lived; but the twig was already bent, and the young man yielded with bad grace to the change of régime; the amusements they offered were either wearisome or repugnant to him. He would wander aimlessly through the salons where they were playing whist, where the ladies played show pieces at the piano, and where they spoke a language he did not understand. He was quite aware of his worldly inaptitude, and that he was considered awkward, dull, and ill-tempered, and the knowledge of this fact paralyzed and frightened him still more. He could not disguise his feeling of *ennui* suficiently to prevent the provincial circles from being greatly offended; they declared unanimously that young de Buxières was a bear, and decided to leave him alone. The death of his father, which happened just as the youth was beginning his official cares, put a sudden end to all this constraint. He took advantage of his season

of mourning to resume his old ways; and returned with
a sigh of relief to his solitude, his books, and his meditations. According to the promise of the *Imitation*, he
found unspeakable joys in his retirement; he rose at
break of day, assisted at early mass, fulfilled, conscientiously, his administrative duties, took his hurried meals
in a boarding-house, where he exchanged a few polite
remarks with his fellow inmates, then shut himself up
in his room to read Pascal or Bossuet until eleven
o'clock.

He thus attained his twenty-seventh year, and it was
into the calm of this serious, cloister-like life, that the
news fell of the death of Claude de Buxières and of the
unexpected inheritance that had accrued to him.

After entering into correspondence with the notary,
M. Arbillot, and becoming assured of the reality of
his rights and of the neccessity of his presence at Vivey,
he had obtained leave of absence from his official duties,
and set out for Haute Marne. On the way, he could not
help marvelling at the providential interposition which
would enable him to leave a career for which he felt he
had no vocation, and to pursue his independent life,
according to his own tastes, and secured from any fear
of outside cares. According to the account given by the
notary, Claude de Buxières's fortune might be valued at
two hundred thousand francs, in furniture and other
movables, without reckoning the château and the adjacent woods. This was a much larger sum than had ever
been dreamed of by Julien de Buxières, whose belongings did not amount in all to three thousand francs. He
made up his mind, therefore, that, as soon as he was

installed at Vivey, he would change his leave of absence to an unlimited furlough of freedom. He contemplated with serene satisfaction this perspective view of calm and solitary retirement in a château lost to view in the depths of the forest, where he could in perfect security give himself up to the studious contemplative life which he loved so much, far from all worldly frivolities and restraint. He already imagined himself at Vivey, shut up in his carefully selected library; he delighted in the thought of having in future to deal only with the country people, whose uncivilized ways would be like his own, and among whom his timidity would not be remarked.

He arrived at Langres in the afternoon of a foggy October day, and inquired immediately at the hotel how he could procure a carriage to take him that evening to Vivey. They found him a driver, but, to his surprise, the man refused to take the journey until the following morning, on account of the dangerous state of the cross-roads, where vehicles might stick fast in the mire if they ventured there after nightfall. Julien vainly endeavored to effect an arrangement with him, and the discussion was prolonged in the courtyard of the hotel. Just as the man was turning away, another, who had overheard the end of the colloquy, came up to young de Buxières, and offered to undertake the journey for twenty francs.

"I have a good horse," said he to Julien; "I know the roads, and will guarantee that we reach Vivey before nightfall."

The bargain was quickly made; and in half an hour, Julien de Buxières was rolling over the plain above Langres, in a shaky old cabriolet, the muddy hood of which bobbed over at every turn of the wheel, while the horse kept up a lively trot over the stones.

The clouds were low, and the road lay across bare and stony prairies, the gray expanse of which became lost in the distant mist. This depressing landscape would have made a disagreeable impression on a less unobserving traveller, but, as we have said, Julien looked only inward, and the phenomena of the exterior world influenced him only unconsciously. Half closing his eyes, and mechanically affected by the rhythmical tintinnabulation of the little bells, hanging around the horse's neck, he had resumed his meditations, and considered how he should arrange his life in this, to him, unknown country, which would probably be his own for some time to come. Nevertheless, when, at the end of the level plain, the road turned off into the wooded region, the unusual aspect of the forest aroused his curiosity. The tufted woods and lofty trees, in endless succession under the fading light, impressed him by their profound solitude and their religious silence. His loneliness was in sympathy with the forest, which seemed contemporary with the Sleeping Beauty of the wood, the verdant walls of which were to separate him forever from the world of cities. Henceforth, he could be himself, could move freely, dress as he wished, or give way to his dreaming, without fearing to encounter the ironical looks of idle and wondering neighbors. For the first time since his departure from his former home, he experienced a feeling of joy and serenity; the influence of the surroundings, so much in harmony with his wishes, unlocked his tongue, and made him communicative.

He made up his mind to speak to the guide, who was smoking at his side and whipping his horse.

"Are we far from Vivey now?"

"That depends, Monsieur—as the crow flies, the distance is not very great, and if we could go by the roads, we should be there in one short hour. Unfortunately, on turning by the Allofroy farm, we shall have to leave the highroad and take the cross path; and then—my gracious! we shall plunge into the ditch down there, and into perdition."

"You told me that you were well acquainted with the roads!"

"I know them, and I do not know them. When it comes to these crossroads, one is sure of nothing. They change every year, and each new superintendent cuts a way out through the woods according to his fancy. The devil himself could not find his way."

"Yet you have been to Vivey before?"

"Oh, yes; five or six years ago; I used often to take parties of hunters to the château. Ah! Monsieur, what a beautiful country it is for hunting; you can not take twenty steps along a trench without seeing a stag or a deer."

"You have doubtless had the opportunity of meeting Monsieur Odouart de Buxières?"

"Yes, indeed, Monsieur, more than once—ah! he is a jolly fellow and a fine man——"

"He was," interrupted Julien, gravely, "for he is dead."

"Ah! excuse me—I did not know it. What! is he really dead? So fine a man! What we must all come

3

to. Careful, now!" added he, pulling in the reins, "we are leaving the highroad, and must keep our eyes open."

The twilight was already deepening, the driver lighted his lantern, and the vehicle turned into a narrow lane, half mud, half stone, and hedged in on both sides with wet brushwood, which flapped noisily against the leathern hood. After fifteen minutes' riding, the paths opened upon a pasture, dotted here and there with juniper bushes, and thence divided into three lines, along which ran the deep track of wagons, cutting the pasturage into small hillocks. After long hesitation, the man cracked his whip and took the right-hand path.

Julien began to fear that the fellow had boasted too much when he declared that he knew the best way. The ruts became deeper and deeper; the road was descending into a hole; suddenly, the wheels became embedded up to the hub in thick, sticky mire, and the horse refused to move. The driver jumped to the ground, swearing furiously; then he called Julien to help him to lift out the wheel. But the young man, slender and frail as he was, and not accustomed to using his muscles, was not able to render much assistance.

"Thunder and lightning!" cried the driver, "it is impossible to get out of this—let go the wheel, Monsieur, you have no more strength than a chicken, and, besides, you don't know how to go about it. What a devil of a road! But we can't spend the night here!"

"If we were to call out," suggested Julien, somewhat mortified at the inefficiency of his assistance, "some one would perhaps come to our aid."

They accordingly shouted with desperation; and after

five or six minutes, a voice hailed back. A woodcutter, from one of the neighboring clearings, had heard the call, and was running toward them.

"This way!" cried the guide, "we are stuck fast in the mud. Give us a lift."

The man came up and walked round the vehicle, shaking his head.

"You've got on to a blind road," said he, "and you'll have trouble in getting out of it, seeing as how there's not light to go by. You had better unharness the horse, and wait for daylight, if you want to get your carriage out."

"And where shall we go for a bed?" growled the driver; "there isn't even a house near in this accursed wild country of yours!"

"Excuse me—you are not far from La Thuilière; the farm people will not refuse you a bed, and to-morrow morning they will help you to get your carriage out of the mud. Unharness, comrade; I will lead you as far as the Planche-au-Vacher; and from there you will see the windows of the farmhouse."

The driver, still grumbling, decided to take his advice. They unharnessed the horse; took one of the lanterns of the carriage as a beacon, and followed slowly the line of pasture-land, under the woodchopper's guidance. At the end of about ten minutes, the forester pointed out a light, twinkling at the extremity of a rustic path, bordered with moss.

"You have only to go straight ahead," said he, "besides, the barking of the dogs will guide you. Ask for Mamselle Vincart. Good-night, gentlemen."

He turned on his heel, while Julien, bewildered, began to reproach himself for not having thanked him enough. The conductor went along with his lantern; young de Buxières followed him with eyes downcast. Thus they continued silently until they reached the termination of the mossy path, where a furious barking saluted their ears.

"Here we are," growled the driver, "fortunately the dogs are not yet let loose, or we should pass a bad quarter of an hour!"

They pushed open a side-wicket and, standing in the courtyard, could see the house. With the exception of the luminous spot that reddened one of the windows of the ground floor, the long, low façade was dark, and, as it were, asleep. On the right, standing alone, outlined against the sky, was the main building of the ancient forge, now used for granaries and stables; inside, the frantic barking of the watch-dogs mingled with the bleating of the frightened sheep, the neighing of horses, and the clanking of wooden shoes worn by the farm hands. At the same moment, the door of the house opened, and a servant, attracted by the uproar, appeared on the threshold, a lantern in her hand.

"Hallo! you people," she exclaimed sharply to the newcomers, who were advancing toward her, "what do you want?"

The driver related, in a few words, the affair of the cabriolet, and asked whether they would house him at the farm until the next day—himself and the gentleman he was conducting to Vivey.

The girl raised the lantern above her head in order to

scrutinize the two strangers; doubtless their appearance and air of respectability reassured her, for she replied, in a milder voice:

"Well, that does not depend on me—I am not the mistress here, but come in, all the same—Mamselle Reine can not be long now, and she will answer for herself."

As soon as the driver had fastened his horse to one of the outside posts of the wicket-gate, the servant brought them into a large, square hall, in which a lamp, covered with a shade, gave a moderate light. She placed two chairs before the fire, which she drew together with the poker.

"Warm yourselves while you are waiting," continued she, "it will not be long, and you must excuse me—I must go and milk the cows—that is work which will not wait."

She reached the courtyard, and shut the gate after her, while Julien turned to examine the room into which they had been shown, and felt a certain serenity creep over him at the clean and cheerful aspect of this homely but comfortable interior. The room served as both kitchen and dining-room. On the right of the flaring chimney, one of the cast-iron arrangements called a cooking-stove was gently humming; the saucepans, resting on the bars, exhaled various appetizing odors. In the centre, the long, massive table of solid beech was already spread with its coarse linen cloth, and the service was laid. White muslin curtains fell in front of the large windows, on the sills of which potted chrysanthemums spread their white, brown, and red blossoms.

ANDRÉ THEURIET

Round the walls a shining battery of boilers, kettles, basins, and copper plates were hung in symmetrical order. On the dresser, near the clock, was a complete service of old Aprey china, in bright and varied colors, and not far from the chimney, which was ornamented with a crucifix of yellow copper, was a set of shelves, attached to the wall, containing three rows of books, in gray linen binding. Julien, approaching, read, not without surprise, some of the titles: *Paul and Virginia*, La Fontaine's *Fables*, Gessner's *Idylls*, *Don Quixote*, and noticed several odd volumes of the *Picturesque Magazine*.

Hanging from the whitened ceiling were clusters of nuts, twisted hemp, strings of yellow maize, and chaplets of golden pippins tied with straw, all harmonizing in the dim light, and adding increased fulness to the picture of thrift and abundance.

"It's jolly here!" said the driver, smacking his lips, "and the smell which comes from that oven makes one hungry. I wish Mamselle Reine would arrive!"

Just as he said this, a mysterious falsetto voice, which seemed to come from behind the copper basins, repeated, in an acrid voice: "Reine! Reine!"

"What in the world is that?" exclaimed the driver, puzzled.

Both looked toward the beams; at the same moment there was a rustling of wings, a light hop, and a black-and white-object flitted by, resting, finally, on one of the shelves hanging from the joists.

"Ha, ha!" said the driver, laughing, "it is only a magpie!"

A WOODLAND QUEEN

He had hardly said it, when, like a plaintive echo, another voice, a human voice this time, childish and wavering, proceeding from a dark corner, faltered: "Rei—eine—Rei—eine!"

"Hark!" murmured Julien, "some one answered."

His companion seized the lamp, and advanced toward the portion of the room left in shadow. Suddenly he stopped short, and stammered some vague excuse.

Julien, who followed him, then perceived, with alarm, in a sort of niche formed by two screens, entirely covered with illustrations from Epinal, a strange-looking being stretched in an easy-chair, which was covered with pillows and almost hidden under various woolen draperies. He was dressed in a long coat of coarse, pale-blue cloth. He was bareheaded, and his long, white hair formed a weird frame for a face of bloodless hue and meagre proportions, from which two vacant eyes stared fixedly. He sat immovable and his arms hung limply over his knees.

"Monsieur," said Julien, bowing ceremoniously, "we are quite ashamed at having disturbed you. Your servant forgot to inform us of your presence, and we were waiting for Mademoiselle Reine, without thinking that——

The old man continued immovable, not seeming to understand; he kept repeating, in the same voice, like a frightened child:

"Rei—eine! Rei—eine!"

The two bewildered travellers gazed at this sepulchral-looking personage, then at each other interrogatively, and began to feel very uncomfortable. The magpie, perched upon the hanging shelf, suddenly flapped his wings, and repeated, in his turn, in falsetto:

"Reine, queen of the woods!"

"Here I am, papa, don't get uneasy!" said a clear, musical voice behind them.

The door had been suddenly opened, and Reine Vincart had entered. She wore on her head a white cape or hood, and held in front of her an enormous bouquet of glistening leaves, which seemed to have been gathered as specimens of all the wild fruit-trees of the forest: the brown beam-berries, the laburnums, and wild cherry, with their red, transparent fruit, the bluish mulberry, the orange-clustered mountain-ash. All this forest vegetation, mingling its black or purple tints with the dark, moist leaves, brought out the whiteness of the young girl's complexion, her limpid eyes, and her brown curls escaping from her hood.

Julien de Buxières and his companion had turned at the sound of Reine's voice. As soon as she perceived them, she went briskly toward them, exclaiming:

"What are you doing here? Don't you see that you are frightening him?"

Julien, humbled and mortified, murmured an excuse, and got confused in trying to relate the incident of the carriage. She interrupted him hurriedly:

"The carriage, oh, yes—La Guitiote spoke to me about it. Well, your carriage will be attended to! Go and sit down by the fire, gentlemen; we will talk about it presently."

She had taken the light from the driver, and placed it on an adjacent table with her plants. In the twinkling of an eye, she removed her hood, unfastened her shawl, and then knelt down in front of the sick man, after kissing him tenderly on the forehead. From the corner where Julien had seated himself, he could hear her soothing voice. Its caressing tones contrasted pleasantly with the harsh accent of a few minutes before.

"You were longing for me, papa," said she, "but you see, I could not leave before all the sacks of potatoes had been laid in the wagon. Now everything has been brought in, and we can sleep in peace. I thought of you on the way, and I have brought you a fine bouquet of wild fruits. We shall enjoy looking them over to-morrow, by daylight. Now, this is the time that you are to drink your bouillon like a good papa, and then as soon as we have had our supper Guite and I will put you to bed nice and warm, and I will sing you a song to send you to sleep."

She rose, took from the sideboard a bowl which she filled from a saucepan simmering on the stove, and then, without taking any notice of her visitors, she returned to the invalid. Slowly and with delicate care she made him swallow the soup by spoonfuls. Julien, notwithstanding the feeling of ill-humor caused by the untoward happenings of the evening, could not help admiring the almost maternal tenderness with which the young girl proceeded in this slow and difficult operation. When the bowl was empty she returned to the stove, and at last bethought herself of her guests.

"Excuse me, Monsieur, but I had to attend to my father first. If I understood Guite aright, you were going to Vivey."

"Yes, Mademoiselle, I had hoped to sleep there to-night."

"You have probably come," continued she, "on business connected with the château. Is not the heir of Monsieur Odouart expected very shortly?"

"I am that heir," replied Julien, coloring.

"You are Monsieur de Buxières?" exclaimed Reine, in astonishment. Then, embarrassed at having shown her surprise too openly, she checked herself, colored in her turn, and finally gave a rapid glance at her interlocutor. She never should have imagined this slender young man, so melancholy in aspect, to be the new proprietor—he was so unlike the late Odouart de Buxières!

"Pardon me, Monsieur," continued she, "you must have thought my first welcome somewhat unceremonious, but my first thought was for my father. He is a great invalid, as you may have noticed, and for the first moment I feared that he had been startled by strange faces."

"It is I, Mademoiselle," replied Julien, with embarrassment, "it is I who ought to ask pardon for having caused all this disturbance. But I do not intend to trouble you any longer. If you will kindly furnish us with a guide who will direct us to the road to Vivey, we will depart to-night and sleep at the château."

"No, indeed," protested Reine, very cordially. "You are my guests, and I shall not allow you to leave us in that manner. Besides, you would probably find the gates closed down there, for I do not think they expected you so soon."

During this interview, the servant who had received

the travellers had returned with her milk-pail; behind her, the other farm-hands, men and women, arranged themselves silently round the table.

"Guitiote," said Reine, "lay two more places at the table. The horse belonging to these gentlemen has been taken care of, has he not?"

"Yes, Mamselle, he is in the stable," replied one of the grooms.

"Good! Bernard, to-morrow you will take Fleuriot with you, and go in search of their carriage which has been swamped in the Planche-au-Vacher. That is settled. Now, Monsieur de Buxieres, will you proceed to table—and your coachman also? Upon my word, I do not know whether our supper will be to your liking. I can only offer you a plate of soup, a chine of pork, and cheese made in the country; but you must be hungry, and when one has a good appetite, one is not hard to please."

Every one had been seated at the table; the servants at the lower end, and Reine Vincart, near the fireplace, between M. de Buxières and the driver. La Guite helped the cabbage-soup all around; soon nothing was heard but the clinking of spoons and smacking of lips. Julien, scarcely recovered from his bewilderment, watched furtively the pretty, robust young girl presiding at the supper, and keeping, at the same time, a watchful eye over all the details of service. He thought her strange; she upset all his ideas. His own imagination and his theories pictured a woman, and more especially a young girl, as a submissive, modest, shadowy creature, with downcast look, only raising her eyes to consult her husband or her mother as to what is allowable and what is forbidden. Now, Reine did not fulfil any of the requirements of this ideal. She seemed to be hardly twenty-two years old, and she acted with the initiative genius, the frankness and the decision of a man, retaining all the while the tenderness and easy grace of a woman. Although it was evident that she was accustomed to govern and command, there was nothing in her look, gesture, or voice which betrayed any assumption of masculinity. She remained a young girl while in the very act of playing the virile part of head of the house. But what astonished Julien quite as much was that she seemed to have received a degree of education superior to that of people of her condition, and he wondered at the amount of will-power by which a nature highly cultivated, relatively speaking, could conform to the unrefined, rough surroundings in which she was placed.

While Julien was immersed in these reflections, and continued eating with an abstracted air, Reine Vincart was rapidly examining the reserved, almost ungainly, young man, who did not dare address any conversation to her, and who was equally stiff and constrained with those sitting near him. She made a mental comparison of him with Claudet, the bold huntsman, alert, resolute, full of dash and spirit, and a feeling of charitable compassion arose in her heart at the thought of the reception which the Séjournant family would give to this new master, so timid and so little acquainted with the ways and dispositions of country folk. Julien did not impress her as being able to defend himself against the ill-will of persons who would consider him an intruder, and would certainly endeavor to make him pay dearly for the inheritance of which he had deprived them.

"You do not take your wine, Monsieur de Buxières!" said she, noticing that her guest's glass was still full.

"I am not much of a wine-drinker," replied he, "and besides, I never take wine by itself—I should be obliged if you would have some water brought."

Reine smiled, and passed him the water-bottle.

"Indeed?" she said, "in that case, you have not fallen among congenial spirits, for in these mountains they like good dinners, and have a special weakness for Burgundy. You follow the chase, at any rate?"

"No, Mademoiselle, I do not know how to handle a gun!"

"I suppose it is not your intention to settle in Vivey?"

"Why not?" replied he; "on the contrary, I intend to inhabit the château, and establish myself there definitely."

"What!" exclaimed Reine, laughing, "you neither drink nor hunt, and you intend to live in our woods! Why, my poor Monsieur, you will die of *ennui*."

"I shall have my books for companions; besides, solitude never has had any terrors for me."

The young girl shook her head incredulously.

"I shouldn't wonder," she continued, "if you do not even play at cards."

"Never; games of chance are repugnant to me."

"Take notice that I do not blame you," she replied, gayly, "but I must give you one piece of advice: don't speak in these neighborhoods of your dislike of hunting, cards, or good wine; our country folk would feel pity for you, and that would destroy your prestige."

Julien gazed at her with astonishment. She turned away to give directions to La Guite about the beds for her guests—then the supper went on silently. As soon as they had swallowed their last mouthful, the menservants repaired to their dormitory, situated in the buildings of the ancient forge. Reine Vincart rose also.

"This is the time when I put my father to bed—I am obliged to take leave of you, Monsieur de Buxières. Guitiote will conduct you to your room. For you, driver, I have had a bed made in a small room next to the furnace; you will be nice and warm. Good-night, gentlemen, sleep well!"

She turned away, and went to rejoin the paralytic sufferer, who, as she approached, manifested his joy by a succession of inarticulate sounds.

The room to which Guitiote conducted Julien was on the first floor, and had a cheerful, hospitable appearance. The walls were whitewashed; the chairs, table, and bed were of polished oak; a good fire of logs crackled in the fireplace, and between the opening of the white window-curtains could be seen a slender silver crescent of moon gliding among the flitting clouds. The young man went at once to his bed; but notwithstanding the fatigues of the day, sleep did not come to him. Through the partition he could hear the clear, sonorous voice of Reine singing her father to sleep with one of the popular ballads of the country, and while turning and twisting in the homespun linen sheets, scented with orris-root, he could not help thinking of this young girl, so original in her ways, whose grace, energy, and frankness fascinated and shocked him at the same time. At last he dozed off; and when the morning stir awoke him, the sun was up and struggling through the foggy atmosphere.

The sky had cleared during the night; there had been a frost, and the meadows were powdered white. The leaves, just nipped with the frost, were dropping softly to the ground, and formed little green heaps at the base of the trees. Julien dressed himself hurriedly, and descended to the courtyard, where the first thing he saw was the cabriolet, which had been brought in the early morning and which one of the farm-boys was in the act of sousing with water in the hope of freeing the hood and wheels from the thick mud which covered them. When he entered the dining-room, brightened by the rosy rays of the morning sun, he found Reine Vincart there before him. She was dressed in a yellow striped woolen skirt, and a jacket of white flannel carelessly belted at the waist. Her dark chestnut hair, parted down the middle and twisted into a loose knot behind, lay in ripples round her smooth, open forehead.

"Good-morning, Monsieur de Buxières," said she, in her cordial tone, "did you sleep well? Yes? I am glad. You find me busy attending to household matters. My father is still in bed, and I am taking advantage of the fact to arrange his little corner. The doctor said he must not be put near the fire, so I have made a place for him here; he enjoys it immensely, and I arranged this nook to protect him from draughts."

And she showed him how she had put the big easy-chair, padded with cushions, in the bright sunlight which streamed through the window, and shielded by the screens, one on each side. She noticed that Julien was examining, with some curiosity, the uncouth pictures from Epinal, with which the screens were covered.

"This," she explained, "is my own invention. My father is a little weak in the head, but he understands a good many things, although he can not talk about them. He used to get weary of sitting still all day in his chair, so I lined the screens with these pictures in order that he might have something to amuse him. He is as pleased as a child with the bright colors, and I explain the subjects to him. I don't tell him much at a time, for fear of fatiguing him. We have got now to Pyramus and Thisbe, so that we shall have plenty to occupy us before we reach the end."

She caught a pitying look from her guest which seemed to say: "The poor man may not last long enough to reach the end." Doubtless she had the same fear, for her dark eyes suddenly glistened, she sighed, and remained for some moments without speaking.

In the mean time the magpie, which Julien had seen the day before, was hopping around its mistress, like a familiar spirit; it even had the audacity to peck at her hair and then fly away, repeating, in its cracked voice: "Reine, queen of the woods!"

"Why 'queen of the woods?'" asked Julien, coloring.

"Ah!" replied the young girl, "it is a nickname which the people around here give me, because I am so fond of the trees. I spend all the time I can in our woods, as much as I can spare from the work of the farm.

A WOODLAND QUEEN

Margot has often heard my father call me by that name; she remembers it, and is always repeating it."

"Do you like living in this wild country?"

"Very much. I was born here, and I like it."

"But you have not always lived here?"

"No; my mother, who had lived in the city, placed me at school in her own country, in Dijon. I received there the education of a young lady, though there is not much to show for it now. I stayed there six years; then my mother died, my father fell ill, and I came home."

"And did you not suffer from so sudden a change?"

"Not at all. You see I am really by nature a country girl. I wish you might not have more trouble than I had, in getting accustomed to your new way of living, in the château at Vivey. But," she added, going toward the fire, "I think they are harnessing the horse, and you must be hungry. Your driver has already primed himself with some toast and white wine. I will not offer you the same kind of breakfast. I will get you some coffee and cream."

He bent his head in acquiescence, and she brought him the coffee herself, helping him to milk and toasted bread. He drank rapidly the contents of the cup, nibbled at a slice of toast, and then, turning to his hostess, said, with a certain degree of embarrassment:

"There is nothing left for me to do, Mademoiselle, but to express my most heartfelt thanks for your kind hospitality. It is a good omen for me to meet with such cordiality on my arrival in an unknown part of the country. May I ask you one more question?" he continued, looking anxiously at her; "why do you think

4 [49]

it will be so difficult for me to get accustomed to the life they lead here?"

"Why?" replied she, shaking her head, "because, to speak frankly, Monsieur, you do not give me the idea of having much feeling for the country. You are not familiar with our ways; you will not be able to speak to the people in their language, and they will not understand yours—you will be, in their eyes, 'the city Monsieur,' whom they will mistrust and will try to circumvent. I should like to find that I am mistaken, but, at present, I have the idea that you will encounter difficulties down there of which you do not seem to have any anticipation——"

She was intercepted by the entrance of the driver, who was becoming impatient. The horse was in harness, and they were only waiting for M. de Buxières. Julien rose, and after awkwardly placing a piece of silver in the hand of La Guite, took leave of Reine Vincart, who accompanied him to the threshold.

"Thanks, once more, Mademoiselle," murmured he, "and *au revoir*, since we shall be neighbors."

He held out his hand timidly and she took it with frank cordiality. Julien got into the cabriolet beside the driver, who began at once to belabor vigorously his mulish animal.

"Good journey and good luck, Monsieur," cried Reine after him, and the vehicle sped joltingly away.

CHAPTER III

CONSCIENCE HIGHER THAN THE LAW

ON leaving La Thuilière, the driver took the straight line toward the pasture-lands of the Planche-au-Vacher.

According to the directions they had received from the people of the farm, they then followed a rocky road, which entailed considerable jolting for the travellers, but which led them without other difficulty to the bottom of a woody dell, where they were able to ford the stream. As soon as they had, with difficulty, ascended the opposite hill, the silvery fog that had surrounded them began to dissipate, and they distinguished a road close by, which led a winding course through the forest.

"Ah! now I see my way!" said the driver, "we have only to go straight on, and in twenty minutes we shall be at Vivey. This devil of a fog cuts into one's skin like a bunch of needles. With your permission, Monsieur de Buxières, and if it will not annoy you, I will light my pipe to warm myself."

Now that he knew he was conducting the proprietor of the château, he repented having treated him so cavalierly the day before; he became obsequious, and endeavored to gain the good-will of his fare by showing himself as loquacious as he had before been cross and sulky. But Julien de Buxières, too much occupied in observing the details of the country, or in ruminating over the impressions he had received during the morning, made but little response to his advances, and soon allowed the conversation to drop.

The sun's rays had by this time penetrated the misty atmosphere, and the white frost had changed to diamond drops, which hung tremblingly on the leafless branches. A gleam of sunshine showed the red tints of the beech-trees, and the bright golden hue of the poplars, and the forest burst upon Julien in all the splendor of its autumnal trappings. The pleasant remembrance of Reine Vincart's hospitality doubtless predisposed him to enjoy the charm of this sunshiny morning, for he became, perhaps for the first time in his life, suddenly alive to the beauty of this woodland scenery. By degrees, toward the left, the brushwood became less dense, and several gray buildings appeared scattered over the glistening prairie. Soon after appeared a park, surrounded by low, crumbling walls, then a group of smoky roofs, and finally, surmounting a massive clump of ash-trees, two round towers with tops shaped like extinguishers. The coachman pointed them out to the young man with the end of his whip.

"There is Vivey," said he, "and here is your property, Monsieur de Buxières."

Julien started, and, notwithstanding his alienation from worldly things, he could not repress a feeling of satisfaction when he reflected that, by legal right, he was about to become master of the woods, the fields, and the old homestead of which the many-pointed slate roofs gleamed in the distance. This satisfaction was mingled with intense curiosity, but it was also somewhat shadowed by a dim perspective of the technical details incumbent on his taking possession. No doubt he should be obliged, in the beginning, to make himself personally recognized, to show the workmen and servants of the château that the new owner was equal to the situation. Now, Julien was not, by nature, a man of action, and the delicately expressed fears of Reine Vincart made him uneasy in his mind. When the carriage, suddenly turning a corner, stopped in front of the gate of entrance, and he beheld, through the cast-iron railing, the long avenue of ash-trees, the grass-grown courtyard, the silent façade, his heart began to beat more rapidly, and his natural timidity again took possession of him.

"The gate is closed, and they don't seem to be expecting you," remarked the driver.

They dismounted. Noticing that the side door was half open, the coachman gave a vigorous pull on the chain attached to the bell. At the sound of the rusty clamor, a furious barking was heard from an adjoining outhouse, but no one inside the house seemed to take notice of the ringing.

"Come, let us get in all the same," said the coachman, giving another pull, and stealing a furtive look at his companion's disconcerted countenance.

He fastened his horse to the iron fence, and both passed through the side gate to the avenue, the dogs all the while continuing their uproar. Just as they reached the courtyard, the door opened and Manette Sèjournant appeared on the doorstep.

"Good-morning, gentlemen," said she, in a slow, drawling voice, "is it you who are making all this noise?"

The sight of this tall, burly woman, whose glance betokened both audacity and cunning, increased still more Julien's embarrassment. He advanced awkwardly, raised his hat and replied, almost as if to excuse himself:

"I beg pardon, Madame—I am the cousin and heir of the late Claude de Buxières. I have come to install myself in the château, and I had sent word of my intention to Monsieur Arbillot, the notary—I am surprised he did not notify you."

"Ah! it is you, Monsieur Julien de Buxières!" exclaimed Madame Séjournant, scrutinizing the newcomer with a mingling of curiosity and scornful surprise which completed the young man's discomfiture. "Monsieur Arbillot was here yesterday—he waited for you all day, and as you did not come, he went away at nightfall."

"I presume you were in my cousin's service?" said Julien, amiably, being desirous from the beginning to evince charitable consideration with regard to his relative's domestic affairs.

"Yes, Monsieur," replied Manette, with dignified sadness; "I attended poor Monsieur de Buxières twenty-six years, and can truly say I served him with devotion! But now I am only staying here in charge of the seals—I and my son Claudet. We have decided to leave as soon as the notary does not want us any more."

A WOODLAND QUEEN

"I regret to hear it, Madame," replied Julien, who was beginning to feel uncomfortable. "There must be other servants around—I should be obliged if you would have our carriage brought into the yard. And then, if you will kindly show us the way, we will go into the house, for I am desirous to feel myself at home—and my driver would not object to some refreshment."

"I will send the cowboy to open the gate," replied the housekeeper. "If you will walk this way, gentlemen, I will take you into the only room that can be used just now, on account of the seals on the property."

Passing in front of them, she directed her steps toward the kitchen, and made way for them to pass into the smoky room, where a small servant was making coffee over a clear charcoal fire. As the travellers entered, the manly form of Claudet Séjournant was outlined against the bright light of the window at his back.

"My son," said Manette, with a meaning side look, especially for his benefit, "here is Monsieur de Buxières, come to take possession of his inheritance."

The *grand chasserot* attempted a silent salutation, and then the young men took a rapid survey of each other.

Julien de Buxières was startled by the unexpected presence of so handsome a young fellow, robust, intelligent, and full of energy, whose large brown eyes gazed at him with a kind of surprised and pitying compassion which was very hard for Julien to bear. He turned uneasily away, making a lame excuse of ordering some wine for his coachman; and while Manette, with an air of martyrdom, brought a glass and a half-empty bottle,

[55]

Claudet continued his surprised and inquiring examination of the legal heir of Claude de Buxières.

The pale, slight youth, buttoned up in a close-fitting, long frock-coat, which gave him the look of a priest, looked so unlike any of the Buxières of the elder branch that it seemed quite excusable to hesitate about the relationship. Claudet maliciously took advantage of the fact, and began to interrogate his would-be deposer by pretending to doubt his identity."

"Are you certainly Monsieur Julien de Buxières?" asked he, surveying him suspiciously from head to foot.

"Do you take me for an impostor?" exclaimed the young man.

"I do not say that," returned Claudet, crossly, "but after all, you do not carry your name written on your face, and, by Jove! as guardian of the seals, I have some responsibility—I want information, that is all!"

Angry at having to submit to these inquiries in the presence of the coachman who had brought him from Langres, Julien completely lost control of his temper.

"Do you require me to show my papers?" he inquired, in a haughty, ironical tone of voice.

Manette, foreseeing a disturbance, hastened to interpose, in her hypocritical, honeyed voice:

"Leave off, Claudet, let Monsieur alone. He would not be here, would he, if he hadn't a right? As to asking him to prove his right, that is not our business —it belongs to the justice and the notary. You had better, my son, go over to Auberive, and ask the gentlemen to come to-morrow to raise the seals."

A WOODLAND QUEEN

At this moment, the cowboy, who had been sent to open the gate, entered the kitchen.

"The carriage is in the courtyard," said he, "and Monsieur's boxes are in the hall. Where shall I put them, Madame Séjournant?"

Julien's eyes wandered from Manette to the young boy, with an expression of intense annoyance and fatigue.

"Why, truly," said Manette, "as a matter of fact, there is only the room of our deceased master, where the seals have been released. Would Monsieur object to taking up his quarters there?"

"I am willing," muttered Julien; "have my luggage carried up there, and give orders for it to be made ready immediately."

The housekeeper gave a sign, and the boy and the servant disappeared.

"Madame," resumed Julien, turning toward Manette, "if I understand you right, I can no longer reckon upon your services to take care of my household. Could you send me some one to supply your place?"

"Oh! as to that matter," replied the housekeeper, still in her wheedling voice, "a day or two more or less! I am not so very particular, and I don't mind attending to the house as long as I remain. At what hour would you wish to dine, Monsieur?"

"At the hour most convenient for you," responded Julien, quickly, anxious to conciliate her; "you will serve my meals in my room."

As the driver had now finished his bottle, they left the room together.

[57]

As soon as the door was closed, Manette and her son exchanged sarcastic looks.

"He a Buxières!" growled Claudet. "He looks like a student priest in vacation."

"He is an *ecrigneule*," returned Manette, shrugging her shoulders.

Ecrigneule is a word of the Langrois dialect, signifying a puny, sickly, effeminate being. In the mouth of Madame Séjournant, this picturesque expression acquired a significant amount of scornful energy.

"And to think," sighed Claudet, twisting his hands angrily in his bushy hair, "that such a slip of a fellow is going to be master here!"

"Master?" repeated Manette, shaking her head, "we'll see about that! He does not know anything at all, and has not what is necessary for ordering about. In spite of his fighting-cock airs, he hasn't two farthings' worth of spunk—it would be easy enough to lead him by the nose. Do you see, Claudet, if we were to manage properly, instead of throwing the handle after the blade, we should be able before two weeks are over to have rain or sunshine here, just as we pleased. We must only have a little more policy."

"What do you mean by policy, mother?"

"I mean—letting things drag quietly on—not breaking all the windows at the first stroke. The lad is as dazed as a young bird that has fallen from its nest. What we have to do is to help him to get control of himself, and accustom him not to do without us. As soon as we have made ourselves necessary to him, he will be at our feet."

A WOODLAND QUEEN

"Would you wish me to become the servant of the man who has cheated me out of my inheritance?" protested Claudet, indignantly.

"His servant—no, indeed! but his companion—why not? And it would be so easy if you would only make up your mind to it, Claude. I tell you again, he is not ill-natured—he looks like a man who is up to his neck in devotion. When he once feels we are necessary to his comfort, and that some reliable person, like the curate, for example, were to whisper to him that you are the son of Claudet de Buxières, he would have scruples, and at last, half on his own account, and half for the sake of religion, he would begin to treat you like a relative."

"No;" said Claudet, firmly, "these tricky ways do not suit me. Monsieur Arbillot proposed yesterday that I should do what you advise. He even offered to inform this gentleman of my relationship to Claude de Buxières. I refused, and forbade the notary to open his mouth on the subject. What! should I play the part of a craven hound before this younger son whom my father detested, and beg for a portion of the inheritance? Thank you! I prefer to take myself out of the way at once!"

"You prefer to have your mother beg her bread at strangers' doors!" replied Manette, bitterly, shedding tears of rage.

"I have already told you, mother, that when one has a good pair of arms, and the inclination to use them, one has no need to beg one's bread. Enough said! I am going to Auberive to notify the justice and the notary."

ANDRÉ THEURIET

While Claudet was striding across the woods, the boy carried the luggage of the newly arrived traveller into the chamber on the first floor, and Zélie, the small servant, put the sheets on the bed, dusted the room, and lighted the fire. In a few minutes, Julien was alone in his new domicile, and began to open his boxes and valises. The chimney, which had not been used since the preceding winter, smoked unpleasantly, and the damp logs only blackened instead of burning. The boxes lay wide open, and the room of the deceased Claude de Buxières had the uncomfortable aspect of a place long uninhabited. Julien had seated himself in one of the large armchairs, covered in Utrecht velvet, and endeavored to rekindle the dying fire. He felt at loose ends and discouraged, and had no longer the courage to arrange his clothes in the open wardrobes, which stood open, emitting a strong odor of decaying mold.

The slight breath of joyous and renewed life which had animated him on leaving the Vincart farm, had suddenly evaporated. His anticipations collapsed in the face of these bristling realities, among which he felt his isolation more deeply than ever before. He recalled the cordiality of Reine's reception, and how she had spoken of the difficulties he should have to encounter. How little he had thought that her forebodings would come true the very same day! The recollection of the cheerful and hospitable interior of La Thuilière contrasted painfully with his cold, bare Vivey mansion, tenanted solely by hostile domestics. Who were these people—this Manette Séjournant with her treacherous smile, and this fellow Claudet, who had, at the very first, subjected him to such offensive questioning? Why did they seem so ill-disposed toward him? He felt as if he were completely enveloped in an atmosphere of contradiction and ill-will. He foresaw what an amount of quiet but steady opposition he should have to encounter from these subordinates, and he became alarmed at the prospect of having to display so much energy in order to establish his authority in the château. He, who had pictured to himself a calm and delightful solitude, wherein he could give himself up entirely to his studious and contemplative tastes. What a contrast to the reality!

Rousing himself at last, he proceeded mechanically to arrange his belongings in the room, formerly inhabited by his cousin de Buxières. He had hardly finished when Zélie made her appearance with some plates and a tablecloth, and began to lay the covers. Seeing the fire had gone out, the little servant uttered an exclamation of dismay.

"Oh!" cried she, "so the wood didn't flare!"

He gazed at her as if she were talking Hebrew, and it was at least a minute before he understood that by "flare" she meant kindle.

"Well, well!" she continued, "I'll go and fetch some splinters."

She returned in a few moments, with a basket filled with the large splinters thrown off by the woodchoppers in straightening the logs: she piled these up on the andirons, and then, applying her mouth vigorously to a long hollow tin tube, open at both ends, which she carried with her, soon succeeded in starting a steady flame.

"Look there!" said she, in a tone implying a certain degree of contempt for the "city Monsieur" who did not even know how to keep up a fire, "isn't that clever? Now I must lay the cloth."

While she went about her task, arranging the plates, the water-bottle, and glasses symmetrically around the table, Julien tried to engage her in conversation. But the little maiden, either because she had been cautioned beforehand, or because she did not very well comprehend M. de Buxières's somewhat literary style of French, would answer only in monosyllables, or else speak only in *patois*, so that Julien had to give up the idea of getting any information out of her. Certainly, Mademoiselle Vincart was right in saying that he did not know the language of these people.

He ate without appetite the breakfast on which Manette had employed all her culinary art, barely tasted the roast partridge, and to Zélie's great astonishment, mingled the old Burgundy wine with a large quantity of water.

"You will inform Madame Séjournant," said he to the girl, as he folded his napkin, "that I am not a great eater, and that one dish will suffice me in future."

He left her to clear away, and went out to look at the domain which he was to call his own. It did not take him very long. The twenty or thirty white houses, which constituted the village and lay sleeping in the wooded hollow like eggs in a nest, formed a curious circular line around the château. In a few minutes he had gone the whole length of it, and the few people he met gave him only a passing glance, in which curiosity seemed to have more share than any hospitable feeling. He entered the narrow church under the patronage of Our Lady; the gray light which entered through the moldy shutters showed a few scattered benches of oak, and the painted wooden altar. He knelt down and endeavored to collect his thoughts, but the rude surroundings of this rustic sanctuary did not tend to comfort his troubled spirit, and he became conscious of a sudden withering of all religious fervor. He turned and left the place, taking a path that led through the forest. It did not interest him more than the village; the woods spoke no language which his heart could understand; he could not distinguish an ash from an oak, and all the different plants were included by him under one general term of "weeds"; but he needed bodily fatigue and violent physical agitation to dissipate the overpowering feeling of discouragement that weighed down his spirits. He walked for several hours without seeing anything, nearly got lost, and did not reach home till after dark. Once more the little servant appeared with his meal, which he ate in an abstracted manner, without even asking whether he were eating veal or mutton; then he went immediately to bed, and fell into an uneasy sleep. And thus ended his first day.

The next morning, about nine o'clock, he was informed that the justice of the peace, the notary, and the clerk, were waiting for him below. He hastened down and found the three functionaries busy conferring in a low voice with Manette and Claudet. The conversation ceased suddenly upon his arrival, and during the embarrassing silence that followed, all eyes were directed toward Julien, who saluted the company and delivered to the justice the documents proving his identity, begging him to proceed without delay to the legal breaking of the seals. They accordingly began operations, and went through all the house without interruption, accompanied by Claudet, who stood stiff and sullen behind the justice, taking advantage of every little opportunity to testify his dislike and ill-feeling toward the legal heir of Claude de Buxières. Toward eleven o'clock, the proceedings came to an end, the papers were signed, and Julien was regularly invested with his rights. But the tiresome formalities were not yet over: he had to invite the three officials to breakfast. This event, however, had been foreseen by Manette. Since early morning she had been busy preparing a bountiful repast, and had even called Julien de Buxières aside in order to instruct him in the hospitable duties which his position and the customs of society imposed upon him.

As they entered the dining-room, young de Buxières noticed that covers were laid for five people; he began to wonder who the fifth guest could be, when an accidental remark of the clerk showed him that the unknown was no other than Claudet. The fact was that Manette could not bear the idea that her son, who had always sat at table with the late Claude de Buxières, should be consigned to the kitchen in presence of these distinguished visitors from Auberive, and had deliberately laid a place for him at the master's table, hoping that the latter would not dare put any public affront upon Claudet. She was not mistaken in her idea. Julien, anxious to show a conciliatory spirit, and making an effort to quell his own repugnance, approached the *grand chasserot*, who was standing at one side by himself, and invited him to take his seat at the table.

"Thank you," replied Claudet, coldly, "I have breakfasted." So saying, he turned his back on M. de Buxières, who returned to the hall, vexed and disconcerted.

The repast was abundant, and seemed of interminable length to Julien. The three guests, whose appetites had been sharpened by their morning exercise, did honor to Madame Séjournant's cooking; they took their wine without water, and began gradually to thaw under the influence of their host's good Burgundy; evincing their increased liveliness by the exchange of heavy country witticisms, or relating noisy and interminable stories of their hunting adventures. Their conversation was very trying to Julien's nerves. Nevertheless, he endeavored to fulfil his duties as master of the house, throwing in a word now and then, so as to appear interested in their gossip, but he ate hardly a mouthful. His features had a pinched expression, and every now and then he caught himself trying to smother a yawn. His companions at the table could not understand a young man of twenty-eight years who drank nothing but water, scorned all enjoyment in eating, and only laughed forcedly under compulsion. At last, disturbed by the continued taciturnity of their host, they rose from the table sooner than their wont, and prepared to take leave. Before their departure, Arbillot the notary, passed his arm familiarly through that of Julien and led him into an adjoining room, which served as billiard-hall and library.

"Monsieur de Buxières," said he, pointing to a pile of law papers heaped upon the green cloth of the table; "see what I have prepared for you; you will find there all the titles and papers relating to the real estate, pictures, current notes, and various matters of your inheritance. You had better keep them under lock and key, and study them at your leisure. You will find them very interesting. I need hardly say," he added, "that I am at your service for any necessary advice or explanation. But, in respect to any minor details, you can apply to Claudet Séjournant, who is very intelligent in such matters, and a good man of business. And, by the way, Monsieur de Buxières, will you allow me to commend the young man especially to your kindly consideration——"

But Julien interrupted him with an imperious gesture, and replied, frowning angrily:

"If you please, Maître Arbillot, we will not enter upon that subject. I have already tried my best to show a kindly feeling toward Monsieur Claudet, but I have been only here twenty-four hours, and he has already found opportunities for affronting me twice. I beg you not to speak of him again."

The notary, who was just lighting his pipe, stopped suddenly. Moved by a feeling of good-fellowship for the *grand chasserot*, who had, however, enjoined him to silence, he had it on the tip of his tongue to inform Julien of the facts concerning the parentage of Claudet de Buxières; but, however much he wished to render Claudet a service, he was still more desirous of respecting the feelings of his client; so, between the hostility of one party and the backwardness of the other, he chose the wise part of inaction.

"That is sufficient, Monsieur de Buxières," replied he, "I will not press the matter."

Thereupon he saluted his client, and went to rejoin the justice and the clerk, and the three comrades wended their way to Auberive through the woods, discussing the incidents of the breakfast, and the peculiarities of the new proprietor.

"This de Buxières," said M. Destourbet, "does not at all resemble his deceased cousin Claude!"

"I can quite understand why the two families kept apart from each other," observed the notary, jocosely.

"Poor *chasserot!*" whined Seurrot the clerk, whom the wine had rendered tender-hearted; "he will not have a penny. I pity him with all my heart!"

As soon as the notary had departed, Julien came to the determination of transforming into a study the hall where he had been conferring with Maître Arbillot, which was dignified with the title of "library," although it contained at the most but a few hundred odd volumes. The hall was spacious, and lighted by two large windows opening on the garden; the floor was of oak, and there was a great fireplace where the largest logs used in a country in which the wood costs nothing could find ample room to blaze and crackle. It took the young man several days to make the necessary changes, and during that time he enjoyed a respite from the petty annoyances worked by the steady hostility of Manette Séjournant and her son. To the great indignation of the inhabitants of the château, he packed off the massive billiard-table, on which Claude de Buxières had so often played in company with his chosen friends, to the garret; after which the village carpenter was instructed to make the bookshelves ready for the reception of Julien's own books, which were soon to arrive by express. When he had got through with these labors, he turned his attention to the documents placed in his hands by the notary, endeavoring to find out by himself the nature of his revenues. He thought this would be a very easy matter, but he soon found that it was encumbered with inextricable difficulties.

A large part of the products of the domain consisted of lumber ready for sale. Claude de Buxières had been in the habit of superintending, either personally or through his intermediate agents, one half of the annual amount of lumber felled for market, the sale of which was arranged with the neighboring forge owners by mutual agreement; the other half was disposed of by notarial act. This latter arrangement was clear and comprehensible; the price of sale and the amounts falling due were both clearly indicated in the deed. But it was quite different with the bargains made by the owner himself, which were often credited by notes payable at sight, mostly worded in confused terms, unintelligible to any but the original writer. Julien became completely bewildered among these various documents, the explanations in which were harder to understand than conundrums. Although greatly averse to following the notary's advice as to seeking Claudet's assistance, he found himself compelled to do so, but was met by such laconic and surly answers that he concluded it would be

more dignified on his part to dispense with the services
of one who was so badly disposed toward him. He
therefore resolved to have recourse to the debtors themselves, whose names he found, after much difficulty, in
the books. These consisted mostly of peasants of the
neighborhood, who came to the château at his summons;
but as soon as they came into Julien's presence, they
discovered, with that cautious perception which is an
instinct with rustic minds, that before them stood a man
completely ignorant of the customs of the country, and
very poorly informed on Claude de Buxières's affairs.
They made no scruple of mystifying this "city gentleman," by means of ambiguous statements and cunning
reticence. The young man could get no enlightenment
from them; all he clearly understood was, that they were
making fun of him, and that he was not able to cope
with these country bumpkins, whose shrewdness would
have done honor to the most experienced lawyer.

After a few days he became discouraged and disgusted. He could see nothing but trouble ahead; he
seemed surrounded by either open enemies or people
inclined to take advantage of him. It was plain that all
the population of the village looked upon him as an
intruder, a troublesome master, a stranger whom they
would like to intimidate and send about his business.
Manette Séjournant, who was always talking about going, still remained in the château, and was evidently
exerting her influence to keep her son also with her.
The fawning duplicity of this woman was unbearable
to Julien; he had not the energy necessary either to
subdue her, or to send her away, and she appeared every

morning before him with a string of hypocritical griev-
ances, and opposing his orders with steady, irritating
inertia.   It seemed as if she were endeavoring to render
his life at Vivey hateful to him, so that he would be
compelled finally to beat a retreat.

One morning in November he had reached such a
state of moral fatigue and depression that, as he sat
listlessly before the library fire, the question arose in his
mind whether it would not be better to rent the château,
place the property in the hands of a manager, and take
himself and his belongings back to Nancy, to his little
room in the Rue Stanislaus, where, at any rate, he could
read, meditate, or make plans for the future without
being every moment tormented by miserable, petty
annoyances. His temper was becoming soured, his
nerves were unstrung, and his mind was so disturbed
that he fancied he had none but enemies around him.   A
cloudy melancholy seemed to invade his brain; he was
seized with a sudden fear that he was about to have an
attack of persecution-phobia, and began to feel his
pulse and interrogate his sensations to see whether he
could detect any of the premonitory symptoms.

While he was immersing himself in this unwholesome
atmosphere of hypochondria, the sound of a door opening and shutting made him start; he turned quickly
around, saw a young woman approaching and smiling
at him, and at last recognized Reine Vincart.

She wore the crimped linen cap and the monk's hood
in use among the peasants of the richer class. Her
wavy, brown hair, simply parted in front, fell in rebellious curls from under the border of her cap, of which

the only decoration was a bow of black ribbon; the end floating gracefully over her shoulders. The sharp November air had imparted a delicate rose tint to her pale complexion, and additional vivacity to her luminous, dark eyes.

"Good-morning, Monsieur de Buxières," said she, in her clear, pleasantly modulated voice; "I think you may remember me? It is not so long since we saw each other at the farm."

"Mademoiselle Vincart!" exclaimed Julien. "Why, certainly I remember you!"

He drew a chair toward the fire, and offered it to her. This charming apparition of his cordial hostess at La Thuilière evoked the one pleasant remembrance in his mind since his arrival in Vivey. It shot, like a ray of sunlight, across the heavy fog of despair which had enveloped the new master of the château. It was, therefore, with real sincerity that he repeated:

"I both know you and am delighted to see you. I ought to have called upon you before now, to thank you for your kind hospitality, but I have had so much to do, and," his face clouding over, "so many annoyances!"

"Really?" said she, softly, gazing pityingly at him; "you must not take offence, but, it is easy to see you have been worried! Your features are drawn and you have an anxious look. Is it that the air of Vivey does not agree with you?"

"It is not the air," replied Julien, in an irritated tone, "it is the people who do not agree with me. And, indeed," sighed he, "I do not think I agree any better with them. But I need not annoy other persons merely

[71]

because I am annoyed myself! Mademoiselle Vincart, what can I do to be of service to you? Have you anything to ask me?"

"Not at all!" exclaimed Reine, with a frank smile; "I not only have nothing to ask from you, but I have brought something for you—six hundred francs for wood we had bought from the late Monsieur de Buxières, during the sale of the Ronces forest." She drew from under her cloak a little bag of gray linen, containing gold, five-franc pieces and bank-notes. "Will you be good enough to verify the amount?" continued she, emptying the bag upon the table; "I think it is correct. You must have somewhere a memorandum of the transaction in writing."

Julien began to look through the papers, but he got bewildered with the number of rough notes jotted down on various slips of paper, until at last, in an impatient fit of vexation, he flung the whole bundle away, scattering the loose sheets all over the floor.

"Who can find anything in such a chaos?" he exclaimed. "I can't see my way through it, and when I try to get information from the people here, they seem to have an understanding among themselves to leave me under a wrong impression, or even to make my uncertainties still greater! Ah! Mademoiselle Reine, you were right! I do not understand the ways of your country folk. Every now and then I am tempted to leave everything just as it stands, and get away from this village, where the people mistrust me and treat me like an enemy!"

Reine gazed at him with a look of compassionate

surprise. Stooping quietly down, she picked up the scattered papers, and while putting them in order on the table, she happened to see the one relating to her own business.

"Here, Monsieur de Buxières," said she, "here is the very note you were looking for. You seem to be somewhat impatient. Our country folk are not so bad as you think; only they do not yield easily to new influences. The beginning is always difficult for them. I know something about it myself. When I returned from Dijon to take charge of the affairs at La Thuilière, I had no more experience than you, Monsieur, and I had great difficulty in accomplishing anything. Where should we be now, if I had suffered myself to be discouraged, like you, at the very outset?"

Julien raised his eyes toward the speaker, coloring with embarrassment to hear himself lectured by this young peasant girl, whose ideas, however, had much more virility than his own.

"You reason like a man, Mademoiselle Vincart," remarked he, admiringly, "pray, how old are you?"

"Twenty-two years; and you, Monsieur de Buxières?"

"I shall soon be twenty-eight."

"There is not much difference between us; still, you are the older, and what I have done, you can do also."

"Oh!" sighed he, "you have a love of action. I have a love of repose—I do not like to act."

"So much the worse!" replied Reine, very decidedly. "A man ought to show more energy. Come now, Monsieur de Buxières, will you allow me to speak frankly to you? If you wish people to come to you, you must first get out of yourself and go to seek them; if you expect your neighbor to show confidence and good-will toward you, you must be open and good-natured toward him."

"That plan has not yet succeeded with two persons around here," replied Julien, shaking his head.

"Which persons?"

"The Séjournants, mother and son. I tried to be pleasant with Claudet, and received from both only rebuffs and insolence."

"Oh! as to Claudet," resumed she, impulsively, "he is excusable. You can not expect he will be very gracious in his reception of the person who has supplanted him——"

"Supplanted?—I do not understand."

"What!" exclaimed Reine, "have they not told you anything, then? That is wrong. Well, at the risk of meddling in what does not concern me, I think it is better to put you in possession of the facts: Your deceased cousin never was married, but he had a child all the same—Claudet is his son, and he intended that he should be his heir also. Every one around the country knows that, for Monsieur de Buxières made no secret of it——"

"Claudet, the son of Claude de Buxières?" ejaculated Julien, with amazement.

"Yes; and if the deceased had had the time to make his will, you would not be here now. But," added the young girl, coloring, "don't tell Claudet I have spoken to you about it. I have been talking here too long.

A WOODLAND QUEEN

Monsieur de Buxières, will you have the goodness to reckon up your money and give me a receipt?"

She had risen, and Julien gazed wonderingly at the pretty country girl who had shown herself so sensible, so resolute, and so sincere. He bent his head, collected the money on the table, scribbled hastily a receipt and handed it to Reine.

"Thank you, Mademoiselle," said he, "you are the first person who has been frank with me, and I am grateful to you for it."

"*Au revoir*, Monsieur de Buxières."

She had already gained the door while he made an awkward attempt to follow her. She turned toward him with a smile on her lips and in her eyes.

"Come, take courage!" she added, and then vanished.

Julien went back dreamily, and sat down again before the hearth. The revelation made by Reine Vincart had completely astounded him. Such was his happy inexperience of life, that he had not for a moment suspected the real position of Manette and her son at the château. And it was this young girl who had opened his eyes to the fact! He experienced a certain degree of humiliation in having had so little perception. Now that Reine's explanation enabled him to view the matter from a different standpoint, he found Claudet's attitude toward him both intelligible and excusable. In fact, the lad was acting in accordance with a very legitimate feeling of mingled pride and anger. After all, he really was Claude de Buxières's son—a natural son, certainly, but one who had been implicitly acknowledged both in private and in public by his father. If the latter had

had time to draw up the incomplete will which had been found, he would, to all appearances, have made Claudet his heir.   Therefore, the fortune of which Julien had become possessed, he owed to some unexpected occurrence, a mere chance.   Public opinion throughout the entire village tacitly recognized and accepted the *grand chasserot* as son of the deceased, and if this recognition had been made legally, he would have been rightful owner of half the property.

"Now that I have been made acquainted with this position of affairs, what is my duty?" asked Julien of himself.   Devout in feeling and in practice, he was also very scrupulous in all matters of conscience, and the reply was not long in coming: that both religion and uprightness commanded him to indemnify Claudet for the wrong caused to him by the carelessness of Claude de Buxières.   Reine had simply told him the facts without attempting to give him any advice, but it was evident that, according to her loyal and energetic way of thinking, there was injustice to be repaired.   Julien was conscious that by acting to that effect he would certainly gain the esteem and approbation of his amiable hostess of La Thuilière, and he felt a secret satisfaction in the idea.   He rose suddenly, and, leaving the library, went to the kitchen, where Manette Séjournant was busy preparing the breakfast.

"Where is your son?" said he.   "I wish to speak with him."

Manette looked inquiringly at him.

"My son," she replied, "is in the garden, fixing up a box to take away his little belongings in—he doesn't want to stay any longer at other peoples' expense. And, by the way, Monsieur de Buxières, have the goodness to provide yourself with a servant to take my place; we shall not finish the week here."

Without making any reply, Julien went out by the door, leading to the garden, and discovered Claudet really occupied in putting together the sides of a packing-case. Although the latter saw the heir of the de Buxières family approaching, he continued driving in the nails without appearing to notice his presence.

"Monsieur Claudet," said Julien, "can you spare me a few minutes? I should like to talk to you."

Claudet raised his head, hesitated for a moment, then, throwing away his hammer and putting on his loose jacket, muttered:

"I am at your service."

They left the outhouse together, and entered an avenue of leafy lime-trees, which skirted the banks of the stream.

"Monsieur," said Julien, stopping in the middle of the walk, "excuse me if I venture on a delicate subject —but I must do so—now that I know all."

"Beg pardon—what do you know?" demanded Claudet, reddening.

"I know that you are the son of my cousin de Buxières," replied the young man with considerable emotion.

The *grand chasserot* knitted his brows.

"Ah!" said he, bitterly, "my mother's tongue has been too long, or else that blind magpie of a notary has been gossiping, notwithstanding my instructions."

"No; neither your mother nor Maître Arbillot has been speaking to me. What I know I have learned from a stranger, and I know also that you would be master here if Claude de Buxières had taken the precaution to write out his will. His negligence on that point has been a wrong to you, which it is my duty to repair."

"What's that!" exclaimed Claudet. Then he muttered between his teeth: "You owe me nothing. The law is on your side."

"I am not in the habit of consulting the law when it is a question of duty. Besides, Monsieur de Buxières treated you openly as his son; if he had done what he ought, made a legal acknowledgment, you would have the right, even in default of a will, to one half of his patrimony. This half I come to offer to you, and beg of you to accept it."

Claudet was astonished, and opened his great, fierce brown eyes with amazement. The proposal seemed so incredible that he thought he must be dreaming, and mistrusted what he heard.

"What! You offer me half the inheritance?" faltered he.

"Yes; and I am ready to give you a certified deed of relinquishment as soon as you wish——"

Claudet interrupted him with a violent shrug of the shoulders.

"I make but one condition," pursued Julien.

"What is it?" asked Claudet, still on the defensive.

"That you will continue to live here, with me, as in your father's time."

Claudet was nearly overcome by this last suggestion, but a lingering feeling of doubt and a kind of innate pride prevented him from giving way, and arrested the expression of gratitude upon his lips.

"What you propose is very generous, Monsieur," said he, "but you have not thought much about it, and later you might regret it. If I were to stay here, I should be a restraint upon you——"

"On the contrary, you would be rendering me a service, for I feel myself incapable of managing the property," replied Julien, earnestly. Then, becoming more confidential as his conscience was relieved of its burden, he continued, pleasantly: "You see I am not vain about admitting the fact. Come, cousin, don't be more proud than I am. Accept freely what I offer with hearty good-will!"

As he concluded these words, he felt his hand seized, and affectionately pressed in a strong, robust grip.

"You are a true de Buxières!" exclaimed Claudet, choking with emotion. "I accept—thanks—but, what have I to give you in exchange?—nothing but my friendship; but that will be as firm as my grip, and will last all my life."

CHAPTER IV

WINTER had come, and with it all the inclement accompaniments usual in this bleak and bitter mountainous country: icy rains, which, mingled with sleet, washed away whirlpools of withered leaves that the swollen streams tossed noisily into the ravines; sharp, cutting winds from the north, bleak frosts hardening the earth and vitrifying the cascades; abundant falls of snow, lasting sometimes an entire week. The roads had become impassable. A thick, white crust covered alike the pasture-lands, the stony levels, and the wooded slopes, where the branches creaked under the weight of their snowy burdens. A profound silence encircled the village, which seemed buried under the successive layers of snowdrifts. Only here and there, occasionally, did a thin line of blue smoke, rising from one of the white roofs, give evidence of any latent life among the inhabitants. The Château de Buxières stood in the midst of a vast carpet of snow on which the sabots of the villagers had outlined a narrow path, leading from the outer steps to the iron gate. Inside, fires blazed on all the hearths, which, however, did not modify the frigid atmosphere of the rudely-built upper rooms.

Julien de Buxières was freezing, both physically and morally, in his abode. His generous conduct toward Claudet had, in truth, gained him the affection of the *grand chasserot*, made Manette as gentle as a lamb, and caused a revulsion of feeling in his favor throughout the village; but, although his material surroundings had become more congenial, he still felt around him the chill of intellectual solitude. The days also seemed longer since Claudet had taken upon himself the management of all details. Julien found that re-reading his favorite books was not sufficient occupation for the weary hours that dragged slowly along between the rising and the setting of the sun. The gossipings of Manette, the hunting stories of Claudet had no interest for young de Buxières, and the acquaintances he endeavored to make outside left only a depressing feeling of *ennui* and disenchantment.

His first visit had been made to the curé of Vivey, where he hoped to meet with some intellectual resources, and a tone of conversation more in harmony with his tastes. In this expectation, also, he had been disappointed. The Abbé Pernot was an amiable quinquagenarian, and a *bon vivant*, whose mind inclined more naturally toward the duties of daily life than toward meditation or contemplative studies. The ideal did not worry him in the least; and when he had said his mass, read his breviary, confessed the devout sinners and visited the sick, he gave the rest of his time to profane but respectable amusements. He was of robust

6   [81]

temperament, with a tendency to corpulency, which he fought against by taking considerable exercise; his face was round and good-natured, his calm gray eyes reflected the tranquillity and uprightness of his soul, and his genial nature was shown in his full smiling mouth, his thick, wavy, gray hair, and his quick and cordial gestures.

When Julien was ushered into the presbytery, he found the curé installed in a small room, which he used for working in, and which was littered up with articles bearing a very distant connection to his pious calling: nets for catching larks, hoops and other nets for fishing, stuffed birds, and a collection of coleopteræ. At the other end of the room stood a dusty bookcase, containing about a hundred volumes, which seemed to have been seldom consulted. The Abbé, sitting on a low chair in the chimney-corner, his cossack raised to his knees, was busy melting glue in an old earthen pot.

"Aha, good-day! Monsieur de Buxières," said he in his rich, jovial voice, "you have caught me in an occupation not very canonical; but what of it? As Saint James says: 'The bow can not be always bent.' I am preparing some lime-twigs, which I shall place in the Bois des Ronces as soon as the snow is melted. I am not only a fisher of souls, but I endeavor also to catch birds in my net, not so much for the purpose of varying my diet, as of enriching my collection!"

"You have a great deal of spare time on your hands, then?" inquired Julien, with some surprise.

"Well, yes—yes—quite a good deal. The parish is not very extensive, as you have doubtless noticed; my parishioners are in the best possible health, thank God! and they live to be very old. I have barely two or three marriages in a year, and as many burials, so that, you see, one must fill up one's time somehow to escape the sin of idleness. Every man must have a hobby. Mine is ornithology; and yours, Monsieur de Buxières?"

Julien was tempted to reply: "Mine, for the moment, is *ennui*." He was just in the mood to unburden himself to the curé as to the mental thirst that was drying up his faculties, but a certain instinct warned him that the Abbé was not a man to comprehend the subtle complexities of his psychological condition, so he contented himself with replying, briefly:

"I read a great deal. I have, over there in the château, a pretty fair collection of historical and religious works, and they are at your service, Monsieur le Curé!"

"A thousand thanks," replied the Abbé Pernot, making a slight grimace; "I am not much of a reader, and my little stock is sufficient for my needs. You remember what is said in the *Imitation: 'Si scires totam Bibliam exterius et omnium philosophorum dicta, quid totum prodesset sine caritate Dei et gratia?'* Besides, it gives me a headache to read too steadily. I require exercise in the open air. Do you hunt or fish, Monsieur de Buxières?"

"Neither the one nor the other."

"So much the worse for you. You will find the time hang very heavily on your hands in this country, where there are so few sources of amusement. But never fear! You can not be always reading, and when the fine weather comes you will yield to the temptation; all the more likely because you have Claudet Séjournant with you. A jolly fellow he is; there is not one like him for killing a snipe or sticking a trout! Our trout here on the Aubette, Monsieur de Buxières, are excellent— of the salmon kind, and very meaty."

Then came an interval of silence. The Abbé began to suspect that this conversation was not one of profound interest to his visitor, and he resumed:

"Speaking of Claudet, Monsieur, allow me to offer you my congratulations. You have acted in a most Christianlike and equitable manner, in making amends for the inconceivable negligence of the deceased Claude de Buxières. Then, on the other hand, Claudet deserves what you have done for him. He is a good fellow, a little too quick-tempered and violent perhaps, but he has a heart of gold. Ah! it would have been no use for the deceased to deny it—the blood of de Buxières runs in his veins!"

"If public rumor is to be believed," said Julien timidly, rising to go, "my deceased cousin Claude was very much addicted to profane pleasures."

"Yes, yes, indeed!" sighed the Abbé, "he was a devil incarnate—but what a magnificent man! What a wonderful huntsman! Notwithstanding his backslidings, there was a great deal of good in him, and I am fain to believe that God has taken him under His protecting mercy."

Julien took his leave, and returned to the château, very much discouraged. "This priest," thought he to himself, "is a man of expediency. He allows himself certain indulgences which are to be regretted, and his mind is becoming clogged by continual association with carnal-minded men. His thoughts are too much given to earthly things, and I have no more faith in him than in the rest of them."

So he shut himself up again in his solitude, with one more illusion destroyed. He asked himself, and his heart became heavy at the thought, whether, in course of time, he also would undergo this stultification, this moral depression, which ends by lowering us to the level of the low-minded people among whom we live.

Among all the persons he had met since his arrival at Vivey, only one had impressed him as being sympathetic and attractive: Reine Vincart—and even her energy was directed toward matters that Julien looked upon as secondary. And besides, Reine was a woman, and he was afraid of women. He believed with Ecclesiastes the preacher, that "they are more bitter than death . . . and whoso pleaseth God shall escape from them." He had therefore no other refuge but in his books or his own sullen reflections, and, consequently, his old enemy, hypochondria, again made him its prey.

Toward the beginning of January, the snow in the valley had somewhat melted, and a light frost made access to the woods possible. As the hunting season seldom extended beyond the first days of February, the huntsmen were all eager to take advantage of the few remaining weeks to enjoy their favorite pastime. Every day the forest resounded with the shouts of beaters-up and the barking of the hounds. From Auberive, Praslay and Grancey, rendezvous were made in the woods of Charbonnière or Maigrefontaine; nothing was thought of but the exploits of certain marksmen, the number of pieces bagged, and the joyous outdoor breakfasts which preceded each occasion. One evening, as Julien, more moody than usual, stood yawning wearily and leaning on the corner of the stove, Claudet noticed him, and was touched with pity for this young fellow, who had so little idea how to employ his time, his youth, or his money. He felt impelled, as a conscientious duty, to draw him out of his unwholesome state of mind, and initiate him into the pleasures of country life.

"You do not enjoy yourself with us, Monsieur Julien," said he, kindly; "I can't bear to see you so downhearted. You are ruining yourself with poring all day long over your books, and the worst of it is, they do not take the frowns out of your face. Take my word for it, you must change your way of living, or you will be ill. Come, now, if you will trust in me, I will undertake to cure your *ennui* before a week is over."

"And what is your remedy, Claudet?" demanded Julien, with a forced smile.

"A very simple one: just let your books go, since they do not succeed in interesting you, and live the life that every one else leads. The de Buxières, your ancestors, followed the same plan, and had no fault to find with it. You are in a wolf country—well, you must howl with the wolves!"

"My dear fellow," replied Julien, shaking his head, "one can not remake one's self. The wolves themselves would discover that I howled out of tune, and would send me back to my books."

"Nonsense! try, at any rate. You can not imagine

what pleasure there is in coursing through the woods, and suddenly, at a sharp turn, catching sight of a deer in the distance, then galloping to the spot where he must pass, and holding him with the end of your gun! You have no idea what an appetite one gets with such exercise, nor how jolly it is to breakfast afterward, all together, seated round some favorite old beech-tree. Enjoy your youth while you have it. Time enough to stay in your chimney-corner and spit in the ashes when rheumatism has got hold of you. Perhaps you will say you never have followed the hounds, and do not know how to handle a gun?"

"That is the exact truth."

"Possibly, but appetite comes with eating, and when once you have tasted of the pleasures of the chase, you will want to imitate your companions. Now, see here: we have organized a party at Charbonnière to-morrow, for the gentlemen of Auberive; there will be some people you know—Destourbet, Justice of the Peace, the clerk Seurrot, Maître Arbillot and the tax-collector, Boucheseiche. Hutinet went over the ground yesterday, and has appointed the meeting for ten o'clock at the Belle-Etoile. Come with us; there will be good eating and merriment, and also some fine shooting, I pledge you my word!"

Julien refused at first, but Claudet insisted, and showed him the necessity of getting more intimately acquainted with the notables of Auberive—people with whom he would be continually coming in contact as representing the administration of justice and various affairs in the canton. He urged so well that young de

Buxières ended by giving his consent. Manette received immediate instructions to prepare eatables for Hutinet, the keeper, to take at early dawn to the Belle-Etoile, and it was decided that the company should start at precisely eight o'clock.

The next morning, at the hour indicated, the *grand chasserot* was already in the courtyard with his two hounds, Charbonneau and Montagnard, who were leaping and barking sonorously around him. Julien, reminded of his promise by the unusual early uproar, dressed himself with a bad grace, and went down to join Claudet, who was bristling with impatience. They started. There had been a sharp frost during the night; some hail had fallen, and the roads were thinly coated with a white dust, called by the country people, in their picturesque language, "a sugar-frost" of snow. A thick fog hung over the forest, so that they had to guess their way; but Claudet knew every turn and every side-path, and thus he and his companion arrived by the most direct line at the rendezvous. They soon began to hear the barking of the dogs, to which Montagnard and Charbonneau replied with emulative alacrity, and finally, through the mist, they distinguished the group of huntsmen from Auberive.

The Belle-Etoile was a circular spot, surrounded by ancient ash-trees, and formed the central point for six diverging alleys which stretched out indefinitely into the forest. The monks of Auberive, at the epoch when they were the lords and owners of the land, had made this place a rendezvous for huntsmen, and had provided a table and some stone benches, which, thirty years ago, were still in existence. The enclosure, which had been chosen for the breakfast on the present occasion, was irradiated by a huge log-fire; a very respectable display of bottles, bread, and various eatables covered the stone table, and the dogs, attached by couples to posts, pulled at their leashes and barked in chorus, while their masters, grouped around the fire, warmed their benumbed fingers over the flames, and tapped their heels while waiting for the last-comers.

At sight of Julien and Claudet, there was a joyous hurrah of welcome. Justice Destourbet exchanged a ceremonious hand-shake with the new proprietor of the château. The scant costume and tight gaiters of the huntsman's attire, displayed more than ever the height and slimness of the country magistrate. By his side, the registrar Seurrot, his legs encased in blue linen spatterdashes, his back bent, his hands crossed comfortably over his "corporation," sat roasting himself at the flame, while grumbling when the wind blew the smoke in his eyes. Arbillot, the notary, as agile and restless as a lizard, kept going from one to the other with an air of mysterious importance. He came up to Claudet, drew him aside, and showed him a little figure in a case.

"Look here!" whispered he, "we shall have some fun; as I passed by the Abbé Pernot's this morning, I stole one of his stuffed squirrels."

He stooped down, and with an air of great mystery poured into his ear the rest of the communication, at the close of which his small black eyes twinkled maliciously, and he passed the end of his tongue over his frozen moustache.

"Come with me," continued he; "it will be a good joke on the collector."

He drew Claudet and Hutinet toward one of the trenches, where the fog hid them from sight.

During this colloquy, Boucheseiche the collector, against whom they were thus plotting, had seized upon Julien de Buxières, and was putting him through a course of hunting lore. Justin Boucheseiche was a man of remarkable ugliness; big, bony, freckled, with red hair, hairy hands, and a loud, rough voice.

He wore a perfectly new hunting costume, cap and gaiters of leather, a havana-colored waistcoat, and had a complete assortment of pockets of all sizes for the cartridges. He pretended to be a great authority on all matters relating to the chase, although he was, in fact, the worst shot in the whole canton; and when he had the good luck to meet with a newcomer, he launched forth on the recital of his imaginary prowess, without any pity for the hearer. So that, having once got hold of Julien, he kept by his side when they sat down to breakfast.

All these country huntsmen were blessed with healthy appetites. They ate heartily, and drank in the same fashion, especially the collector Boucheseiche, who justified his name by pouring out numerous bumpers of white wine. During the first quarter of an hour nothing could be heard but the noise of jaws masticating, glasses and forks clinking; but when the savory pastries, the cold game and the hams had disappeared, and had been replaced by goblets of hot Burgundy and boiling coffee, then tongues became loosened. Julien, to his infinite disgust, was forced again to be present at a conversation similar to the one at the time of the raising of the seals, the coarseness of which had so astonished and shocked him. After the anecdotes of the chase were exhausted, the guests began to relate their experiences among the fair sex, losing nothing of the point from the effect of the numerous empty bottles around. All the scandalous cases in the courts of justice, all the coarse jokes and adventures of the district, were related over again. Each tried to surpass his neighbor. To hear these men of position boast of their gallantries with all classes, one would have thought that the entire canton underwent periodical changes and became one vast Saturnalia, where rustic satyrs courted their favorite nymphs. But nothing came of it, after all; once the feast was digested, and they had returned to the conjugal abode, all these terrible gay Lotharios became once more chaste and worthy fathers of families. Nevertheless, Julien, who was unaccustomed to such bibulous festivals and such unbridled license of language, took it all literally, and reproached himself more than ever with having yielded to Claudet's entreaties.

At last the table was deserted, and the marking of the limits of the hunt began.

As they were following the course of the trenches, the notary stopped suddenly at the foot of an ash-tree, and took the arm of the collector, who was gently humming out of tune.

"Hush! Collector," he whispered, "do you see that fellow up there, on the fork of the tree? He seems to be jeering at us."

At the same time he pointed out a squirrel, sitting perched upon a branch, about halfway up the tree. The animal's tail stood up behind like a plume, his ears were upright, and he had his front paws in his mouth, as if cracking a nut.

"A squirrel!" cried the impetuous Boucheseiche, immediately falling into the snare; "let no one touch him, gentlemen—I will settle his account for him."

The rest of the hunters had drawn back in a circle, and were exchanging sly glances. The collector loaded his gun, shouldered it, covered the squirrel, and then let go.

"Hit!" exclaimed he, triumphantly, as soon as the smoke had dispersed.

In fact, the animal had slid down the branch, head first, but, somehow, he did not fall to the ground.

"He has caught hold of something," said the notary, facetiously.

"Ah! you will hold on, you rascal, will you?" shouted Boucheseiche, beside himself with excitement, and the next moment he sent a second shot, which sent the hair flying in all directions.

The creature remained in the same position. Then there was a general roar.

"He is quite obstinate!" remarked the clerk, slyly.

Boucheseiche, astonished, looked attentively at the tree, then at the laughing crowd, and could not understand the situation.

"If I were in your place, Collector," said Claudet, in an insinuating manner, "I should climb up there, to see——"

But Justin Boucheseiche was not a climber. He called a youngster, who followed the hunt as beater-up.

"I will give you ten sous," said he; "to mount that tree and bring me my squirrel!"

The young imp did not need to be told twice. In the twinkling of an eye he threw his arms around the tree, and reached the fork. When there, he uttered an exclamation.

"Well?" cried the collector, impatiently, "throw him down!"

"I can't, Monsieur," replied the boy, "the squirrel is fastened by a wire." Then the laughter burst forth more boisterously than before.

"A wire, you young rascal! Are you making fun of me?" shouted Boucheseiche; "come down this moment!"

"Here he is, Monsieur," replied the lad, throwing himself down with the squirrel which he tossed at the collector's feet.

When Boucheseiche verified the fact that the squirrel was a stuffed specimen, he gave a resounding oath.

"In the name of—! who is the miscreant that has perpetrated this joke?"

No one could reply for laughing. Then ironical cheers burst forth from all sides.

"Brave Boucheseiche! That's a kind of game one doesn't often get hold of!"

"We never shall see any more of that kind!"

"Let us carry Boucheseiche in triumph!"

And so they went on, marching around the tree. Arbillot seized a slip of ivy and crowned Boucheseiche, while all the others clapped their hands and capered in front of the collector, who, at last, being a good fellow at heart, joined in the laugh at his own expense.

Julien de Buxières alone could not share the general hilarity. The uproar caused by this simple joke did not even chase the frown from his brow. He was provoked at not being able to bring himself within the diapason of this somewhat vulgar gayety: he was aware that his melancholy countenance, his black clothes, his want of sympathy jarred unpleasantly on the other jovial guests. He did not intend any longer to play the part of a kill-joy. Without saying anything to Claudet, therefore, he waited until the huntsmen had scattered in the brush-wood, and then, diving into a trench, in an opposite direction, he gave them all the slip, and turned in the direction of Planche-au-Vacher.

As he walked slowly, treading under foot the dry frosty leaves, he reflected how the monotonous crackling of this foliage, once so full of life, now withered and rendered brittle by the frost, seemed to represent his own deterioration of feeling. It was a sad and suitable accompaniment of his own gloomy thoughts.

He was deeply mortified at the sorry figure he had presented at the breakfast-table. He acknowledged sorrowfully to himself that, at twenty-eight years of age, he was less young and less really alive than all these country squires, although all, except Claudet, had passed their fortieth year. Having missed his season of childhood, was he also doomed to have no youth? Others found delight in the most ordinary amusements, why, to him, did life seem so insipid and colorless?

A WOODLAND QUEEN

Why was he so unfortunately constituted that all human joys lost their sweetness as soon as he opened his heart to them? Nothing made any powerful impression on him; everything that happened seemed to be a perpetual reiteration, a song sung for the hundredth time, a story a hundred times related.

He was like a new vase, cracked before it had served its use, and he felt thoroughly ashamed of the weakness and infirmity of his inner self. Thus pondering, he traversed much ground, hardly knowing where he was going. The fog, which now filled the air and which almost hid the trenches with its thin bluish veil, made it impossible to discover his bearings. At last he reached the border of some pasture-land, which he crossed, and then he perceived, not many steps away, some buildings with tiled roofs, which had something familiar to him in their aspect. After he had gone a few feet farther he recognized the court and façade of La Thuilière; and, as he looked over the outer wall, a sight altogether novel and unexpected presented itself.

Standing in the centre of the courtyard, her outline showing in dark relief against the light "sugar-frosting," stood Reine Vincart, her back turned to Julien. She held up a corner of her apron with one hand, and with the other took out handfuls of grain, which she scattered among the birds fluttering around her. At each moment the little band was augmented by a new arrival. All these little creatures were of species which do not emigrate, but pass the winter in the shelter of the wooded dells. There were blackbirds with yellow bills, who advanced boldly over the snow up to the very feet

[95]

of the distributing fairy; robin redbreasts, nearly as tame, hopping gayly over the stones, bobbing their heads and puffing out their red breasts; and tomtits, prudently watching awhile from the tops of neighboring trees, then suddenly taking flight, and with quick, sharp cries, seizing the grain on the wing. It was charming to see all these little hungry creatures career around Reine's head, with a joyous fluttering of wings. When the supply was exhausted, the young girl shook her apron, turned around, and recognized Julien.

"Were you there, Monsieur de Buxières?" she exclaimed; "come inside the courtyard! Don't be afraid; they have finished their meal. Those are my boarders," she added, pointing to the birds, which, one by one, were taking their flight across the fields. "Ever since the first fall of snow, I have been distributing grain to them once a day. I think they must tell one another under the trees there, for every day their number increases. But I don't complain of that. Just think, these are not birds of passage; they do not leave us at the first cold blast, to find a warmer climate; the least we can do is to recompense them by feeding them when the weather is too severe! Several know me already, and are very tame. There is a blackbird in particular, and a blue tomtit, that are both extremely saucy!"

These remarks were of a nature to please Julien. They went straight to the heart of the young mystic; they recalled to his mind St. Francis of Assisi, preaching to the fish and conversing with the birds, and he felt an increase of sympathy for this singular young girl. He would have liked to find a pretext for remaining longer with her, but his natural timidity in the presence of women paralyzed his tongue, and, already, fearing he should be thought intruding, he had raised his hat to take leave, when Reine addressed him:

"I do not ask you to come into the house, because I am obliged to go to the sale of the Ronces woods, in order to speak to the men who are cultivating the little lot that we have bought. I wager, Monsieur de Buxières, that you are not yet acquainted with our woods?"

"That is true," he replied, smiling.

"Very well, if you will accompany me, I will show you the canton they are about to develop. It will not be time lost, for it will be a good thing for the people who are working for you to know that you are interested in their labors."

Julien replied that he should be happy to be under her guidance.

"In that case," said Reine, "wait for me here. I shall be back in a moment."

She reappeared a few minutes later, wearing a white hood with a cape, and a knitted woolen shawl over her shoulders.

"This way!" said she, showing a path that led across the pasture-lands.

They walked along silently at first. The sky was clear, the wind had freshened. Suddenly, as if by enchantment, the fog, which had hung over the forest, became converted into needles of ice. Each tree was powdered over with frozen snow, and on the hillsides overshadowing the valley the massive tufts of forest were veiled in a bluish-white vapor.

7

Never had Julien de Buxières been so long in tête-à-tête with a young woman. The extreme solitude, the surrounding silence, rendered this dual promenade more intimate and also more embarrassing to a young man who was alarmed at the very thought of a female countenance. His ecclesiastical education had imbued Julien with very rigorous ideas as to the careful and reserved behavior which should be maintained between the sexes, and his intercourse with the world had been too infrequent for the idea to have been modified in any appreciable degree. It was natural, therefore, that this walk across the fields in the company of Reine should assume an exaggerated importance in his eyes. He felt himself troubled and yet happy in the chance afforded him to become more closely acquainted with this young girl, toward whom a secret sympathy drew him more and more. But he did not know how to begin conversation, and the more he cudgelled his brains to find a way of opening the attack, the more he found himself at sea. Once more Reine came to his assistance.

"Well, Monsieur de Buxières," said she, "do matters go more to your liking now? You have acted most generously toward Claudet, and he ought to be pleased."

"Has he spoken to you, then?"

"No; not himself, but good news, like bad, flies fast, and all the villagers are singing your praises."

"I only did a very simple and just thing," replied Julien.

"Precisely, but those are the very things that are the hardest to do. And according as they are done well or ill, so is the person that does them judged by others."

"You have thought favorably of me then, Mademoiselle Vincart," he ventured, with a timid smile.

"Yes; but my opinion is of little importance. You must be pleased with yourself—that is more essential. I am sure that it must be pleasanter now for you to live at Vivey?"

"Hm!—more bearable, certainly."

The conversation languished again. As they approached the confines of the farm they heard distant barking, and then the voices of human beings. Finally two gunshots broke on the air.

"Ha, ha!" exclaimed Reine, listening, "the Auberive Society is following the hounds, and Claudet must be one of the party. How is it you were not with them?"

"Claudet took me there, and I was at the breakfast—but, Mademoiselle, I confess that that kind of amusement is not very tempting to me. At the first opportunity I made my escape, and left the party to themselves."

"Well, now, to be frank with you, you were wrong. Those gentlemen will feel aggrieved, for they are very sensitive. You see, when one has to live with people, one must yield to their customs, and not pooh-pooh their amusements."

"You are saying exactly what Claudet said last night."

"Claudet was right."

"What am I to do? The chase has no meaning for me. I can not feel any interest in the butchery of miserable animals that are afterward sent back to their quarters."

ANDRÉ THEURIET

"I can understand that you do not care for the chase for its own sake; but the ride in the open air, in the open forest? Our forests are so beautiful—look there, now! does not that sight appeal to you?"

From the height they had now gained, they could see all over the valley, illuminated at intervals by the pale rays of the winter sun. Wherever its light touched the brushwood, the frosty leaves quivered like diamonds, while a milky cloud enveloped the parts left in shadow. Now and then, a slight breeze stirred the branches, causing a shower of sparkling atoms to rise in the air, like miniature rainbows. The entire forest seemed clothed in the pure, fairy-like robes of a virgin bride.

"Yes, that is beautiful," admitted Julien, hesitatingly; "I do not think I ever saw anything similar: at any rate, it is you who have caused me to notice it for the first time. But," continued he, "as the sun rises higher, all this phantasmagoria will melt and vanish. The beauty of created things lasts only a moment, and serves as a warning for us not to set our hearts on things that perish."

Reine gazed at him with astonishment.

"Do you really think so?" exclaimed she: "that is very sad, and I do not know enough to give an opinion. All I know is, that if God has created such beautiful things it is in order that we may enjoy them. And that is the reason why I worship these woods with all my heart. Ah! if you could only see them in the month of June, when the foliage is at its fulness. Flowers everywhere—yellow, blue, crimson! Music also everywhere—the song of birds, the murmuring of waters, and the balmy scents in the air. Then there are the lime-trees, the wild cherry, and the hedges red with strawberries—it is intoxicating. And, whatever you may say, Monsieur de Buxières, I assure you that the beauty of the forest is not a thing to be despised. Every season it is renewed: in autumn, when the wild fruits and tinted leaves contribute their wealth of color; in winter, with its vast carpets of snow, from which the tall ash springs to such a stately height—look, now! up there!"

They were in the depths of the forest. Before them were colonnades of slim, graceful trees, rising in one unbroken line toward the skies, their slender branches forming a dark network overhead, and their lofty proportions lessening in the distance, until lost in the solemn gloom beyond. A religious silence prevailed, broken only by the occasional chirp of the wren, or the soft pattering of some smaller four-footed race.

"How beautiful!" exclaimed Reine, with animation; "one might imagine one's self in a cathedral! Oh! how I love the forest; a feeling of awe and devotion comes over me, and makes me want to kneel down and pray!"

Julien looked at her with an uneasy kind of admiration. She was walking slowly now, grave and thoughtful, as if in church. Her white hood had fallen on her shoulders, and her hair, slightly stirred by the wind, floated like a dark aureole around her pale face. Her luminous eyes gleamed between the double fringes of her eyelids, and her mobile nostrils quivered with suppressed emotion. As she passed along, the brambles from the wayside, intermixed with ivy and other hardy plants, caught on the hem of her dress and formed a verdant train, giving her the appearance of the high-priestess of some mysterious temple of Nature. At this moment, she identified herself so perfectly with her nickname, "queen of the woods," that Julien, already powerfully affected by her peculiar and striking style of beauty, began to experience a superstitious dread of her influence. His Catholic scruples, or the remembrance of certain pious lectures administered in his childhood, rendered him distrustful, and he reproached himself for the interest he took in the conversation of this seductive creature. He recalled the legends of temptations to which the Evil One used to subject the anchorites of old, by causing to appear before them the attractive but illusive forms of the heathen deities. He wondered whether he were not becoming the sport of the same baleful influence; if, like the Lamias and Dryads of antiquity, this queen of the woods were not some spirit of the elements, incarnated in human form and sent to him for the purpose of dragging his soul down to perdition.

In this frame of mind he followed in her footsteps, cautiously, and at a distance, when she suddenly turned, as if waiting for him to rejoin her. He then perceived that they had reached the end of the copse, and before them lay an open space, on which the cut lumber lay in cords, forming dark heaps on the frosty ground. Here and there were allotments of chosen trees and poles, among which a thin spiral of smoke indicated the encampment of the cutters. Reine made straight for them, and immediately presented the new owner of the château to the workmen. They made their awkward obeisances, scrutinizing him in the mistrustful manner customary with the peasants of mountainous regions when they meet strangers. The master workman then turned to Reine, replying to her remarks in a respectful but familiar tone:

"Make yourself easy, mamselle, we shall do our best and rush things in order to get through with the work. Besides, if you will come this way with me, you will see that there is no idling; we are just now going to fell an oak, and before a quarter of an hour is over it will be lying on the ground, cut off as neatly as if with a razor."

They drew near the spot where the first strokes of the axe were already resounding. The giant tree did not seem affected by them, but remained haughty and immovable. Then the blows redoubled until the trunk began to tremble from the base to the summit, like a living thing. The steel had made the bark, the sapwood, and even the core of the tree, fly in shivers; but the oak had resumed its impassive attitude, and bore stoically the assaults of the workmen. Looking upward, as it reared its proud and stately head, one would have affirmed that it never could fall. Suddenly the woodsmen fell back; there was a moment of solemn and terrible suspense; then the enormous trunk heaved and plunged down among the brushwood with an alarming crash of breaking branches. A sound as of lamentation rumbled through the icy forest, and then all was still.

The men, with unconscious emotion, stood contemplating the monarch oak lying prostrate on the ground.

Reine had turned pale; her dark eyes glistened with tears.

"Let us go," murmured she to Julien; "this death of a tree affects me as if it were that of a Christian."

They took leave of the woodsmen, and reëntered the forest. Reine kept silence and her companion was at a loss to resume the conversation; so they journeyed along together quietly until they reached a border line, whence they could perceive the smoke from the roofs of Vivey.

"You have only to go straight down the hill to reach your home," said she, briefly; "*au revoir*, Monsieur de Buxières."

Thus they quitted each other, and, looking back, he saw that she slackened her speed and went dreamily on in the direction of Planche-au-Vacher.

CHAPTER V

IN the mountainous region of Langres, spring can hardly be said to appear before the end of May. Until that time the cold weather holds its own; the white frosts, and the sharp, sleety April showers, as well as the sudden windstorms due to the malign influence of the ice-gods, arrest vegetation, and only a few of the more hardy plants venture to put forth their trembling shoots until later. But, as June approaches and the earth becomes warmed through by the sun, a sudden metamorphosis is effected. Sometimes a single night is sufficient for the floral spring to burst forth in all its plenitude. The hedges are alive with lilies and woodruffs; the blue columbines shake their foolscap-like blossoms along the green side-paths; the milky spikes of the Virgin plant rise slender and tall among the bizarre and many-colored orchids. Mile after mile, the forest unwinds its fairy show of changing scenes. Sometimes one comes upon a spot of perfect verdure; at other times one wanders in almost complete darkness under the thick interlacing boughs of the ash-trees, through which occasional gleams of light fall on the dark soil or on the spreading ferns. Now the wanderer emerges upon an open space so full of sunshine that the strawberries are already ripening; near them are stacked the tender young trees, ready for spacing, and the billets of wood piled up and half covered with thistle and burdock leaves; and a little farther away, half hidden by tall weeds, teeming with insects, rises the peaked top of the woodsman's hut. Here one walks beside deep, grassy trenches, which appear to continue without end, along the forest level; farther, the wild mint and the centaurea perfume the shady nooks, the oaks and lime-trees arch their spreading branches, and the honeysuckle twines itself round the knotty shoots of the hornbeam, whence the thrush gives forth her joyous, sonorous notes.

Not only in the forest, but also in the park belonging to the château, and in the village orchards, spring had donned a holiday costume. Through the open windows, between the massive bunches of lilacs, hawthorn, and laburnum blossoms, Julien de Buxières caught glimpses of rolling meadows and softly tinted vistas. The gentle twittering of the birds and the mysterious call of the cuckoo, mingled with the perfume of flowers, stole into his study, and produced a sense of enjoyment as novel to him as it was delightful. Having until the present time lived a sedentary life in cities, he had had no opportunity of experiencing this impression of nature in her awakening and luxuriant aspect; never had he felt so completely under the seductive influence of the goddess Maïa than at this season when the abundant sap exudes in a white foam from the trunk of the willow; when between the plant world and ourselves a magnetic current seems to exist, which seeks to wed their fraternizing emanations with our own personality. He was oppressed by the vividness of the verdure, intoxicated with the odor of vegetation, agitated by the confused music of the birds, and in this May fever of excitement, his thoughts wandered with secret delight to Reine Vincart, to this queen of the woods, who was the personification of all the witchery of the forest. Since their January promenade in the glades of Charbonnière, he had seen her at a distance, sometimes on Sundays in the little church at Vivey, sometimes like a fugitive apparition at the turn of a road. They had also exchanged formal salutations, but had not spoken to each other. More than once, after the night had fallen, Julien had stopped in front of the courtyard of La Thuilière, and watched the lamps being lighted inside. But he had not ventured to knock at the door of the house; a foolish timidity had prevented him; so he had returned to the château, dissatisfied and reproaching himself for allowing his awkward shyness to interpose, as it were, a wall of ice between himself and the only person whose acquaintance seemed to him desirable.

At other times he would become alarmed at the large place a woman occupied in his thoughts, and he congratulated himself on having resisted the dangerous temptation of seeing Mademoiselle Vincart again. He acknowledged that this singular girl had for him an attraction against which he ought to be on his guard. Reine might be said to live alone at La Thuilière, for her father could hardly be regarded seriously as a protector. Julien's visits might have compromised her, and the young man's severe principles of rectitude forbade him to cause scandal which he could not repair. He was not thinking of marriage, and even had his thoughts inclined that way, the proprieties and usages of society which he had always in some degree respected, would not allow him to wed a peasant girl. It was evident, therefore, that both prudence and uprightness would enjoin him to carry on any future relations with Mademoiselle Vincart with the greatest possible reserve.

Nevertheless, and in spite of these sage reflections, the enchanting image of Reine haunted him more than was at all reasonable. Often, during his hours of watchfulness, he would see her threading the avenues of the forest, her dark hair half floating in the breeze, and wearing her white hood and her skirt bordered with ivy. Since the spring had returned, she had become associated in his mind with all the magical effects of nature's renewal. He discovered the liquid light of her dark eyes in the rippling darkness of the streams; the lilies recalled the faintly tinted paleness of her cheeks; the silène roses, scattered throughout the hedges, called forth the remembrance of the young maiden's rosy lips, and the vernal odor of the leaves appeared to him like an emanation of her graceful and wholesome nature.

This state of feeling began to act like an obsession, a sort of witchcraft, which alarmed him. What was she really, this strange creature? A peasant indeed, apparently; but there was also something more refined and cultivated about her, due, doubtless, to her having received her education in a city school. She both felt and expressed herself differently from ordinary country girls, although retaining the frankness and untutored charm of rustic natures. She exercised an uneasy fascination over Julien, and at times he returned to the superstitious impression made upon him by Reine's behavior and discourse in the forest. He again questioned with himself whether this female form, in its untamed beauty, did not enfold some spirit of temptation, some insidious fairy, similar to the Melusine, who appeared to Count Raymond in the forest of Poitiers.

Most of the time he would himself laugh at this extravagant supposition, but, while endeavoring to make light of his own cowardice, the idea still haunted and tormented him. Sometimes, in the effort to rid himself of the persistence of his own imagination, he would try to exorcise the demon who had got hold of him, and this exorcism consisted in despoiling the image of his temptress of the veil of virginal purity with which his admiration had first invested her. Who could assure him, after all, that this girl, with her independent ways, living alone at her farm, running through the woods at all hours, was as irreproachable as he had imagined? In the village, certainly, she was respected by all; but people were very tolerant—very easy, in fact—on the question of morals in this district, where the gallantries of Claude de Buxières were thought quite natural, where the illegitimacy of Claudet offended no one's sense of the proprieties, and where the after-dinner conversations, among the class considered respectable, were such as Julien had listened to with repugnance. Nevertheless, even in his most suspicious moods, Julien had never dared broach the subject to Claudet.

Every time that the name of Reine Vincart had come
to his lips, a feeling of bashfulness, in addition to his
ordinary timidity, had prevented him from interrogating Claudet concerning the character of this mysterious
queen of the woods. Like all novices in love-affairs
Julien dreaded that his feelings should be divined, at
the mere mention of the young girl's name. He preferred to remain isolated, concentrating in himself his
desires, his trouble and his doubts.

Yet, whatever efforts he made, and however firmly
he adhered to his resolution of silence, the hypochondria from which he suffered could not escape the notice
of the *grand chasserot*. He was not clear-sighted enough
to discern the causes, but he could observe the effects.
It provoked him to find that all his efforts to enliven his
cousin had proved futile. He had cudgelled his brains
to comprehend whence came these fits of terrible melancholy, and, judging Julien by himself, came to the
conclusion that his *ennui* proceeded from an excess of
strictness and good behavior.

"Monsieur de Buxières," said he, one evening when
they were walking silently, side by side, in the avenues
of the park, which resounded with the song of the nightingales, "there is one thing that troubles me, and that
is that you do not confide in me."

"What makes you think so, Claudet?" demanded
Julien, with surprise.

"*Parbleu!* the way you act. You are, if I may say so,
too secretive. When you wanted to make amends for
Claude de Buxières's negligence, and proposed that I
should live here with you, I accepted without any cere-

mony. I hoped that in giving me a place at your fire
and your table, you would also give me one in your
affections, and that you would allow me to share your
sorrows, like a true brother comrade——"

"I assure you, my dear fellow, that you are mistaken.
If I had any serious trouble on my mind, you should be
the first to know it."

"Oh! that's all very well to say; but you are unhappy
all the same—one can see it in your mien, and shall I
tell you the reason? It is that you are too sedate, Monsieur de Buxières; you have need of a sweetheart to
brighten up your days."

"Ho, ho!" replied Julien, coloring, "do you wish to
have me married, Claudet?"

"Ah! that's another affair. No; but still I should
like to see you take some interest in a woman—some
gay young person who would rouse you up and make
you have a good time. There is no lack of such in the
district, and you would only have the trouble of choosing."

M. de Buxières's color deepened, and he was visibly
annoyed.

"That is a singular proposition," exclaimed he, after
awhile; "do you take me for a libertine?"

"Don't get on your high horse, Monsieur de Buxières! There would be no one hurt. The girls I allude
to are not so difficult to approach."

"That has nothing to do with it, Claudet; I do not
enjoy that kind of amusement."

"It is the kind that young men of our age indulge in,
all the same. Perhaps you think there would be diffi-

culties in the way. They would not be insurmountable, I can assure you; those matters go smoothly enough here. You slip your arm round her waist, give her a good, sounding salute, and the acquaintance is begun. You have only to improve it!"

"Enough of this," interrupted Julien, harshly, "we never can agree on such topics!"

"As you please, Monsieur de Buxières; since you do not like the subject, we will not bring it up again. If I mentioned it at all, it was that I saw you were not interested in either hunting or fishing, and thought you might prefer some other kind of game. I do wish I knew what to propose that would give you a little pleasure," continued Claudet, who was profoundly mortified at the ill-success of his overtures. "Now! I have it. Will you come with me to-morrow, to the Ronces woods? The charcoal-dealers who are constructing their furnaces for the sale, will complete their dwellings this evening and expect to celebrate in the morning. They call it watering the bouquet, and it is the occasion of a little festival, to which we, as well at the presiding officials of the cutting, are invited. Naturally, the guests pay their share in bottles of wine. You can hardly be excused from showing yourself among these good people. It is one of the customs of the country. I have promised to be there, and it is certain that Reine Vincart, who has bought the Ronces property, will not fail to be present at the ceremony."

Julien had already the words on his lips for declining Claudet's offer, when the name of Reine Vincart produced an immediate change in his resolution. It just crossed his mind that perhaps Claudet had thrown out her name as a bait and an argument in favor of his theories on the facility of love-affairs in the country. However that might be, the allusion to the probable presence of Mademoiselle Vincart at the coming *fête*, rendered young Buxières more tractable, and he made no further difficulties about accompanying his cousin.

The next morning, after partaking hastily of breakfast, they started on their way toward the cutting. The charcoal-dealers had located themselves on the border of the forest, not far from the spot where, in the month of January, Reine and Julien had visited the woodcutters. Under the sheltering branches of a great ash-tree, the newly erected hut raised its peaked roof covered with clods of turf, and two furnaces, just completed, occupied the ground lately prepared. One of them, ready for use, was covered with the black earth called *frazil*, which is extracted from the site of old charcoal-works; the other, in course of construction, showed the successive layers of logs ranged in circles inside, ready for the fire. The workmen moved around, going and coming; first, the head-man or patron, a man of middle age, of hairy chest, embrowned visage, and small beady eyes under bushy eyebrows; his wife, a little, shrivelled, elderly woman; their daughter, a thin awkward girl of seventeen, with fluffy hair and a cunning, hard expression; and finally, their three boys, robust young fellows, serving their apprenticeship at the trade. This party was reënforced by one or two more single men, and some of the daughters of the woodchoppers, attracted by the prospect of a day of dancing and joyous feasting.

These persons were sauntering in and out under the trees, waiting for the dinner, which was to be furnished mainly by the guests, the contribution of the charcoal-men being limited to a huge pot of potatoes which the patroness was cooking over the fire, kindled in front of the hut.

The arrival of Julien and Claudet, attended by the small cowboy, puffing and blowing under a load of provisions, was hailed with exclamations of gladness and welcome. While one of the assistants was carefully unrolling the big loaves of white bread, the enormous meat pastry, and the bottles encased in straw, Reine Vincart appeared suddenly on the scene, accompanied by one of the farm-hands, who was also tottering under the weight of a huge basket, from the corners of which peeped the ends of bottles, and the brown knuckle of a smoked ham. At sight of the young proprietress of La Thuilière, the hurrahs burst forth again, with redoubled and more sustained energy. As she stood there smiling, under the greenish shadow cast by the ash-trees, Reine appeared to Julien even more seductive than among the frosty surroundings of the previous occasion. Her simple and rustic spring costume was marvellously becoming: a short blue-and-yellow striped skirt, a tight jacket of light-colored material, fitted closely to the waist, a flat linen collar tied with a narrow blue ribbon, and a bouquet of woodruff at her bosom. She wore stout leather boots, and a large straw hat, which she threw carelessly down on entering the hut. Among so many faces of a different type, all somewhat disfigured by hardships of exposure, this lovely face with its olive

complexion, lustrous black eyes, and smiling red lips,
framed in dark, soft, wavy hair resting on her plump
shoulders, seemed to spread a sunshiny glow over the
scene. It was a veritable portrayal of the "queen of the
woods," appearing triumphant among her rustic subjects. As an emblem of her royal prerogative, she held
in her hand an enormous bouquet of flowers she had
gathered on her way: honeysuckles, columbine, all sorts
of grasses with shivering spikelets, black alder blossoms
with their white centres, and a profusion of scarlet pop-
pies. Each of these exhaled its own salubrious spring-
like perfume, and a light cloud of pollen, which covered
the eyelashes and hair of the young girl with a delicate
white powder.

"Here, Père Théotime," said she, handing her collection over to the master charcoal-dealer, "I gathered
these for you to ornament the roof of your dwelling."

She then drew near to Claudet; gave him her hand
in comrade fashion, and saluted Julien:

"Good-morning, Monsieur de Buxières, I am very
glad to see you here. Was it Claudet who brought you,
or did you come of your own accord?"

While Julien, dazed and bewildered, was seeking a
reply, she passed quickly to the next group, going from
one to another, and watching with interest the placing
of the bouquet on the summit of the hut. One of the
men brought a ladder and fastened the flowers to a
spike. When they were securely attached and began
to nod in the air, he waved his hat and shouted: "Hou,
houp!" This was the signal for going to table.

The food had been spread on the tablecloth under

the shade of the ash-trees, and all the guests sat around on sacks of charcoal; for Reine and Julien alone they had reserved two stools, made by the master, and thus they found themselves seated side by side. Soon a profound, almost religious, silence indicated that the attack was about to begin; after which, and when the first fury of their appetites had been appeased, the tongues began to be loosened: jokes and anecdotes, seasoned with loud bursts of laughter, were bandied to and fro under the spreading branches, and presently the wine lent its aid to raise the spirits of the company to an exuberant pitch. But there was a certain degree of restraint observed by these country folk. Was it owing to Reine's presence? Julien noticed that the remarks of the working-people were in a very much better tone than those of the Auberive gentry, with whom he had breakfasted; the gayety of these children of the woods, although of a common kind, was always kept within decent limits, and he never once had occasion to feel ashamed. He felt more at ease among them than among the notables of the borough, and he did not regret having accepted Claudet's invitation.

"I am glad I came," murmured he in Reine's ear, "and I never have eaten with so much enjoyment!"

"Ah! I am glad of it," replied the young girl, gayly, "perhaps now you will begin to like our woods."

When nothing was left on the table but bones and empty bottles, Père Théotime took a bottle of sealed wine, drew the cork, and filled the glasses.

"Now," said he, "before christening our bouquet, we will drink to Monsieur de Buxières, who has brought

us his good wine, and to our sweet lady, Mademoiselle
Vincart."

The glasses clinked, and the toasts were drunk with
fervor.

"Mamselle Reine," resumed Père Théotime, with a
certain amount of solemnity, "you can see, the hut is
built; it will be occupied to-night, and I trust good work
will be done. You can perceive from here our first furnace, all decorated and ready to be set alight. But, in
order that good luck shall attend us, you yourself must
set light to the fire. I ask you, therefore, to ascend to
the top of the chimney and throw in the first embers;
may I ask this of your good-nature?"

"Why, certainly!" replied Reine, "come, Monsieur
de Buxières, you must see how we light a charcoal furnace."

All the guests jumped from their seats; one of the
men took the ladder and leaned it against the sloping
side of the furnace. Meanwhile, Père Théotime was
bringing an earthen vase full of burning embers. Reine
skipped lightly up the steps, and when she reached the
top, stood erect near the orifice of the furnace.

Her graceful outline came out in strong relief against
the clear sky; one by one, she took the embers handed
her by the charcoal-dealer, and threw them into the
opening in the middle of the furnace. Soon there was a
crackling inside, followed by a dull rumbling; the chips
and rubbish collected at the bottom had caught fire,
and the air-holes left at the base of the structure facili-
tated the passage of the current, and hastened the kin-
dling of the wood.

"Bravo; we've got it!" exclaimed Père Théotime.

"Bravo!" repeated the young people, as much exhilarated with the open air as with the two or three glasses of white wine they had drunk. Lads and lasses joined hands and leaped impetuously around the furnace.

"A song, Reine! Sing us a song!" cried the young girls.

She stood at the foot of the ladder, and, without further solicitation, intoned, in her clear and sympathetic voice, a popular song, with a rhythmical refrain:

> My father bid me
>   Go sell my wheat.
> To the market we drove—
>   "Good-morrow, my sweet!
> How much, can you say,
>   Will its value prove?"
>
>   The embroidered rose
>   Lies on my glove.
>
> "A hundred francs
>   Will its value prove."
> "When you sell your wheat,
>   Do you sell your love?"
>
>   The embroidered rose
>   Lies on my glove!
>
> "My heart, Monsieur,
>   Will never rove,
> I have promised it
>   To my own true love."
>
>   The embroidered rose
>   Lies on my glove.

A WOODLAND QUEEN

"For me he braves
The wind and the rain;
For me he weaves
A silver chain."

On my 'broidered glove.
Lies the rose again.

Repeating the refrain in chorus, boys and girls danced
and leaped in the sunlight. Julien leaned against the
trunk of a tree, listening to the sonorous voice of Reine,
and could not take his eyes off the singer. When she
had ended her song, Reine turned in another direction;
but the dancers had got into the spirit of it and could
not stand still; one of the men came forward, and
started another popular air, which all the rest repeated in
unison:

Up in the woods
Sleeps the fairy to-day:
The king, her lover,
Has strolled that way!
Will those who are young
Be married or nay?
Yea, yea!

Carried away by the rhythm, and the pleasure of
treading the soft grass under their feet, the dancers
quickened their pace. The chain of young folks disconnected for a moment, was reformed, and twisted in
and out among the trees; sometimes in light, sometimes in shadow, until they disappeared, singing, into
the very heart of the forest. With the exception of Père
Théotime and his wife, who had gone to superintend

the furnace, all the guests, including Claudet, had joined the gay throng. Reine and Julien, the only ones remaining behind, stood in the shade near the border-line of the forest. It was high noon, and the sun's rays, shooting perpendicularly down, made the shade desirable. Reine proposed to her companion to enter the hut and rest, while waiting for the return of the dancers. Julien accepted readily; but not without being surprised that the young girl should be the first to suggest a tête-à-tête in the obscurity of a remote hut. Although more than ever fascinated by the unusual beauty of Mademoiselle Vincart, he was astonished, and occasionally shocked, by the audacity and openness of her action toward him. Once more the spirit of doubt took possession of him, and he questioned whether this freedom of manners was to be attributed to innocence or effrontery. After the pleasant friendliness of the mid-day repast, and the enlivening effect of the dance round the furnace, he was both glad and troubled to find himself alone with Reine. He longed to let her know what tender admiration she excited in his mind; but he did not know how to set about it, nor in what style to address a girl of so strange and unusual a disposition. So he contented himself with fixing an enamored gaze upon her, while she stood leaning against one of the inner posts, and twisted mechanically between her fingers a branch of wild honeysuckle. Annoyed at his taciturnity, she at last broke the silence:

"You are not saying anything, Monsieur de Buxières; do you regret having come to this *fête?*"

"Regret it, Mademoiselle?" returned he; "it is a

long time since I have had so pleasant a day, and I thank you, for it is to you I owe it."

"To me? You are joking. It is the good-humor of the people, the spring sunshine, and the pure air of the forest that you must thank. I have no part in it."

"You are everything in it, on the contrary," said he, tenderly. "Before I knew you, I had met with country people, seen the sun and trees, and so on, and nothing made any impression on me. But, just now, when you were singing over there, I felt gladdened and inspired; I felt the beauty of the woods, I sympathized with these good people, and these grand trees, all these things among which you live so happily. It is you who have worked this miracle. Ah! you are well named. You are truly the fairy of the feast, the queen of the woods!"

Astonished at the enthusiasm of her companion, Reine looked at him sidewise, half closing her eyes, and perceived that he was altogether transformed. He appeared to have suddenly thawed. He was no longer the awkward, sickly youth, whose every movement was paralyzed by timidity, and whose words froze on his tongue; his slender frame had become supple, his blue eyes enlarged and illuminated; his delicate features expressed refinement, tenderness, and passion. The young girl was moved and won by so much emotion, the first that Julien had ever manifested toward her. Far from being offended at this species of declaration, she replied, gayly:

"As to the queen of the woods working miracles, I know none so powerful as these flowers."

She unfastened the bouquet of white starry woodruff from her corsage, and handed them over to him in their envelope of green leaves.

"Do you know them?" said she; "see how sweet they smell! And the odor increases as they wither."

Julien had carried the bouquet to his lips, and was inhaling slowly the delicate perfume.

"Our woodsmen," she continued, "make with this plant a broth which cures from ill effects of either cold or heat as if by enchantment; they also infuse it into white wine, and convert it into a beverage which they call May wine, and which is very intoxicating."

Julien was no longer listening to these details. He kept his eyes steadily fixed on Mademoiselle Vincart, and continued to inhale rapturously the bouquet, and to experience a kind of intoxication.

"Let me keep these flowers," he implored, in a choking voice.

"Certainly," replied she, gayly; "keep them, if it will give you pleasure."

"Thank you," he murmured, hiding them in his bosom.

Reine was surprised at his attaching such exaggerated importance to so slight a favor, and a sudden flush overspread her cheeks. She almost repented having given him the flowers when she saw what a tender reception he had given them, so she replied, suggestively:

"Do not thank me; the gift is not significant. Thousands of similar flowers grow in the forest, and one has only to stoop and gather them."

A WOODLAND QUEEN

He dared not reply that this bouquet, having been worn by her, was worth much more to him than any other, but he thought it, and the thought aroused in his mind a series of new ideas. As Reine had so readily granted this first favor, was she not tacitly encouraging him to ask for others? Was he dealing with a simple, innocent girl, or a village coquette, accustomed to be courted? And on this last supposition should he not pass for a simpleton in the eyes of this experienced girl, if he kept himself at too great a distance. He remembered the advice of Claudet concerning the method of conducting love-affairs smoothly with certain women of the country. Whether she was a coquette or not, Reine had bewitched him. The charm had worked more powerfully still since he had been alone with her in this obscure hut, where the cooing of the wild pigeons faintly reached their ears, and the penetrating odors of the forest pervaded their nostrils. Julien's gaze rested lovingly on Reine's wavy locks, falling heavily over her neck, on her half-covered eyes with their luminous pupils full of golden specks of light, on her red lips, on the two little brown moles spotting her somewhat décolleté neck. He thought her adorable, and was dying to tell her so; but when he endeavored to formulate his declaration, the words stuck fast in his throat, his veins swelled, his throat became dry, his head swam. In this disorder of his faculties he brought to mind the recommendation of Claudet: "One arm round the waist, two sounding kisses, and the thing is done." He rose abruptly, and went up to the young girl:

"Since you have given me these flowers," he began,

[123]

in a husky voice, "will you also, in sign of friendship, give me your hand, as you gave it to Claudet?"

After a moment's hesitation, she held out her hand; but, hardly had he touched it when he completely lost control of himself, and slipping the arm which remained free around Reine's waist, he drew her toward him and lightly touched with his lips her neck, the beauty of which had so magnetized him.

The young girl was stronger than he; in the twinkling of an eye she tore herself from his audacious clasp, threw him violently backward, and with one bound reached the door of the hut. She stood there a moment, pale, indignant, her eyes blazing, and then exclaimed, in a hollow voice:

"If you come a step nearer, I will call the charcoal-men!"

But Julien had no desire to renew the attack; already sobered, cowed, and repentant, he had retreated to the most obscure corner of the dwelling.

"Are you mad?" she continued, with vehemence, "or has the wine got into your head? It is rather early for you to be adopting the ways of your deceased cousin! I give you notice that they will not succeed with me!" And, at the same moment, tears of humiliation filled her eyes. "I did not expect this of you, Monsieur de Buxières!"

"Forgive me!" faltered Julien, whose heart smote him at the sight of her tears; "I have behaved like a miserable sinner and a brute! It was a moment of madness—forget it and forgive me!"

"Nobody ever treated me with disrespect before,"

returned the young girl, in a suffocated voice; "I was wrong to allow you any familiarity, that is all. It shall not happen to me again!"

Julien remained mute, overpowered with shame and remorse. Suddenly, in the stillness around, rose the voices of the dancers returning and singing the refrain of the rondelay:

> I had a rose—
>   On my heart it lay—
> Will those who are young
>   Be married, or nay?
>   Yea, yea!

"There are our people," said Reine, softly, "I am going to them; adieu—do not follow me!"

She left the hut and hastened toward the furnace, while Julien, stunned with the rapidity with which this unfortunate scene had been enacted, sat down on one of the benches, a prey to confused feelings of shame and angry mortification. No, certainly, he did not intend to follow her! He had no desire to show himself in public with this young girl whom he had so stupidly insulted, and in whose face he never should be able to look again. Decidedly, he did not understand women, since he could not even tell a virtuous girl from a frivolous coquette! Why had he not been able to see that the good-natured, simple familiarity of Reine Vincart had nothing in common with the enticing allurements of those who, to use Claudet's words, had "thrown their caps over the wall." How was it that he had not read, in those eyes, pure as the fountain's source, the candor and uprightness of a maiden heart which had nothing to conceal. This cruel evidence of his inability to conduct himself properly in the affairs of life exasperated and humiliated him, and at the same time that he felt his self-love most deeply wounded, he was conscious of being more hopelessly enamored of Reine Vincart. Never had she appeared so beautiful as during the indignant movement which had separated her from him. Her look of mingled anger and sadness, the expression of her firm, set lips, the quivering nostrils, the heaving of her bosom, he recalled it all, and the image of her proud beauty redoubled his grief and despair.

He remained a long time concealed in the shadow of the hut. Finally, when he heard the voices dying away in different directions, and was satisfied that the charcoal-men were attending to their furnace work, he made up his mind to come out. But, as he did not wish to meet any one, instead of crossing through the cutting he plunged into the wood, taking no heed in what direction he went, and being desirous of walking alone as long as possible, without meeting a single human visage.

As he wandered aimlessly through the deepening shadows of the forest, crossed here and there by golden bars of light from the slanting rays of the setting sun, he pondered over the probable results of his unfortunate behavior. Reine would certainly keep silence on the affront she had received, but would she be indulgent enough to forget or forgive the insult? The most evident result of the affair would be that henceforth all friendly relations between them must cease. She certainly would maintain a severe attitude toward the person who had so grossly insulted her, but would she be altogether pitiless in her anger? All through his dismal feelings of self-reproach, a faint hope of reconciliation kept him from utter despair. As he reviewed the details of the shameful occurrence, he remembered that the expression of her countenance had been one more of sorrow than of anger. The tone of melancholy reproach in which she had uttered the words: "I did not expect this from you, Monsieur de Buxières!" seemed to convey the hope that he might, one day, be forgiven. At the same time, the poignancy of his regret showed him how much hold the young girl had taken upon his affections, and how cheerless and insipid his life would be if he were obliged to continue on unfriendly terms with the woodland queen.

He had come to this conclusion in his melancholy reflections, when he reached the outskirts of the forest.

He stood above the calm, narrow valley of Vivey; on the right, over the tall ash-trees, peeped the pointed turrets of the château; on the left, and a little farther behind, was visible a whitish line, contrasting with the surrounding verdure, the winding path to La Thuilière, through the meadow-land of Planche-au-Vacher. Suddenly, the sound of voices reached his ears, and, looking more closely, he perceived Reine and Claudet walking side by side down the narrow path. The evening air softened the resonance of the voices, so that the words themselves were not audible, but the intonation of the alternate speakers, and their confidential and friendly gestures, evinced a very animated, if not tender, exchange of sentiments. At times the conversation was enlivened by Claudet's bursts of laughter, or an amicable gesture from Reine. At one moment, Julien saw the young girl lay her hand familiarly on the shoulder of the *grand chasserot*, and immediately a pang of intense jealousy shot through his heart. At last the young pair arrived at the banks of a stream, which traversed the path and had become swollen by the recent heavy rains. Claudet took Reine by the waist and lifted her in his vigorous arms, while he picked his way across the stream; then they resumed their way toward the bottom of the pass, and the tall brushwood hid their retreating forms from Julien's eager gaze, although it was long before the vibrations of their sonorous voices ceased echoing in his ears.

"Ah!" thought he, quite overcome by this new development, "she stands less on ceremony with him than with me! How close they kept to each other in that lonely path! With what animation they conversed! with what abandon she allowed herself to be carried in his arms! All that indicates an intimacy of long standing, and explains a good many things!"

He recalled Reine's visit to the château, and how cleverly she had managed to inform him of the parentage existing between Claudet and the deceased Claude de Buxières; how she had by her conversation raised a feeling of pity in his mind for Claudet, and a desire to repair the negligence of the deceased.

"How could I be so blind!" thought Julien, with secret scorn of himself; "I did not see anything, I comprehended none of their artifices! They love each other, that is sure, and I have been playing throughout the part of a dupe. I do not blame him. He was in love, and allowed himself to be persuaded. But she! whom I thought so open, so true, so loyal! Ah! she is no better than others of her class, and she was coquetting with me in order to insure her lover a position! Well! one more illusion is destroyed. Ecclesiastes was right. *Inveni amarivrem morte mulierem*, 'woman is more bitter than death'!"

Twilight had come, and it was already dark in the forest. Slowly and reluctantly, Julien descended the slope leading to the château, and the gloom of the woods entered his heart.

CHAPTER VI

EALOUSY is a maleficent deity of the harpy tribe; she embitters everything she touches.

Ever since the evening that Julien had witnessed the crossing of the brook by Reine and Claudet, a secret poison had run through his veins, and embittered every moment of his life. Neither the glowing sun of June, nor the glorious development of the woods had any charm for him. In vain did the fields display their golden treasures of ripening corn; in vain did the pale barley and the silvery oats wave their luxuriant growth against the dark background of the woods; all these fairylike effects of summer suggested only prosaic and misanthropic reflections in Julien's mind. He thought of the tricks, the envy and hatred that the possession of these little squares of ground brought forth among their rapacious owners. The prolific exuberance of forest vegetation was an exemplification of the fierce and destructive activity of the blind forces of Nature. All the earth was a hateful theatre for the continual enactment of bloody and monotonous dramas; the worm consuming the plant; the bird mangling the insect, the deer fighting among themselves, and man, in his turn, pursuing all kinds of game. He identified nature with woman, both possessing in his eyes an equally deceiving appearance, the same beguiling beauty, and the same spirit of ambuscade and perfidy. The people around him inspired him only with mistrust and suspicion. In every peasant he met he recognized an enemy, prepared to cheat him with wheedling words and hypocritical lamentations. Although during the few months he had experienced the delightful influence of Reine Vincart, he had been drawn out of his former prejudices, and had imagined he was rising above the littleness of every-day worries; he now fell back into hard reality; his feet were again embedded in the muddy ground of village politics, and consequently village life was a burden to him.

He never went out, fearing to meet Reine Vincart. He fancied that the sight of her might aggravate the malady from which he suffered and for which he eagerly sought a remedy.

But, notwithstanding the cloistered retirement to which he had condemned himself, his wound remained open. Instead of solitude having a healing effect, it seemed to make his sufferings greater. When, in the evening, as he sat moodily at his window, he would hear Claudet whistle to his dog, and hurry off in the direction of La Thuilière, he would say to himself: "He is going to keep an appointment with Reine." Then a feeling of blind rage would overpower him; he felt tempted to leave his room and follow his rival secretly—a moment afterward he would be ashamed of his meanness. Was it not enough that he had once, although involuntarily, played the degrading part of a spy! What satisfaction could he derive from such a course? Would he be much benefited when he returned home with rage in his heart and senses, after watching a love-scene between the young pair? This consideration kept him in his seat, but his imagination ran riot instead; it went galloping at the heels of Claudet, and accompanied him down the winding paths, moistened by the evening dew. As the moon rose above the trees, illuminating the foliage with her mild bluish rays, he pictured to himself the meeting of the two lovers on the flowery turf bathed in the silvery light. His brain seemed on fire. He saw Reine in white advancing like a moonbeam, and Claudet passing his arm around the yielding waist of the maiden. He tried to substitute himself in idea, and to imagine the delight of the first words of welcome, and the ecstasy of the prolonged embrace. A shiver ran through his whole body; a sharp pain transfixed his heart; his throat closed convulsively; half fainting, he leaned against the window-frame, his eyes closed, his ears stopped, to shut out all sights or sounds, longing only for oblivion and complete torpor of body and mind.

He did not realize his longing. The enchanting image of the woodland queen, as he had beheld her in the dusky light of the charcoal-man's hut, was ever before him. He put his hands over his eyes. She was there still, with her deep, dark eyes and her enticing cherry lips. Even the odor of the honeysuckle arising from the garden assisted the reality of the vision, by recalling the sprig of the same flower which Reine was twisting round her fingers at their last interview. This sweet breath of flowers in the night seemed like an emanation from the young girl herself, and was as fleeting and intangible as the remembrance of vanished happiness. Again and again did his morbid nature return to past events, and make his present position more unbearable.

"Why," thought he, "did I ever entertain so wild a hope? This wood-nymph, with her robust yet graceful figure, her clear-headedness, her energy and will-power, could she ever have loved a being so weak and unstable as myself? No, indeed; she needs a lover full of life and vigor; a huntsman, with a strong arm, able to protect her. What figure should I cut by the side of so hearty and well-balanced a fellow?"

In these fits of jealousy, he was not so angry with Claudet for being loved by Reine as for having so carefully concealed his feelings. And yet, while inwardly blaming him for this want of frankness, he did not realize that he himself was open to a similar accusation, by hiding from Claudet what was troubling him so grievously.

Since the evening of the inauguration festival, he had become sullen and taciturn. Like all timid persons, he took refuge in a moody silence, which could not but irritate his cousin. They met every day at the same table; to all appearance their intimacy was as great as ever, but, in reality, there was no mutual exchange of feeling. Julien's continued ill-humor was a source of anxiety to Claudet, who turned his brain almost inside out in endeavoring to discover its cause. He knew he had done nothing to provoke any coolness; on the contrary, he had set his wits to work to show his gratitude by all sorts of kindly offices.

By dint of thinking the matter over, Claudet came to the conclusion that perhaps Julien was beginning to repent of his generosity, and that possibly this coolness was a roundabout way of manifesting his change of feeling. This seemed to be the only plausible solution of his cousin's behavior. "He is probably tired," thought he, "of keeping us here at the château, my mother and myself."

Claudet's pride and self-respect revolted at this idea. He did not intend to be an incumbrance on any one, and became offended in his turn at the mute reproach which he imagined he could read in his cousin's troubled countenance. This misconception, confirmed by the obstinate silence of both parties, and aggravated by its own continuance, at last produced a crisis.

It happened one night, after they had taken supper together, and Julien's ill-humor had been more evident than usual. Provoked at his persistent taciturnity, and more than ever convinced that it was his presence that young de Buxières objected to, Claudet resolved to force an explanation. Instead, therefore, of quitting the dining-room after dessert, and whistling to his dog to accompany him in his habitual promenade, the *grand chasserot* remained seated, poured out a small glass of brandy, and slowly filled his pipe. Surprised to see that he was remaining at home, Julien rose and began to pace the floor, wondering what could be the reason of this unexpected change. As suspicious people are usually prone to attribute complicated motives for the most simple actions, he imagined that Claudet, becoming aware of the jealous feeling he had excited, had given up his promenade solely to mislead and avert suspicion. This idea irritated him still more, and halting suddenly in his walk, he went up to Claudet and said, brusquely:

"You are not going out, then?"

"No;" replied Claudet, "if you will permit me, I will stay and keep you company. Shall I annoy you?"

"Not in the least; only, as you are accustomed to walk every evening, I should not wish you to inconvenience yourself on my account. I am not afraid of being alone, and I am not selfish enough to deprive you of society more agreeable than mine."

"What do you mean by that?" cried Claudet, pricking up his ears.

"Nothing," muttered Julien, between his set teeth, "except that your fancied obligation of keeping me company ought not to prevent you missing a pleasant engagement, or keeping a rendezvous."

"A rendezvous," replied his interlocutor, with a forced laugh, "so you think, when I go out after supper, I go to seek amusement. A rendezvous! And with whom, if you please?"

"With your mistress, of course," replied Julien, sarcastically, "from what you said to me, there is no scarcity here of girls inclined to be good-natured, and you have only the trouble of choosing among them. I supposed you were courting some woodman's young daughter, or some pretty farmer girl, like—like Reine Vincart."

"Reine Vincart!" repeated Claudet, sternly, "what business have you to mix up her name with those creatures to whom you refer? Mademoiselle Vincart," added he, "has nothing in common with that class, and you have no right, Monsieur de Buxières, to use her name so lightly!"

The allusion to Reine Vincart had agitated Claudet to such a degree that he did not notice that Julien, as he pronounced her name, was as much moved as himself.

The vehemence with which Claudet resented the insinuation increased young de Buxières's irritation.

"Ha, ha!" said he, laughing scornfully, "Reine Vincart is an exceedingly pretty girl!"

"She is not only pretty, she is good and virtuous, and deserves to be respected."

"How you uphold her! One can see that you are interested in her."

".I uphold her because you are unjust toward her. But I wish you to understand that she has no need of any one standing up for her—her good name is sufficient to protect her. Ask any one in the village—there is but one voice on that question."

"Come," said Julien, huskily, "confess that you are in love with her."

"Well! suppose I am," said Claudet, angrily, "yes, I love her! There, are you satisfied now?"

Although de Buxières knew what he had to expect, he was not the less affected by so open an avowal thrust at him, as it were. He stood for a moment, silent; then, with a fresh burst of rage:

A WOODLAND QUEEN

"You love her, do you? Why did you not tell me before? Why were you not more frank with me?"

As he spoke, gesticulating furiously, in front of the open window, the deep red glow of the setting sun, piercing through the boughs of the ash-trees, threw its bright reflections on his blazing eyeballs and convulsed features. His interlocutor, leaning against the opposite corner of the window-frame, noticed, with some anxiety, the extreme agitation of his behavior, and wondered what could be the cause of such emotion.

"I? Not frank with you! Ah, that is a good joke, Monsieur de Buxières! Naturally, I should not go proclaiming on the housetops that I have a tender feeling for Mademoiselle Vincart, but, all the same, I should have told you had you asked me sooner. I am not reserved; but, you must excuse my saying it, you are walled in like a subterranean passage. One can not get at the color of your thoughts. I never for a moment imagined that you were interested in Reine, and you never have made me sufficiently at home to entertain the idea of confiding in you on that subject."

Julien remained silent. He had reseated himself at the table, where, leaning his head in his hands, he pondered over what Claudet had said. He placed his hand so as to screen his eyes, and bit his lips as if a painful struggle was going on within him. The splendors of the setting sun had merged into the dusky twilight, and the last piping notes of the birds sounded faintly among the sombre trees. A fresh breeze had sprung up, and filled the darkening room with the odor of honeysuckle.

Under the soothing influence of the falling night,

Julien slowly raised his head, and addressing Claudet in a low and measured voice like a father confessor interrogating a penitent, said:

"Does Reine know that you love her?"

"I think she must suspect it," replied Claudet, "although I never have ventured to declare myself squarely. But girls are very quick, Reine especially. They soon begin to suspect there is some love at bottom, when a young man begins to hang around them too frequently."

"You see her often, then?"

"Not as often as I should like. But, you know, when one lives in the same district, one has opportunities of meeting—at the beech harvest, in the woods, at the church door. And when you meet, you talk but little, making the most of your time. Still, you must not suppose, as I think you did, that we have rendezvous in the evening. Reine respects herself too much to go about at night with a young man as escort, and besides, she has other fish to fry. She has a great deal to do at the farm, since her father has become an invalid."

"Well, do you think she loves you?" said Julien, with a movement of nervous irritation.

"I can not tell," replied Claudet shrugging his shoulders, "she has confidence in me, and shows me some marks of friendship, but I never have ventured to ask her whether she feels anything more than friendship for me. Look here, now. I have good reasons for keeping back; she is rich and I am poor. You can understand that I would not, for any consideration, allow her to think that I am courting her for her money——"

"Still, you desire to marry her, and you hope that she

will not say no—you acknowledge that!" cried Julien, vociferously.

Claudet, struck with the violence and bitterness of tone of his companion, came up to him.

"How angrily you say that, Monsieur de Buxières!" exclaimed he in his turn; "upon my word, one might suppose the affair is very displeasing to you. Will you let me tell you frankly an idea that has already entered my head several times these last two or three days, and which has come again now, while I have been listening to you? It is that perhaps you, yourself, are also in love with Reine?"

"I!" protested Julien. He felt humiliated at Claudet's perspicacity; but he had too much pride and self-respect to let his preferred rival know of his unfortunate passion. He waited a moment to swallow something in his throat that seemed to be choking him, and then, trying in vain to steady his voice, he added:

"You know that I have an aversion for women; and for that matter, I think they return it with interest. But, at all events, I am not foolish enough to expose myself to their rebuffs. Rest assured, I shall not follow at your heels!"

Claudet shook his head incredulously.

"You doubt it," continued de Buxières; "well, I will prove it to you. You can not declare your wishes because Reine is rich and you are poor? I will take charge of the whole matter."

"I—I do not understand you," faltered Claudet, bewildered at the strange turn the conversation was taking.

"You will understand—soon," asserted Julien, with a gesture of both decision and resignation.

The truth was, he had made one of those resolutions which seem illogical and foolish at first sight, but are natural to minds at once timid and exalted. The suffering caused by Claudet's revelations had become so acute that he was alarmed. He recognized with dismay the disastrous effects of this hopeless love, and determined to employ a heroic remedy to arrest its further ravages. This was nothing less than killing his love, by immediately getting Claudet married to Reine Vincart. Sacrifices like this are easier to souls that have been subjected since their infancy to Christian discipline, and accustomed to consider the renunciation of mundane joys as a means of securing eternal salvation. As soon as this idea had developed in Julien's brain, he seized upon it with the precipitation of a drowning man, who distractedly lays hold of the first object that seems to offer him a means of safety, whether it be a dead branch or a reed.

"Listen," he resumed; "at the very first explanation that we had together, I told you I did not intend to deprive you of your right to a portion of your natural father's inheritance. Until now, you have taken my word for it, and we have lived at the château like two brothers. But now that a miserable question of money alone prevents you from marrying the woman you love, it is important that you should be legally provided for. We will go to-morrow to Monsieur Arbillot, and ask him to draw up the deed, making over to you from me one half of the fortune of Claude de Buxières. You will then be, by law, and in the eyes of all, one of the desirable matches of the canton, and you can demand the hand of Mademoiselle Vincart, without any fear of being thought presumptuous or mercenary."

Claudet, to whom this conclusion was wholly unexpected, was thunderstruck. His emotion was so great that it prevented him from speaking. In the obscurity of the room his deep-set eyes seemed larger, and shone with the tears he could not repress.

"Monsieur Julien," said he, falteringly, "I can not find words to thank you. I am like an idiot. And to think that only a little while ago I suspected you of being tired of me, and regretting your benefits toward me! What an animal I am! I measure others by myself. Well! can you forgive me? If I do not express myself well, I feel deeply, and all I can say is that you have made me very happy!" He sighed heavily. "The question is now," continued he, "whether Reine will have me! You may not believe me, Monsieur de Buxières, but though I may seem very bold and resolute, I feel like a wet hen when I get near her. I have a dreadful panic that she will send me away as I came. I don't know whether I can ever find courage to ask her."

"Why should she refuse you?" said Julien, sadly, "she knows that you love her. Do you suppose she loves any one else?"

"That I don't know. Although Reine is very frank, she does not let every one know what is passing in her mind, and with these young girls, I tell you, one is never sure of anything. That is just what I fear may be possible."

"If you fear the ordeal," said de Buxières, with a visible effort, "would you like me to present the matter for you?"

"I should be very glad. It would be doing me a great service. It would be adding one more kindness to those I have already received, and some day I hope to make it all up to you."

The next morning, according to agreement, Julien accompanied Claudet to Auberive, where Maître Arbillot drew up the deed of gift, and had it at once signed and recorded. Afterward the young men adjourned to breakfast at the inn. The meal was brief and silent. Neither seemed to have any appetite. As soon as they had drunk their coffee, they turned back on the Vivey road; but, when they had got as far as the great lime-tree, standing at the entrance to the forest, Julien touched Claudet lightly on the shoulder.

"Here," said he, "we must part company. You will return to Vivey, and I shall go across the fields to La Thuilière. I shall return as soon as I have had an interview with Mademoiselle Vincart. Wait for me at the château."

"The time will seem dreadfully long to me," sighed Claudet; "I shall not know how to dispose of my body until you return."

"Your affair will be all settled within two or three hours from now. Stay near the window of my room, and you will catch first sight of me coming along in the distance. If I wave my hat, it will be a sign that I bring a favorable answer."

Claudet pressed his hand; they separated, and Julien

descended the newly mown meadow, along which he walked under the shade of trees scattered along the border line of the forest.

The heat of the midday sun was tempered by a breeze from the east, which threw across the fields and woods the shadows of the white fleecy clouds. The young man, pale and agitated, strode with feverish haste over the short-cropped grass, while the little brooklet at his side seemed to murmur a flute-like, soothing accompaniment to the tumultuous beatings of his heart. He was both elated and depressed at the prospect of submitting his already torn and lacerated feelings to so severe a trial. The thought of beholding Reine again, and of sounding her feelings, gave him a certain amount of cruel enjoyment. He would speak to her of love—love for another, certainly—but he would throw into the declaration he was making, in behalf of another, some of his own tenderness; he would have the supreme and torturing satisfaction of watching her countenance, of anticipating her blushes, of gathering the faltering avowal from her lips. He would once more drink of the intoxication of her beauty, and then he would go and shut himself up at Vivey, after burying at La Thuilière all his dreams and profane desires. But, even while the courage of this immolation of his youthful love was strong within him, he could not prevent a dim feeling of hope from crossing his mind. Claudet was not certain that he was beloved; and possibly Reine's answer would be a refusal. Then he should have a free field.

By a very human, but very illogical impulse, Julien

de Buxières had hardly concluded the arrangement with Claudet which was to strike the fatal blow to his own happiness when he began to forestall the possibilities which the future might have in store for him. The odor of the wild mint and meadow-sweet, dotting the banks of the stream, again awoke vague, happy anticipations. Longing to reach Reine Vincart's presence, he hastened his steps, then stopped suddenly, seized with an over-powering panic. He had not seen her since the painful episode in the hut, and it must have left with her a very sorry impression. What could he do, if she refused to receive him or listen to him?

While revolving these conflicting thoughts in his mind, he came to the fields leading directly to La Thuilière, and just beyond, across a waving mass of oats and rye, the shining tops of the farm-buildings came in sight. A few minutes later, he pushed aside a gate and entered the yard.

The shutters were closed, the outer gate was closed inside, and the house seemed deserted. Julien began to think that the young girl he was seeking had gone into the fields with the farm-hands, and stood uncertain and disappointed in the middle of the courtyard. At this sudden intrusion into their domain, a brood of chickens, who had been clucking sedately around, and picking up nourishment at the same time, scattered screaming in every direction, heads down, feet sprawling, until by unanimous consent they made a bee-line for a half-open door, leading to the orchard. Through this manœuvre, the young man's attention was brought to the fact that through this opening he could reach the rear façade of the building. He therefore entered a grassy lane, winding round a group of stones draped with ivy; and leaving the orchard on his left, he pushed on toward the garden itself—a real country garden with square beds bordered by mossy clumps alternating with currant-bushes, rows of raspberry-trees, lettuce and cabbage beds, beans and runners climbing up their slender supports, and, here and there, bunches of red carnations and peasant roses.

Suddenly, at the end of a long avenue, he discovered Reine Vincart, seated on the steps before an arched door, communicating with the kitchen. A plum-tree, loaded with its violet fruit, spread its light shadow over the young girl's head, as she sat shelling fresh-gathered peas and piling the faint green heaps of color around her. The sound of approaching steps on the grassy soil caused her to raise her head, but she did not stir. In his intense emotion, Julien thought the alley never would come to an end. He would fain have cleared it with a single bound, so as to be at once in the presence of Mademoiselle Vincart, whose immovable attitude rendered his approach still more difficult. Nevertheless, he had to get over the ground somehow at a reasonable pace, under penalty of making himself ridiculous, and he therefore found plenty of time to examine Reine, who continued her work with imperturbable gravity, throwing the peas as she shelled them into an ash-wood pail at her feet.

She was bareheaded, and wore a striped skirt and a white jacket fitted to her waist. The checkered shadows cast by the tree made spots of light and darkness over her face and her uncovered neck, the top button of her camisole being unfastened on account of the heat. De Buxières had been perfectly well recognized by her, but an emotion, at least equal to that experienced by the young man, had transfixed her to the spot, and a subtle feminine instinct had urged her to continue her employment, in order to hide the sudden trembling of her fingers. During the last month, ever since the adventure in the hut, she had thought often of Julien; and the remembrance of the audacious kiss which the young de Buxières had so impetuously stolen from her neck, invariably brought the flush of shame to her brow. But, although she was very indignant at the fiery nature of his caress, as implying a want of respect little in harmony with Julien's habitual reserve, she was astonished at herself for not being still more angry. At first, the affront put upon her had roused a feeling of indignation, but now, when she thought of it, she felt only a gentle embarrassment, and a soft beating of the heart. She began to reflect that to have thus broken loose from all restraint before her, this timid youth must have been carried away by an irresistible burst of passion, and any woman, however high-minded she may be, will forgive such violent homage rendered to the sovereign power of her beauty. Besides his feeding of her vanity, another independent and more powerful motive predisposed her to indulgence: she felt a tender and secret attraction toward Monsieur de Buxières. This healthy and energetic girl had been fascinated by the delicate charm of a nature so unlike her own in its sensitiveness and disposition to self-blame. Julien's melancholy blue eyes had, unknown to himself, exerted a magnetic influence on Reine's dark, liquid orbs, and, without endeavoring to analyze the sympathy that drew her toward a nature refined and tender even to weakness, without asking herself where this unreflecting instinct might lead her, she was conscious of a growing sentiment toward him, which was not very much unlike love itself.

Julien de Buxières's mood was not sufficiently calm to observe anything, or he would immediately have perceived the impression that his sudden appearance had produced upon Reine Vincart. As soon as he found himself within a few steps of the young girl, he saluted her awkwardly, and she returned his bow with marked coldness. Extremely disconcerted at this reception, he endeavored to excuse himself for having invaded her dwelling in so unceremonious a manner.

"I am all the more troubled," added he, humbly, "that after what has happened, my visit must appear to you indiscreet, if not improper."

Reine, who had more quickly recovered her self-possession, pretended not to understand the unwise allusion that had escaped the lips of her visitor. She rose, pushed away with her foot the stalks and pods, which encumbered the passage, and replied, very shortly:

"You are excused, Monsieur. There is no need of an introduction to enter La Thuilière. Besides, I suppose that the motive which has brought you here can only be a proper one."

While thus speaking, she shook her skirt down, and without any affectation buttoned up her camisole.

"Certainly, Mademoiselle," faltered Julien, "it is a

most serious and respectable motive that causes me to wish for an interview, and—if—I do not disturb you——"

"Not in the least, Monsieur; but, if you wish to speak with me, it is unnecessary for you to remain standing. Allow me to fetch you a chair."

She went into the house, leaving the young man over-whelmed with the coolness of his reception; a few minutes later she reappeared, bringing a chair, which she placed under the tree. "Sit here, you will be in the shade."

She seated herself on the same step as before, lean-ing her back against the wall, and her head on her hand.

"I am ready to listen to you," she said.

Julien, much less under his own control than she, discovered that his mission was more difficult than he had imagined it would be; he experienced a singular amount of embarrassment in unfolding his subject; and was obliged to have recourse to prolonged inquiries con-cerning the health of Monsieur Vincart.

"He is still in the same condition," said Reine, "neither better nor worse, and, with the illness which afflicts him, the best I can hope for is that he may remain in that condition. But," continued she, with a slight inflection of irony; "doubtless it is not for the purpose of inquiring after my father's health that you have come all the way from Vivey?"

"That is true, Mademoiselle," replied he, coloring. "What I have to speak to you about is a very delicate matter. You will excuse me, therefore, if I am somewhat embarrassed. I beg of you, Mademoiselle, to listen to me with indulgence."

"What can he be coming to?" thought Reine, wondering why he made so many preambles before beginning. And, at the same time, her heart began to beat violently.

Julien took the course taken by all timid people after meditating for a long while on the best way to prepare the young girl for the communication he had taken upon himself to make—he lost his head and inquired abruptly:

"Mademoiselle Reine, do you not intend to marry?"

Reine started, and gazed at him with a frightened air.

"I!" exclaimed she, "Oh, I have time enough and I am not in a hurry." Then, dropping her eyes: "Why do you ask that?"

"Because I know of some one who loves you and who would be glad to marry you."

She became very pale, took up one of the empty pods, twisted it nervously around her finger without speaking.

"Some one belonging to our neighborhood?" she faltered, after a few moments' silence.

"Yes; some one whom you know, and who is not a recent arrival here. Some one who possesses, I believe, sterling qualities sufficient to make a good husband, and means enough to do credit to the woman who will wed him. Doubtless you have already guessed to whom I refer?"

She sat motionless, her lips tightly closed, her features

rigid, but the nervous twitching of her fingers as she bent the green stem back and forth, betrayed her inward agitation.

"No; I can not tell," she replied at last, in an almost inaudible voice.

"Truly?" he exclaimed, with an expression of astonishment, in which was a certain amount of secret satisfaction; "you can not tell whom I mean? You have never thought of the person of whom I am speaking in that light?"

"No; who is that person?"

She had raised her eyes toward his, and they shone with a deep, mysterious light.

"It is Claudet Séjournant," replied Julien, very gently, and in an altered tone.

The glow that had illumined the dark orbs of the young girl faded away, her eyelids dropped, and her countenance became as rigid as before; but Julien did not notice anything. The words he had just uttered had cost him too much agony, and he dared not look at his companion, lest he should behold her joyful surprise, and thereby aggravate his suffering.

"Ah!" said Reine, coldly, "in that case, why did not Claudet come himself and state his own case?"

"His courage failed him at the last moment—and so——"

"And so," continued she, with sarcastic bitterness of tone, "you took upon yourself to speak for him?"

"Yes; I promised him I would plead his cause. I was sure, moreover, that I should not have much difficulty in gaining the suit. Claudet has loved you for a long time. He is good-hearted, and a fine fellow to look at. And as to worldly advantages, his position is now equal to your own. I have made over to him, by legal contract, the half of his father's estate. What answer am I to take back?"

He spoke with difficulty in broken sentences, without turning his eyes toward Mademoiselle Vincart. The silence that followed his last question seemed to him unbearable, and the contrasting chirping of the noisy grasshoppers, and the buzzing of the flies in the quiet sunny garden, resounded unpleasantly in his ears.

Reine remained speechless. She was disconcerted and well-nigh overpowered by the unexpected announcement, and her brain seemed unable to bear the crowd of tumultuous and conflicting emotions which presented themselves. Certainly, she had already suspected that Claudet had a secret liking for her, but she never had thought of encouraging the feeling. The avowal of his hopes neither surprised nor hurt her; that which pained her was the intervention of Julien, who had taken in hand the cause of his relative. Was it possible that this same M. de Buxières, who had made so audacious a display of his tender feeling in the hut, could now come forward as Claudet's advocate, as if it were the most natural thing in the world for him to do? In that case, his astonishing behavior at the *fête*, which had caused her so much pain, and which she had endeavored to excuse in her own mind as the untutored outbreak of his pent-up love, that fiery caress, was only the insulting manifestation of a brutal caprice? The transgressor thought so little of her, she was of such small importance in his eyes, that he had no hesitation in proposing that she marry Claudet? She beheld herself scorned, humiliated, insulted by the only man in whom she ever had felt interested. In the excess of her indignation she felt herself becoming hard-hearted and violent; a profound discouragement, a stony indifference to all things, impelled her to extreme measures, and, not being able at the moment to find any one on whom she could put them in operation, she was almost tempted to lay violent hands on herself.

"What shall I say to Claudet?" repeated Julien, endeavoring to conceal the suffering which was devouring his heart by an assumption of outward frigidity.

She turned slowly round, fixed her searching eyes, which had become as dark as waters reflecting a stormy sky, upon his face, and demanded, in icy tones:

"What do you advise me to say?"

Now, if Julien had been less of a novice, he would have understood that a girl who loves never addresses such a question; but the feminine heart was a book in which he was a very poor speller. He imagined that Reine was only asking him as a matter of form, and that it was from a feeling of maidenly reserve that she adopted this passive method of escaping from openly declaring her wishes. She no doubt desired his friendly aid in the matter, and he felt as if he ought to grant her that satisfaction.

"I have the conviction," stammered he, "that Claudet will make a good husband, and you will do well to accept him."

Reine bit her lip, and her paleness increased so as to

set off still more the fervid lustre of her eyes. The two little brown moles stood out more visibly on her white neck, and added to her attractions.

"So be it!" exclaimed she, "tell Claudet that I consent, and that he will be welcome at La Thuilière."

"I will tell him immediately." He bent gravely and sadly before Reine, who remained standing and motionless against the door. "Adieu, Mademoiselle!"

He turned away abruptly; plunged into the first avenue he came to, lost his way twice and finally reached the courtyard, and thence escaped at breakneck speed across the fields.

Reine maintained her statue-like pose as long as the young man's footsteps resounded on the stony paths; but when they died gradually away in the distance, when nothing could be heard save the monotonous trill of the grasshoppers basking in the sun, she threw herself down on the green heap of rubbish; she covered her face with her hands and gave way to a passionate outburst of tears and sobs.

In the meanwhile, Julien de Buxières, angry with himself, irritated by the speedy success of his mission, was losing his way among the pasturages, and getting entangled in the thickets. All the details of the interview presented themselves before his mind with remorseless clearness. He seemed more lonely, more unfortunate, more disgusted with himself and with all else than he ever had been before. Ashamed of the wretched part he had just been enacting, he felt almost childish repugnance to returning to Vivey, and tried to pick out the paths that would take him there by the longest way. But he was not sufficiently accustomed to laying out a route for himself, and when he thought he had a league farther to go, and had just leaped over an intervening hedge, the pointed roofs of the château appeared before him at a distance of not more than a hundred feet, and at one of the windows on the first floor he could distinguish Claudet, leaning for ward, as if to interrogate him.

He remembered then the promise he had made the young huntsman; and faithful to his word, although with rage and bitterness in his heart, he raised his hat, and with effort, waved it three times above his head. At this signal, the forerunner of good news, Claudet replied by a triumphant shout, and disappeared from the window. A moment later, Julien heard the noise of furious galloping down the enclosures of the park. It was the lover, hastening to learn the particulars of the interview.

CHAPTER VII

THE STRANGE, DARK SECRET

F Julien had once entertained the hope that Claudet's marriage with Reine would act as a kind of heroic remedy for the cure of his unfortunate passion, he very soon perceived that he had been wofully mistaken. As soon as he had informed the *grand chasserot* of the success of his undertaking, he became aware that his own burden was considerably heavier. Certainly it had been easier for him to bear uncertainty than the boisterous rapture evinced by his fortunate rival. His jealousy rose against it, and that was all. Now that he had torn from Reine the avowal of her love for Claudet, he was more than ever oppressed by his hopeless passion, and plunged into a condition of complete moral and physical disintegration. It mingled with his blood, his nerves, his thoughts, and possessed him altogether, dwelling within him like an adored and tyrannical mistress. Reine appeared constantly before him as he had contemplated her on the outside steps of the farmhouse, in her never-to-be-forgotten negligée of the short skirt and the half-open bodice. He again beheld the silken treasure of her tresses, gliding playfully around her shoulders, the clear, honest look of her limpid eyes, the expressive smile of her enchanting lips, and with a sudden revulsion of feeling he reflected that perhaps before a month was over, all these charms would belong to Claudet. Then, almost at the same moment, like a swallow, which, with one rapid turn of its wing, changes its course, his thoughts went in the opposite direction, and he began to imagine what would have happened if, instead of replying in the affirmative, Reine had objected to marrying Claudet. He could picture himself kneeling before her as before the Madonna, and in a low voice confessing his love. He would have taken her hands so respectfully, and pleaded so eloquently, that she would have allowed herself to be convinced. The little hands would have remained prisoners in his own; he would have lifted her tenderly, devotedly, in his arms, and under the influence of this feverish dream, he fancied he could feel the beating heart of the young girl against his own bosom. Suddenly he would wake up out of his illusions, and bite his lips with rage on finding himself in the dull reality of his own dwelling.

. One day he heard footsteps on the gravel; a sonorous and jovial voice met his ear. It was Claudet, starting for La Thuilière. Julien bent forward to see him, and ground his teeth as he watched his joyous departure. The sharp sting of jealousy entered his soul, and he rebelled against the evident injustice of Fate. How had he deserved that life should present so dismal and forbidding an aspect to him? He had had none of the joys of infancy; his youth had been spent wearily under the peevish discipline of a cloister; he had entered on his young manhood with all the awkwardness and timidity of a night-bird that is made to fly in the day. Up to the age of twenty-seven years, he had known neither love nor friendship; his time had been given entirely to earning his daily bread, and to the cultivation of religious exercises, which consoled him in some measure for his apparently useless way of living. Latterly, it is true, Fortune had seemed to smile upon him, by giving him a little more money and liberty, but this smile was a mere mockery, and a snare more hurtful than the pettinesses and privations of his past life. The fickle goddess, continuing her part of mystifier, had opened to his enraptured sight a magic window through which she had shown him a charming vision of possible happiness; but while he was still gazing, she had closed it abruptly in his face, laughing scornfully at his discomfiture. What sense was there in this perversion of justice, this perpetual mockery of Fate? At times the influence of his early education would resume its sway, and he would ask himself whether all this apparent contradiction were not a secret admonition from on high, warning him that he had not been created to enjoy the fleeting pleasures of this world, and ought, therefore, to turn his attention toward things eternal, and renounce the perishable delights of the flesh?

"If so," thought he, irreverently, "the warning comes rather late, and it would have answered the purpose better had I been allowed to continue in the narrow way of obscure poverty!" Now that the enervating influence of a more prosperous atmosphere had weakened his courage, and cooled the ardor of his piety, his faith began to totter like an old wall. His religious beliefs seemed to have been wrecked by the same storm which had destroyed his passionate hopes of love, and left him stranded and forlorn without either haven or pilot, blown hither and thither solely by the violence of his passion.

By degrees he took an aversion to his home, and would spend entire days in the woods. Their secluded haunts, already colored by the breath of autumn, became more attractive to him as other refuge failed him. They were his consolation; his doubts, weakness, and amorous regrets, found sympathy and indulgence under their silent shelter. He felt less lonely, less humiliated, less prosaic among these great forest depths, these lofty ash-trees, raising their verdant branches to heaven. He found he could more easily evoke the seductive image of Reine Vincart in these calm solitudes, where the recollections of the previous springtime mingled with the phantoms of his heated imagination and clothed themselves with almost living forms. He seemed to see the young girl rising from the mists of the distant valleys. The least fluttering of the leaves heralded her fancied approach. At times the hallucination was so complete that he could see, in the interlacing of the branches, the undulations of her supple form, and the graceful outlines of her profile. Then he would be seized by an insane desire to reach the fugitive and speak to her once more, and would go tearing along the brushwood for that purpose. Now and then, in the half light formed by the hanging boughs, he would see rays of golden light, coming straight down to the ground, and resting there lightly like diaphanous apparitions. Sometimes the rustling of birds taking flight, would sound in his ears like the timid *frou-frou* of a skirt, and Julien, fascinated by the mysterious charm of these indefinite objects, and following the impulse of their mystical suggestions, would fling himself impetuously into the jungle, repeating to himself the words of the "Canticle of Canticles": "I hear the voice of my beloved; behold! she cometh leaping upon the mountains, skipping upon the hills." He would continue to press forward in pursuit of the intangible apparition, until he sank with exhaustion near some stream or fountain. Under the influence of the fever, which was consuming his brain, he would imagine the trickling water to be the song of a feminine voice. He would wind his arms around the young saplings, he would tear the berries from the bushes, pressing them against his thirsty lips, and imagining their odoriferous sweetness to be a fond caress from the loved one.

He would return from these expeditions exhausted but not appeased. Sometimes he would come across Claudet, also returning home from paying his court to Reine Vincart; and the unhappy Julien would scrutinize his rival's countenance, seeking eagerly for some trace of the impressions he had received during the loving interview. His curiosity was nearly always baffled; for Claudet seemed to have left all his gayety and conversational powers at La Thuilière. During their tête-à-tête meals, he hardly spoke at all, maintaining a reserved attitude and a taciturn countenance. Julien, provoked at this unexpected sobriety, privately accused his cousin of dissimulation, and of trying to conceal his happiness. His jealousy so blinded him that he considered the silence of Claudet as pure hypocrisy not recognizing that it was assumed for the purpose of concealing some unpleasantness rather than satisfaction.

The fact was that Claudet, although rejoicing at the turn matters had taken, was verifying the poet's saying: "Never is perfect happiness our lot." When Julien brought him the good news, and he had flown so joyfully to La Thuilière, he had certainly been cordially received by Reine, but, nevertheless, he had noticed with surprise an absent and dreamy look in her eyes, which did not agree with his idea of a first interview of lovers. When he wished to express his affection in the vivacious and significant manner ordinarily employed among the peasantry, that is to say, by vigorous embracing and resounding kisses, he met with unexpected resistance.

"Keep quiet!" was the order, "and let us talk rationally!"

He obeyed, although not agreeing in her view of the reserve to be maintained between lovers; but, he made up his mind to return to the charge and triumph over her bashful scruples. In fact, he began again the very next day, and his impetuous ardor encountered the same refusal in the same firm, though affectionate manner. He ventured to complain, telling Reine that she did not love him as she ought.

"If I did not feel friendly toward you," replied the young girl, laconically, "should I have allowed you to talk to me of marriage?"

Then, seeing that he looked vexed and worried, and

realizing that she was perhaps treating him too roughly, she continued, more gently:

"Remember, Claudet, that I am living all alone at the farm. That obliges me to have more reserve than a girl whose mother is with her. So you must not be offended if I do not behave exactly as others might, and rest assured that it will not prevent me from being a good wife to you, when we are married."

"Well, now," thought Claudet, as he was returning despondently to Vivey: "I can't help thinking that a little caress now and then wouldn't hurt any one!"

Under these conditions it is not to be supposed he was in a mood to relate any of the details of such meagre love-making. His self-love was wounded by Reine's coldness. Having always been "cock-of-the-walk," he could not understand why he had such poor success with the only one about whom he was in earnest. He kept quiet, therefore, hiding his anxiety under the mask of careless indifference. Moreover, a certain primitive instinct of prudence made him circumspect. In his innermost soul, he still entertained doubts of Julien's sincerity. Sometimes he doubted whether his cousin's conduct had not been dictated by the bitterness of rejected love, rather than a generous impulse of affection, and he did not care to reveal Reine's repulse to one whom he vaguely suspected of being a former lover. His simple, ardent nature could not put up with opposition, and he thought only of hastening the day when Reine would belong to him altogether. But, when he broached this subject, he had the mortification to find that she was less impatient than himself.

"There is no hurry," she replied, "our affairs are not in order, our harvests are not housed, and it would be better to wait till the dull season."

In his first moments of joy and effervescence, Claudet had evinced the desire to announce immediately the betrothal throughout the village. This Reine had opposed; she thought they should avoid awakening public curiosity so long beforehand, and she extracted from Claudet a promise to say nothing until the date of the marriage should be settled. He had unwillingly consented, and thus, during the last month, the matter had been dragging on indefinitely.

With Julien de Buxières, this interminable delay, these incessant comings and goings from the château to the farm, as well as the mysterious conduct of the bridegroom-elect, became a subject of serious irritation, amounting almost to obsession. He would have wished the affair hurried up, and the sacrifice consummated without hindrance. He believed that when once the newly-married pair had taken up their quarters at La Thuilière, the very certainty that Reine belonged in future to another would suffice to effect a radical cure in him, and chase away the deceptive phantoms by which he was pursued.

One evening, as Claudet was returning home, more out of humor and silent than usual, Julien asked him, abruptly:

"Well! how are you getting along? When is the wedding?"

"Nothing is decided yet," replied Claudet, "we have time enough!"

"You think so?" exclaimed de Buxières, sarcastically; "you have considerable patience for a lover!"

The remark and the tone provoked Claudet.

"The delay is not of my making," returned he.

"Ah!" replied the other, quickly, "then it comes from Mademoiselle Vincart?" And a sudden gleam came into his eyes, as if Claudet's assertion had kindled a spark of hope in his breast. The latter noticed the momentary brightness in his cousin's usually stormy countenance, and hastened to reply:

"Nay, nay; we both think it better to postpone the wedding until the harvest is in."

"You are wrong. A wedding should not be postponed. Besides, this prolonged love-making, these daily visits to the farm—all that is not very proper. It is compromising for Mademoiselle Vincart!"

Julien shot out these remarks with a degree of fierceness and violence that astonished Claudet.

"You think, then," said he, "that we ought to rush matters, and have the wedding before winter?"

"Undoubtedly!"

The next day, at La Thuilière, the *grand chasserot*, as he stood in the orchard, watching Reine spread linen on the grass, entered bravely on the subject.

"Reine," said he, coaxingly, "I think we shall have to decide upon a day for our wedding."

She set down the watering-pot with which she was wetting the linen, and looked anxiously at her betrothed.

"I thought we had agreed to wait until the later season. Why do you wish to change that arrangement?"

"That is true; I promised not to hurry you, Reine,

but it is beyond me to wait—you must not be vexed with me if I find the time long. Besides, they know nothing, around the village, of our intentions, and my coming here every day might cause gossip and make it unpleasant for you. At any rate, that is the opinion of Monsieur de Buxières, with whom I was conferring only yesterday evening."

At the name of Julien, Reine frowned and bit her lip.

"Aha!" said she, "it is he who has been advising you?"

"Yes; he says the sooner we are married, the better it will be."

"Why does he interfere in what does not concern him?" said she, angrily, turning her head away. She stood a moment in thought, absently pushing forward the roll of linen with her foot. Then, shrugging her shoulders and raising her head, she said slowly, while still avoiding Claudet's eyes:

"Perhaps you are right—both of you. Well, let it be so! I authorize you to go to Monsieur le Curé and arrange the day with him."

"Oh, thanks, Reine!" exclaimed Claudet, rapturously; "you make me very happy!"

He pressed her hands in his, but though absorbed in his own joyful feelings, he could not help remarking that the young girl was trembling in his grasp. He even fancied that there was a suspicious, tearful glitter in her brilliant eyes.

He left her, however, and repaired at once to the curé's house, which stood near the château, a little behind the church.

A WOODLAND QUEEN

The servant showed him into a small garden separated by a low wall from the cemetery. He found the Abbé Pernot seated on a stone bench, sheltered by a trellised vine. He was occupied in cutting up pieces of hazel-nuts to make traps for small birds.

"Good-evening, Claudet!" said the curé, without moving from his work; "you find me busy preparing my nets; if you will permit me, I will continue, for I should like to have my two hundred traps finished by this evening. The season is advancing, you know! The birds will begin their migrations, and I should be greatly provoked if I were not equipped in time for the opportune moment. And how is Monsieur de Buxières? I trust he will not be less good-natured than his deceased cousin, and that he will allow me to spread my snares on the border hedge of his woods. But," added he, as he noticed the flurried, impatient countenance of his visitor, "I forgot to ask you, my dear young fellow, to what happy chance I owe your visit? Excuse my neglect!"

"Don't mention it, Monsieur le Curé. You have guessed rightly. It is a very happy circumstance which brings me. I am about to marry."

"Aha!" laughed the Abbé, "I congratulate you, my dear young friend. This is really delightful news. It is not good for man to be alone, and I am glad to know you must give up the perilous life of a bachelor. Well, tell me quickly the name of your betrothed. Do I know her?"

"Of course you do, Monsieur le Curé; there are few you know so well. It is Mademoiselle Vincart."

"Reine?"

The Abbé flung away the pruning-knife and branch that he was cutting, and gazed at Claudet with a stupefied air. At the same time, his jovial face became shadowed, and his mouth assumed an expression of consternation.

"Yes, indeed, Reine Vincart," repeated Claudet, somewhat vexed at the startled manner of his reverence; "are you surprised at my choice?"

"Excuse me—and—is it all settled?" stammered the Abbé, with bewilderment, "and—and do you really love each other?"

"Certainly; we agree on that point; and I have come here to arrange with you about having the banns published."

"What! already?" murmured the curé, buttoning and unbuttoning the top of his coat in his agitation, "you seem to be in a great hurry to go to work. The union of the man and the woman—ahem—is a serious matter, which ought not to be undertaken without due consideration. That is the reason why the Church has instituted the sacrament of marriage. Hast thou well considered, my son?"

"Why, certainly, I have reflected," exclaimed Claudet with some irritation, "and my mind is quite made up. Once more, I ask you, Monsieur le Curé, are you displeased with my choice, or have you anything to say against Mademoiselle Vincart?"

"I? no, absolutely nothing. Reine is an exceedingly good girl."

"Well, then?"

"Well, my friend, I will go over to-morrow and see

your fiancée, and we will talk matters over. I shall act for the best, in the interests of both of you, be assured of that. In the meantime, you will both be united this evening in my prayers; but, for to-day, we shall have to stop where we are. Good-evening, Claudet! I will see you again."

With these enigmatic words, he dismissed the young lover, who returned to the château, vexed and disturbed by his strange reception.

The moment the door of the presbytery had closed behind Claudet, the Abbé Pernot, flinging to one side all his preparations, began to pace nervously up and down the principal garden-walk. He appeared completely unhinged. His features were drawn, through an unusual tension of ideas forced upon him. He had hurriedly caught his skull-cap from his head, as if he feared the heat of his meditation might cause a rush of blood to the head. He quickened his steps, then stopped suddenly, folded his arms with great energy, then opened them again abruptly to thrust his hands into the pockets of his gown, searching through them with feverish anxiety, as if he expected to find something which might solve obscure and embarrassing questions.

"Good Lord! Good Lord! What a dreadful piece of business; and right in the bird season, too! But I can say nothing to Claudet. It is a secret that does not belong to me. How can I get out of it? Tutt! tutt! tutt!"

These monosyllabic ejaculations broke forth like the vexed clucking of a frightened blackbird; after which relief, the Abbé resumed his fitful striding up and down the box-bordered alley. This lasted until the hour of twilight, when Augustine, the servant, as soon as the Angelus had sounded, went to inform her master that they were waiting prayers for him in the church. He obeyed the summons, although in a somewhat absent mood, and hurried over the services in a manner which did not contribute to the edification of the assistants. As soon as he got home, he ate his supper without appetite, mumbled his prayers, and shut himself up in the room he used as a study and workshop. He remained there until the night was far advanced, searching through his scanty library to find two dusty volumes treating of "cases of conscience," which he looked eagerly over by the feeble light of his study lamp. During this laborious search he emitted frequent sighs, and only left off reading occasionally in order to dose himself plentifully with snuff. At last, as he felt that his eyes were becoming inflamed, his ideas conflicting in his brain, and as his lamp was getting low, he decided to go to bed. But he slept badly, turned over at least twenty times, and was up with the first streak of day to say his mass in the chapel. He officiated with more dignity and piety than was his wont; and after reading the second gospel he remained for a long while kneeling on one of the steps of the altar. After he had returned to the sacristy, he divested himself quickly of his sacerdotal robes, reached his room by a passage of communication, breakfasted hurriedly, and putting on his three-cornered hat, and seizing his knotty, cherry-wood cane, he shot out of doors as if he had been summoned to a fire.

Augustine, amazed at his precipitate departure, went

up to the attic, and, from behind the shelter of the sky-light, perceived her master striding rapidly along the road to Planche-au-Vacher. There she lost sight of him—the underwood was too thick. But, after a few minutes, the gaze of the inquisitive woman was re-warded by the appearance of a dark object emerging from the copse, and defining itself on the bright pasture land beyond. "Monsieur le Curé is going to La Thuilière," thought she, and with this half-satisfaction she descended to her daily occupations.

It was true, the Abbé Pernot was walking, as fast as he could, to the Vincart farm, as unmindful of the dew that tarnished his shoe-buckles as of the thorns which attacked his calves. He had that within him which spurred him on, and rendered him unconscious of the accidents on his path. Never, during his twenty-five years of priestly office, had a more difficult question embarrassed his conscience. The case was a grave one, and moreover, so urgent that the Abbé was quite at a loss how to proceed. How was it that he never had foreseen that such a combination of circumstances might occur? A priest of a more fervent spirit, who had the salvation of his flock more at heart, could not have been taken so unprepared. Yes; that was surely the cause! The profane occupations in which he had al-lowed himself to take so much enjoyment, had distracted his watchfulness and obscured his perspicacity. Provi-dence was now punishing him for his lukewarmness, by interposing across his path this stumbling-block, which was probably sent to him as a salutary warning, but which he saw no way of getting over.

While he was thus meditating and reproaching himself, the thrushes were calling to one another from the branches of their favorite trees; whole flights of yellowhammers burst forth from the hedges red with haws; but he took no heed of them and did not even give a single thought to his neglected nests and snares.

He went straight on, stumbling over the juniper bushes, and wondering what he should say when he reached the farm, and how he should begin. Sometimes he addressed himself, thus: "Have I the right to speak? What a revelation! And to a young girl! Oh, Lord, lead me in the straight way of thy truth, and instruct me in the right path!"

As he continued piously repeating this verse of the Psalmist, in order to gain spiritual strength, the gray roofs of La Thuilière rose before him; he could hear the crowing of the cocks and the lowing of the cows in the stable. Five minutes after, he had pushed open the door of the kitchen where La Guite was arranging the bowls for breakfast.

"Good-morning, Guitiote," said he, in a choking voice; "is Mademoiselle Vincart up?"

"Holy Virgin! Monsieur le Curé! Why, certainly Mademoiselle is up. She was on foot before any of us, and now she is trotting around the orchard. I will go fetch her."

"No, do not stir. I know the way, and I will go and find her myself."

She was in the orchard, was she? The Abbé preferred it should be so; he thought the interview would be less painful, and that the surrounding trees would give him ideas. He walked across the kitchen, descended the steps leading from the ground floor to the garden, and ascended the slope in search of Reine, whom he soon perceived in the midst of a bower formed by clustering filbert-trees.

At sight of the curé, Reine turned pale; he had doubtless come to tell her the result of his interview with Claudet, and what day had been definitely chosen for the nuptial celebration. She had been troubled all night by the reflection that her fate would soon be irrevocably sealed; she had wept, and her eyes betrayed it. Only the day before, she had looked upon this project of marriage, which she had entertained in a moment of anger and injured feeling, as a vague thing, a vaporous eventuality of which the realization was doubtful; now, all was arranged, settled, cruelly certain; there was no way of escaping from a promise which Claudet, alas! was bound to consider a serious one. These thoughts traversed her mind, while the curé was slowly approaching the filbert-trees; she felt her heart throb, and her eyes again filled with tears. Yet her pride would not allow that the Abbé should witness her irresolution and weeping; she made an effort, overcame the momentary weakness, and addressed the priest in an almost cheerful voice:

"Monsieur le Curé, I am sorry that they have made you come up this hill to find me. Let us go back to the farm, and I will offer you a cup of coffee."

"No, my child," replied the Abbé, motioning with his hand that she should stay where she was, "no, thank you! I will not take anything. Remain where you are.

I wish to talk to you, and we shall be less liable to be disturbed here."

There were two rustic seats under the nut-trees; the curé took one and asked Reine to take the other, opposite to him. There they were, under the thick, verdant branches, hidden from indiscreet passers-by, surrounded by silence, installed as in a confessional.

The morning quiet, the solitude, the half light, all invited meditation and confidence; nevertheless the young girl and the priest sat motionless; both agitated and embarrassed and watching each other without uttering a sound. It was Reine who first broke the silence.

"You have seen Claudet, Monsieur le Curé?"

"Yes, yes!" replied the Abbé, sighing deeply.

"He—spoke to you of our—plans," continued the young girl, in a quavering voice, "and you fixed the day?"

"No, my child, we settled nothing. I wanted to see you first, and converse with you about something very important."

The Abbé hesitated, rubbed a spot of mud off his soutane, raised his shoulders like a man lifting a heavy burden, then gave a deep cough.

"My dear child," continued he at length, prudently dropping his voice a tone lower, "I will begin by repeating to you what I said yesterday to Claudet Séjournant: the marriage, that is to say, the indissoluble union, of man and woman before God, is one of the most solemn and serious acts of life. The Church has constituted it a sacrament, which she administers only on certain formal conditions. Before entering into this bond, one ought, as we are taught by Holy Writ, to sound the heart, subject the very inmost of the soul to searching examinations. I beg of you, therefore, answer my questions freely, without false shame, just as if you were at the tribunal of repentance. Do you love Claudet?"

Reine trembled. This appeal to her sincerity renewed all her perplexities and scruples. She raised her full, glistening eyes to the curé, and replied, after a slight hesitation:

"I have a sincere affection for Claudet—and—much esteem."

"I understand that," replied the priest, compressing his lips, "but—excuse me if I press the matter—has the engagement you have made with him been determined simply by considerations of affection and suitableness, or by more interior and deeper feelings?"

"Pardon, Monsieur le Curé," returned Reine, coloring, "it seems to me that a sentiment of friendship, joined to a firm determination to prove a faithful and devoted wife, should be, in your eyes as they are in mine, a sufficient assurance that——"

"Certainly, certainly, my dear child; and many husbands would be contented with less. However, it is not only a question of Claudet's happiness, but of yours also. Come now! let me ask you: is your affection for young Séjournant so powerful that in the event of any unforeseen circumstance happening, to break off the marriage, you would be forever unhappy?"

"Ah!" replied Reine, more embarrassed than ever, "you ask too grave a question, Monsieur le Curé! If it were broken off without my having to reproach myself for it, it is probable that I should find consolation in time."

"Very good! Consequently, you do not love Claudet, if I may take the word *love* in the sense understood by people of the world. You only like, you do not love him? Tell me. Answer frankly."

"Frankly, Monsieur le Curé, no!"

"Thanks be to God! We are saved!" exclaimed the Abbé, drawing a long breath, while Reine, amazed, gazed at him with wondering eyes.

"I do not understand you," faltered she; "what is it?"

"It is this: the marriage can not take place."

"Can not? why?"

"It is impossible, both in the eyes of the Church and in those of the world."

The young girl looked at him with increasing amazement.

"You alarm me!" cried she. "What has happened? What reasons hinder me from marrying Claudet?"

"Very powerful reasons, my dear child. I do not feel at liberty to reveal them to you, but you must know that I am not speaking without authority, and that you may rely on the statement I have made."

Reine remained thoughtful, her brows knit, her countenance troubled.

"I have every confidence in you, Monsieur le Curé, but——"

"But you hesitate about believing me," interrupted the Abbé, piqued at not finding in one of his flock the blind obedience on which he had reckoned. "You must know, nevertheless, that your pastor has no interest in deceiving you, and that when he seeks to influence you, he has in view only your well-being in this world and in the next."

"I do not doubt your good intentions," replied Reine, with firmness, "but a promise can not be annulled without sufficient cause. I have given my word to Claudet, and I am too loyal at heart to break faith with him without letting him know the reason."

"You will find some pretext."

"And supposing that Claudet would be content with such a pretext, my own conscience would not be," objected the young girl, raising her clear, honest glance toward the priest; "your words have entered my soul, they are troubling me now, and it will be worse when I begin to think this matter over again. I can not bear uncertainty. I must see my way clearly before me. I entreat you then, Monsieur le Curé, not to do things by halves. You have thought it your duty to tell me I can not wed with Claudet; now tell me why not?"

"Why not? why not?" repeated the Abbé, angrily. "I distress myself in telling you that I am not authorized to satisfy your unwise curiosity! You must humble your intelligence and believe without arguing."

"In matters of faith, that may be possible," urged Reine, obstinately, "but my marriage has nothing to do with discussing the truths of our holy religion. I therefore respectfully ask to be enlightened, Monsieur le Curé; otherwise——"

"Otherwise?" repeated the Abbé Pernot, inquiringly, rolling his eyes uneasily.

"Otherwise, I shall keep my word respectably, and I shall marry Claudet."

"You will not do that?" said he, imploringly, joining his hands as if in supplication; "after being openly warned by me, you dare not burden your soul with such a terrible responsibility. Come, my child, does not the possibility of committing a mortal sin alarm your conscience as a Christian?"

"I can not sin if I am in ignorance, and as to my conscience, Monsieur le Curé, do you think it is acting like a Christian to alarm without enlightening?"

"Is that your last word?" inquired the Abbé, completely aghast.

"It is my last word," she replied, vehemently, moved both by a feeling of self-respect, and a desire to force the hand of her interlocutor.

"You are a proud, obstinate girl!" exclaimed the Abbé, rising abruptly, "you wish to compel me to reveal this secret! Well, have your way! I will tell you. May the harm which may result from it fall lightly upon you, and do not hereafter reproach me for the pain I am about to inflict upon you."

He checked himself for a moment, again joined his hands, and raising his eyes toward heaven ejaculated fervently, as if repeating his devotions in the oratory: "O Lord, thou knowest I would have spared her this bitter cup, but, between two evils, I have avoided the greater. If I forfeit my solemn promise, consider, O Lord, I pray thee, that I do it to avoid disgrace and exposure for her, and deign to forgive thy servant!"

He seated himself again, placed one of his hands be-

fore his eyes, and began, in a hollow voice, Reine, all
the while gazing nervously at him:

"My child, you are forcing me to violate a secret
which has been solemnly confided to me. It concerns
a matter not usually talked about before young girls,
but you are, I believe, already a woman in heart and
understanding, and you will hear resignedly what I have
to tell you, however much the recital may trouble you.
I have already informed you that your marriage with
Claudet is impossible. I now declare that it would be
criminal, for the reason that incest is an abomination."

"Incest!" repeated Reine, pale and trembling, "what
do you mean?"

"I mean," sighed the curé, "that you are Claudet's
sister, not having the same mother, but the same father:
Claude-Odouart de Buxières."

"Oh! you are mistaken! that can not be!"

"I am stating facts. It grieves me to the heart, my
dear child, that in speaking of your deceased mother,
I should have to reveal an error over which she lamented,
like David, with tears of blood. She confessed her sin,
not to the priest, but to a friend, a few days before her
death. In justice to her memory, I ought to add that,
like most of the unfortunates seduced by this untama-
ble de Buxières, she succumbed to his wily misrepre-
sentations. She was a victim rather than an accom-
plice. The man himself acknowledged as much in a
note entrusted to my care, which I have here."

And the Abbé drew from his pocket an old, worn
letter, the writing yellow with age, and placed it before
Reine. In this letter, written in Claude de Buxières's

12   [177]

coarse, sprawling hand, doubtless in reply to a reproach-ful appeal from his mistress, he endeavored to offer some kind of honorable amends for the violence he had used, and to calm Madame Vincart's remorse by promising, as was his custom, to watch over the future of the child which should be born to her.

"That child was yourself, my poor girl," continued the Abbé, picking up the letter which Reine had thrown down, after reading it, with a gesture of sickened disgust.

She appeared not to hear him. She had buried her face in her hands, to hide the flushing of her cheeks, and sat motionless, altogether crushed beneath the shameful revelation; convulsive sobs and tremblings occasionally agitating her frame.

"You can now understand," continued the priest, "how the announcement of this projected marriage stunned and terrified me. I could not confide to Claudet the reason for my stupefaction, and I should have been thankful if you could have understood so that I could have spared you this cruel mortification, but you would not take any intimation from me. And now, forgive me for inflicting this cross upon you, and bear it with courage, with Christian fortitude."

"You have acted as was your duty," murmured Reine, sadly, "and I thank you, Monsieur le Curé!"

"And will you promise me to dismiss Claudet at once —to-day?"

"I promise you."

The Abbé Pernot advanced to take her hand, and administer some words of consolation; but she evaded, with a stern gesture, the good man's pious sympathy, and escaped toward the dwelling.

The spacious kitchen was empty when she entered. The shutters had been closed against the sun, and it had become cool and pleasant. Here and there, among the copper utensils, and wherever a chance ray made a gleam of light, the magpie was hopping about, uttering short, piercing cries. In the recess of the niche containing the colored prints, sat the old man Vincart, dozing, in his usual supine attitude, his hands spread out, his eyelids drooping, his mouth half open. At the sound of the door, his eyes opened wide. He rather guessed at, than saw, the entrance of the young girl, and his pallid lips began their accustomed refrain: "Reine! Rei—eine!"

Reine flew impetuously toward the paralytic old man, threw herself on her knees before him, sobbing bitterly, and covered his hands with kisses. Her caresses were given in a more respectful, humble, contrite manner than ever before.

"Oh! father—father!" faltered she; "I loved you always, I shall love you now with all my heart and soul!"

CHAPTER VIII

THE kitchen was bright with sunshine, and the industrious bees were buzzing around the flowers on the window-sills, while Reine was listlessly attending to culinary duties, and preparing her father's meal. The humiliating disclosures made by the Abbé Pernot weighed heavily upon her mind. She foresaw that Claudet would shortly be at La Thuilière in order to hear the result of the curé's visit; but she did not feel sufficiently mistress of herself to have a decisive interview with him at such short notice, and resolved to gain at least one day by absenting herself from the farm. It seemed to her necessary that she should have that length of time to arrange her ideas, and evolve some way of separating Claudet and herself without his suspecting the real motive of rupture. So, telling La Guite to say that unexpected business had called her away, she set out for the woods of Maigrefontaine.

Whenever she had felt the need of taking counsel with herself before deciding on any important matter, the forest had been her refuge and her inspiration. The refreshing solitude of the valleys, watered by living streams, acted as a strengthening balm to her irresolute

[180]

will; her soul inhaled the profound peace of these leafy
retreats. By the time she had reached the inmost shade
of the forest her mind had become calmer, and better
able to unravel the confusion of thoughts that surged
like troubled waters through her brain. The dominant
idea was, that her self-respect had been wounded; the
shock to her maidenly modesty, and the shame attendant
upon the fact, affected her physically, as if she had been
belittled and degraded by a personal stain; and this
downfall caused her deep humiliation. By slow degrees,
however, and notwithstanding this state of abject despair, she felt, cropping up somewhere in her heart, a
faint germ of gladness, and, by close examination, discovered its origin: she was now loosed from her obligations toward Claudet, and the prospect of being once
more free afforded her immediate consolation.

She had so much regretted, during the last few weeks,
the feeling of outraged pride which had incited her to
consent to this marriage; her loyal, sincere nature had
revolted at the constraint she had imposed upon herself;
her nerves had been so severely taxed by having to
receive her fiancé with sufficient warmth to satisfy his
expectations, and yet not afford any encouragement to
his demonstrative tendencies, that the certainty of her
newly acquired freedom created a sensation of relief and
well-being. But, hardly had she analyzed and acknowledged this sensation when she reproached herself for
harboring it when she was about to cause Claudet such
affliction.

Poor Claudet! what a cruel blow was in store for him!
He was so guilelessly in love, and had such unbounded

confidence in the success of his projects! **Reine was** overcome by tender reminiscences. She had always experienced, as if divining by instinct the natural bonds which united them, a sisterly affection for Claudet. Since their earliest infancy, at the age when they learned their catechism under the church porch, they had been united in a bond of friendly fellowship. With Reine, this tender feeling had always remained one of friendship, but, with Claudet, it had ripened into love; and now, after allowing the poor young fellow to believe that his love was reciprocated, she was forced to disabuse him. It was useless for her to try to find some way of softening the blow; there was none. Claudet was too much in love to remain satisfied with empty words; he would require solid reasons; and the only conclusive one which would convince him, without wounding his self-love, was exactly the one which the young girl could not give him. She was, therefore, doomed to send Claudet away with the impression that he had been jilted by a, heartless and unprincipled coquette. And yet something must be done. The *grand chasserot* had been too long already in the toils; there was something barbarously cruel in not freeing him from his illusions.

In this troubled state of mind, Reine gazed appealingly at the silent witnesses of her distress. She heard a voice within her saying to the tall, vaulted ash, "Inspire me!" to the little rose-colored centaurea of the wayside, "Teach me a charm to cure the harm I have done!" But the woods, which in former days had been her advisers and instructors, remained deaf to her invocation. For the first time, she felt herself isolated and abandoned to her own resources, even in the midst of her beloved forest.

It is when we experience these violent mental crises, that we become suddenly conscious of Nature's cold indifference to our sufferings. She really is nothing more than the reflex of our own sensations, and can only give us back what we lend her. Beautiful but selfish, she allows herself to be courted by novices, but presents a freezing, emotionless aspect to those who have out-lived their illusions.

Reine did not reach home until the day had begun to wane. La Guite informed her that Claudet had waited for her during part of the afternoon, and that he would come again the next day at nine o'clock. Notwithstanding her bodily fatigue, she slept uneasily, and her sleep was troubled by feverish dreams. Every time she closed her eyes, she fancied herself conversing with Claudet, and woke with a start at the sound of his angry voice.

She arose at dawn, descended at once to the lower floor, to get through her morning tasks, and as soon as the big kitchen clock struck nine, she left the house and took the path by which Claudet would come. A feeling of delicate consideration toward her lover had impelled her to choose for her explanation any other place than the one where she had first received his declaration of love, and consented to the marriage. Very soon he came in sight, his stalwart figure outlined against the gray landscape. He was walking rapidly; her heart smote her, her hands became like ice, but she summoned all her fortitude, and went bravely forward to meet him.

When he came within forty or fifty feet, he recognized Reine, and took a short cut across the stubble studded with cobwebs glistening with dew.

"Aha! my Reine, my queen, good-morning!" cried he, joyously, "it is sweet of you to come to meet me!"

"Good-morning, Claudet. I came to meet you because I wish to speak with you on matters of importance, and I preferred not to have the conversation take place in our house. Shall we walk as far as the Planche-au-Vacher?"

He stopped short, astonished at the proposal and also at the sad and resolute attitude of his betrothed. He examined her more closely, noticed her deep-set eyes, her cheeks, whiter than usual.

"Why, what is the matter, Reine?" he inquired; "you are not yourself; do you not feel well?"

"Yes, and no. I have passed a bad night, thinking over matters that are troubling me, and I think that has produced some fever."

"What matters? Any that concern us?"

"Yes;" replied she, laconically.

Claudet opened his eyes. The young girl's continued gravity began to alarm him; but, seeing that she walked quickly forward, with an absent air, her face lowered, her brows bent, her mouth compressed, he lost courage and refrained from asking her any questions. They walked on thus in silence, until they came to the open level covered with juniper-bushes, from which solitary place, surrounded by hawthorn hedges, they could trace the narrow defile leading to Vivey, and the faint mist beyond.

A WOODLAND QUEEN

"Let us stop here," said Reine, seating herself on a flat, mossy stone, "we can talk here without fear of being disturbed."

"No fear of that," remarked Claudét, with a forced smile, "with the exception of the shepherd of Vivey, who comes here sometimes with his cattle, we shall not see many passers-by. It must be a secret that you have to tell me, Reine?" he added.

"No;" she returned, "but I foresee that my words will give you pain, my poor Claudet, and I prefer you should hear them without being annoyed by the farm-people passing to and fro."

"Explain yourself!" he exclaimed, impetuously. "For heaven's sake, don't keep me in suspense!"

"Listen, Claudet. When you asked my hand in marriage, I answered yes, without taking time to reflect. But, since I have been thinking over our plans, I have had scruples. My father is becoming every day more of an invalid, and in his present state I really have no right to live for any one but him. One would think he was aware of our intentions, for since you have been visiting at the farm, he is more agitated and suffers more. I think that any change in his way of living would bring on a stroke, and I never should forgive myself if I thought I had shortened his life. That is the reason why, as long as I have him with me, I do not see that it will be possible for me to dispose of myself. On the other hand, I do not wish to abuse your patience. I therefore ask you to take back your liberty and give me back my promise."

"That is to say, you won't have me!" he exclaimed.

[185]

"No; my poor friend, it means only that I shall not marry so long as my father is living, and that I can not ask you to wait until I am perfectly free. Forgive me for having entered into the engagement too carelessly, and do not on that account take your friendship from me."

"Reine," interrupted Claudet, angrily, "don't turn your brain inside out to make me believe that night is broad day. I am not a child, and I see very well that your father's health is only a pretext. You don't want me, that's all, and, with all due respect, you have changed your mind very quickly! Only the day before yesterday you authorized me to arrange about the day for the ceremony with the Abbé Pernot. Now that you have had a visit from the curé, you want to put the affair off until the week when two Sundays come together! I am a little curious to know what that confounded old abbé has been babbling about me, to turn you inside out like a glove in such a short time."

Claudet's conscience reminded him of several rare frolics, chance love-affairs, meetings in the woods, and so on, and he feared the priest might have told Reine some unfavorable stories about him. "Ah!" he continued, clenching his fists, "if this old poacher in a cassock has done me an ill turn with you, he will not have much of a chance for paradise!"

"Undeceive yourself," said Reine, quickly, "Monsieur le Curé is your friend, like myself; he esteems you highly, and never has said anything but good of you."

"Oh, indeed!" sneered the young man, "as you are

both so fond of me, how does it happen that you have given me my dismissal the very day after your interview with the curé?"

Reine, knowing Claudet's violent disposition, and wishing to avoid trouble for the curé, thought it advisable to have recourse to evasion.

"Monsieur le Curé," said she, "has had no part in my decision. He has not spoken against you, and deserves no reproaches from you."

"In that case, why do you send me away?"

"I repeat again, the comfort and peace of my father are paramount with me, and I do not intend to marry so long as he may have need of me."

"Well," said Claudet, persistently, "I love you, and I will wait."

"It can not be."

"Why?"

"Because," replied she, sharply, "because it would be kind neither to you, nor to my father, nor to me. Because marriages that drag along in that way are never good for anything!"

"Those are bad reasons!" he muttered, gloomily.

"Good or bad," replied the young girl, "they appear valid to me, and I hold to them."

"Reine," said he, drawing near to her and looking straight into her eyes, "can you swear, by the head of your father, that you have given me the true reason for your rejecting me?"

She became embarrassed, and remained silent.

"See!" he exclaimed, "you dare not take the oath!"

"My word should suffice," she faltered.

"No; it does not suffice. But your silence says a great deal, I tell you! You are too frank, Reine, and you don't know how to lie. I read it in your eyes, I do. The true reason is that you do not love me."

She shrugged her shoulders and turned away her head.

"No, you do not love me. If you had any love for me, instead of discouraging me, you would hold out some hope to me, and advise me to have patience. You never have loved me, confess now!"

By dint of this persistence, Reine by degrees lost her self-confidence. She could realize how much Claudet was suffering, and she reproached herself for the torture she was inflicting upon him. Driven into a corner, and recognizing that the avowal he was asking for was the only one that would drive him away, she hesitated no longer.

"Alas!" she murmured, lowering her eyes, "since you force me to tell you some truths that I would rather have kept from you, I confess you have guessed. I have a sincere friendship for you, but that is all. I have concluded that to marry a person one ought to love him differently, more than everything else in the world, and I feel that my heart is not turned altogether toward you."

"No," said Claudet, bitterly, "it is turned elsewhere."

"What do you mean? I do not understand you."

"I mean that you love some one else."

"That is not true," she protested.

"You are blushing—a proof that I have hit the nail!"

"Enough of this!" cried she, imperiously.

"You are right. Now that you have said you don't want me any longer, I have no right to ask anything further. Adieu!"

He turned quickly on his heel. Reine was conscious of having been too hard with him, and not wishing him to go away with such a grief in his heart, she sought to retain him by placing her hand upon his arm.

"Come, Claudet," said she, entreatingly, "do not let us part in anger. It pains me to see you suffer, and I am sorry if I have said anything unkind to you. Give me your hand in good fellowship, will you?"

But Claudet drew back with a fierce gesture, and glancing angrily at Reine, he replied, rudely:

"Thanks for your regrets and your pity; I have no use for them." She understood that he was deeply hurt; gave up entreating, and turned away with eyes full of tears.

He remained motionless, his arms crossed, in the middle of the road. After some minutes, he turned his head. Reine was already nothing more than a dark speck against the gray of the increasing fog. Then he went off, haphazard, across the pasture-lands. The fog was rising slowly, and the sun, shorn of its beams, showed its pale face faintly through it. To the right and the left, the woods were half hidden by moving white billows, and Claudet walked between fluid walls of vapor. This hidden sky, these veiled surroundings, harmonized with his mental condition. It was easier for him to hide his chagrin. "Some one else! Yes; that's it. She loves some other fellow! how was it I

did not find that out the very first day?" Then he recalled how Reine shrank from him when he solicited
a caress; how she insisted on their betrothal being kept
secret, and how many times she had postponed the date
of the wedding. It was evident that she had received
him only in self-defence, and on the pleading of Julien
de Buxières. Julien! the name threw a gleam of light
across his brain, hitherto as foggy as the country around
him. Might not Julien be the fortunate rival on whom
Reine's affections were so obstinately set? Still, if she
had always loved Monsieur de Buxières, in what spirit
of perversity or thoughtlessness had she suffered the
advances of another suitor?

Reine was no coquette; and such a course of action
would be repugnant to her frank, open nature. It was
a profound enigma, which Claudet, who had plenty of
good common sense, but not much insight, was unable
to solve. But grief has, among its other advantages, the
power of rendering our perceptions more acute; and by
dint of revolving the question in his mind, Claudet at last
became enlightened. Had not Reine simply followed
the impulse of her wounded feelings? She was very
proud, and when the man whom she secretly loved had
come coolly forward to plead the cause of one who was
indifferent to her, would not her self-respect be lowered,
and would she not, in a spirit of bravado, accept the
proposition, in order that he might never guess the sufferings of her spurned affections? There was no doubt,
that, later, recognizing that the task was beyond her
strength, she had felt ashamed of deceiving Claudet any
longer, and, acting on the advice of the Abbé Pernot,

had made up her mind to break off a union that was repugnant to her.

"Yes;" he repeated, mournfully to himself, "that must have been the way it happened." And with this kind of explanation of Reine's actions, his irritation seemed to lessen. Not that his grief was less poignant, but the first burst of rage had spent itself like a great wind-storm, which becomes lulled after a heavy fall of rain; the bitterness was toned down, and he was enabled to reason more clearly.

Julien—well, what was the part of Julien in all this disturbance? "If what I imagine is true," thought he, "Monsieur de Buxières knows that Reine loves him, but has he any reciprocal feeling for her? With a man as mysterious as my cousin, it is not easy to find out what is going on in his heart. Anyhow, I have no right to complain of him; as soon as he discovered my love for Reine, did he not, besides ignoring his own claim, offer spontaneously to take my message? Still, there is something queer at the bottom of it all, and whatever it costs me, I am going to find it out."

At this moment, through the misty air, he heard faintly the village clock strike eleven. "Already so late! how the time flies, even when one is suffering!" He bent his course toward the château, and, breathless and excited, without replying to Manette's inquiries, he burst into the hall where his cousin was pacing up and down, waiting for breakfast. At this sudden intrusion Julien started, and noted Claudet's quick breathing and disordered state.

"Ho, ho!" exclaimed he, in his usual sarcastic tone,

"what a hurry you are in! I suppose you have come to say the wedding-day is fixed at last?"

"No!" replied Claudet, briefly, "there will be no wedding."

Julien tottered, and turned to face his cousin.

"What's that? Are you joking?"

"I am in no mood for joking. Reine will not have me; she has taken back her promise."

While pronouncing these words, he scrutinized attentively his cousin's countenance, full in the light from the opposite window. He saw his features relax, and his eyes glow with the same expression which he had noticed a few days previous, when he had referred to the fact that Reine had again postponed the marriage.

"Whence comes this singular change?" stammered de Buxières, visibly agitated; "what reasons does Mademoiselle Vincart give in explanation?"

"Idle words: her father's health, disinclination to leave him. You may suppose I take such excuses for what they are worth. The real cause of her refusal is more serious and more mortifying."

"You know it, then?" exclaimed Julien, eagerly.

"I know it, because I forced Reine to confess it."

"And the reason is?"

"That she does not love me."

"Reine—does not love you!"

Again a gleam of light irradiated the young man's large, blue eyes. Claudet was leaning against the table, in front of his cousin; he continued slowly, looking him steadily in the face:

"That is not all. Not only does Reine not love me, but she loves some one else."

Julien changed color; the blood coursed over his cheeks, his forehead, his ears; he drooped his head.

"Did she tell you so?" he murmured, at last, feebly.

"She did not, but I guessed it. Her heart is won, and I think I know by whom."

Claudet had uttered these last words slowly and with a painful effort, at the same time studying Julien's countenance with renewed inquiry. The latter became more and more troubled, and his physiognomy expressed both anxiety and embarrassment.

"Whom do you suspect?" he stammered.

"Oh!" replied Claudet, employing a simple artifice to sound the obscure depth of his cousin's heart, "it is useless to name the person; you do not know him."

"A stranger?"

Julien's countenance had again changed. His hands were twitching nervously, his lips compressed, and his dilated pupils were blazing with anger, instead of triumph, as before.

"Yes; a stranger, a clerk in the iron-works at Grancey, I think."

"You think!—you think!" cried Julien, fiercely, "why don't you have more definite information before you accuse Mademoiselle Vincart of such treachery?"

He resumed pacing the hall, while his interlocutor, motionless, remained silent, and kept his eyes steadily upon him.

"It is not possible," resumed Julien, "Reine can not have played us such a trick! When I spoke to

her for you, it was so easy to say she was already betrothed!"

"Perhaps," objected Claudet, shaking his head, "she
had reasons for not letting you know all that was in her
mind."

"What reasons?"

"She doubtless believed at that time that the man
she preferred did not care for her. There are some
people who, when they are vexed, act in direct contradiction to their own wishes. I have the idea that Reine
accepted me only for want of some one better, and afterward, being too open-hearted to dissimulate for any
length of time, she thought better of it, and sent me
about my business."

"And you," interrupted Julien, sarcastically, "you,
who had been accepted as her betrothed, did not know
better how to defend your rights than to suffer yourself
to be ejected by a rival, whose intentions, even, you have
not clearly ascertained!"

"By Jove! how could I help it? A fellow that takes
an unwilling bride is playing for too high stakes. The
moment I found there was another she preferred, I had
but one course before me—to take myself off."

"And you call that loving!" shouted de Buxières,
"you call that losing your heart! God in heaven! if I
had been in your place, how differently I should have
acted! Instead of leaving, with piteous protestations, I
should have stayed near Reine, I should have surrounded
her with tenderness. I should have expressed my passion with so much force that its flame should pass from
my burning soul to hers, and she would have been forced

to love me! Ah! If I had only thought! if I had dared! how different it would have been!"

He jerked out his sentences with unrestrained frenzy. He seemed hardly to know what he was saying, or that he had a listener. Claudet stood contemplating him in sullen silence: "Aha!" thought he, with bitter resignation; "I have sounded you at last. I know what is in the bottom of your heart."

Manette, bringing in the breakfast, interrupted their colloquy, and both assumed an air of indifference, according to a tacit understanding that a prudent amount of caution should be observed in her presence. They ate hurriedly, and as soon as the cloth was removed, and they were again alone, Julien, glancing with an indefinable expression at Claudet, muttered savagely:

"Well! what do you decide?"

"I will tell you later," responded the other, briefly.

He quitted the room abruptly, told Manette that he would not be home until late, and strode out across the fields, his dog following. He had taken his gun as a blind, but it was useless for Montagnard to raise his bark; Claudet allowed the hares to scamper away without sending a single shot after them. He was busy inwardly recalling the details of the conversation he had had with his cousin. The situation now was simplified: Julien was in love with Reine, and was vainly combating his overpowering passion. What reason had he for concealing his love? What motive or reasoning had induced him, when he was already secretly enamored of the girl, to push Claudet in front and interfere to procure her acceptance of him as a fiancé? This point alone remained obscure. Was Julien carrying out certain theories of the respect due his position in society, and did he fear to contract a misalliance by marrying a mere farmer's daughter? Or did he, with his usual timidity and distrust of himself, dread being refused by Reine, and, half through pride, half through backwardness, keep away for fear of a humiliating rejection? With de Buxières's proud and suspicious nature, each of these suppositions was equally likely. The conclusion most undeniable was, that notwithstanding his set ideas and his moral cowardice, Julien had an ardent and overpowering love for Mademoiselle Vincart. As to Reine herself, Claudet was more than ever convinced that she had a secret inclination toward somebody, although she had denied the charge. But for whom was her preference? Claudet knew the neighborhood too well to believe the existence of any rival worth talking about, other than his cousin de Buxières. None of the boys of the village or the surrounding towns had ever come courting old Father Vincart's daughter, and de Buxières himself possessed sufficient qualities to attract Reine. Certainly, if he were a girl, he never should fix upon Julien for a lover; but women often have tastes that men can not comprehend, and Julien's refinement of nature, his bashfulness, and even his reserve, might easily have fascinated a girl of such strong will and somewhat peculiar notions. It was probable, therefore, that she liked him, and perhaps had done so for a long time; but, being clear-sighted and impartial, she could see that he never would marry her, because her condition in life was not equal to his own. Afterward, when the man she loved had flaunted his indifference so far as to plead the cause of another, her pride had revolted, and in the blind agony of her wounded feelings, she had thrown herself into the arms of the first comer, as if to punish herself for entertaining loving thoughts of a man who could so disdain her affection.

So, by means of that lucid intuition which the heart alone can furnish, Claudet at last succeeded in evolving the naked truth. But the fatiguing labor of so much thinking, to which his brain was little accustomed, and the sadness which continued to oppress him, overcame him to such an extent that he was obliged to sit down and rest on a clump of brushwood. He gazed over the woods and the clearings, which he had so often traversed light of heart and of foot, and felt mortally unhappy. These sheltering lanes and growing thickets, where he had so frequently encountered Reine, the beautiful hunting-grounds in which he had taken such delight, only awakened painful sensations, and he felt as if he should grow to hate them all if he were obliged to pass the rest of his days in their midst. As the day waned, the sinuosities of the forest became more blended; the depth of the valleys was lost in thick vapors. The wind had risen. The first falling leaves of the season rose and fell like wounded birds; heavy clouds gathered in the sky, and the night was coming on apace. Claudet was grateful for the sudden darkness, which would blot out a view now so distasteful to him. Shortly, on the Auberive side, along the winding Aubette, feeble lights became visible, as if inviting the young man to profit by their guidance. He arose, took the path indicated, and went to supper, or rather, to a pretence of supper, in the same inn where he had breakfasted with Julien, whence the latter had gone on his mission to Reine. This remembrance alone would have sufficed to destroy his appetite.

He did not remain long at table; he could not, in fact, stay many minutes in one place, and so, notwithstanding the urgent insistence of the hostess, he started on the way back to Vivey, feeling his way through the profound darkness. When he reached the château, every one was in bed. Noiselessly, his dog creeping after him, he slipped into his room, and, overcome with fatigue, fell into a heavy slumber.

The next morning his first visit was to Julien. He found him in a nervous and feverish condition, having passed a sleepless night. Claudet's revelations had entirely upset his intentions, and planted fresh thorns of jealousy in his heart. On first hearing that the marriage was broken off, his heart had leaped for joy, and hope had revived within him; but the subsequent information that Mademoiselle Vincart was probably interested in some lover, as yet unknown, had grievously sobered him. He was indignant at Reine's duplicity, and Claudet's cowardly resignation. The agony caused by Claudet's betrothal was a matter of course, but this love-for-a-stranger episode was an unexpected and mortal wound. He was seized with violent fits of rage; he was sometimes tempted to go and reproach the young girl with what he called her breach of faith, and then go and throw himself at her feet and avow his own passion.

But the mistrust he had of himself, and his incurable bashfulness, invariably prevented these heroic resolutions from being carried out. He had so long cultivated a habit of minute, fatiguing criticism upon every inward emotion that he had almost incapacitated himself for vigorous action.

He was in this condition when Claudet came in upon him. At the noise of the opening door, Julien raised his head, and looked dolefully at his cousin.

"Well?" said he, languidly.

"Well!" retorted Claudet, bravely, "on thinking over what has been happening during the last month, I have made sure of one thing of which I was doubtful."

"Of what were you doubtful?" returned de Buxières, quite ready to take offence at the answer.

"I am about to tell you. Do you remember the first conversation we had together concerning Reine? You spoke of her with so much earnestness that I then suspected you of being in love with her."

"I—I—hardly remember," faltered Julien, coloring.

"In that case, my memory is better than yours, Monsieur de Buxières. To-day, my suspicions have become certainties. You are in love with Reine Vincart!"

"I?" faintly protested his cousin.

"Don't deny it, but rather, give me your confidence; you will not be sorry for it. You love Reine, and have loved her for a long while. You have succeeded in hiding it from me because it is hard for you to unbosom yourself; but, yesterday, I saw it quite plainly. You dare not affirm the contrary!"

Julien, greatly agitated, had hidden his face in his

hands. After a moment's silence, he replied, defiantly: "Well, and supposing it is so? What is the use of talking about it, since Reine's affections are placed elsewhere?"

"Oh! that's another matter. Reine has declined to have me, and I really think she has some other affair in her head. Yet, to confess the truth, the clerk at the iron-works was a lover of my own imagining; she never thought of him."

"Then why did you tell such a lie?" cried Julien, impetuously.

"Because I thought I would plead the lie to get at the truth. Forgive me for having made use of this old trick to put you on the right track. It wasn't such a bad idea, for I succeeded in finding out what you took so much pains to hide from me."

"To hide from you? Yes, I did wish to hide it from you. Wasn't that right, since I was convinced that Reine loved you?" exclaimed Julien, in an almost stifled voice, as if the avowal were choking him. "I have always thought it idle to parade one's feelings before those who do not care about them."

"You were wrong," returned poor Claudet, sighing deeply, "if you had spoken for yourself, I have an idea you would have been better received, and you would have spared me a terrible heart-breaking."

He said it with such profound sadness that Julien, notwithstanding the absorbing nature of his own thoughts, was quite overcome, and almost on the point of confessing, openly, the intensity of his feeling toward Reine Vincart. But, accustomed as he was, by long habit, to concentrate every emotion within himself, he found it impossible to become, all at once, communicative; he felt an invincible and almost maidenly bashfulness at the idea of revealing the secret sentiments of his soul, and contented himself with saying, in a low voice:

"Do you not love her any more, then?"

"I? oh, yes, indeed! But to be refused by the only girl I ever wished to marry takes all the spirit out of me. I am so discouraged, I feel like leaving the country. If I were to go, it would perhaps be doing you a service, and that would comfort me a little. You have treated me as a friend, and that is a thing one doesn't forget. I have not the means to pay you back for your kindness, but I think I should be less sorry to go if my departure would leave the way more free for you to return to La Thuilière."

"You surely would not leave on my account?" exclaimed Julien, in alarm.

"Not solely on your account, rest assured. If Reine had loved me, it never would have entered my head to make such a sacrifice for you, but she will not have me. I am good for nothing here. I am only in your way."

"But that is a wild idea! Where would you go?"

"Oh! there would be no difficulty about that. One plan would be to go as a soldier. Why not? I am hardy, a good walker, a good shot, can stand fatigue; I have everything needed for military life. It is an occupation that I should like, and I could earn my epaulets as well as my neighbor. So that perhaps,

Monsieur de Buxières, matters might in that way be arranged to suit everybody."

"Claudet!" stammered Julien, his voice thick with sobs, "you are a better man than I! Yes; you are a better man than I!"

And, for the first time, yielding to an imperious longing for expansion, he sprang toward the *grand chasserot*, clasped him in his arms, and embraced him fraternally.

"I will not let you expatriate yourself on my account," he continued; "do not act rashly, I entreat!"

"Don't worry," replied Claudet, laconically, "if I so decide, it will not be without deliberation."

In fact, during the whole of the ensuing week, he debated in his mind this question of going away. Each day his position at Vivey seemed more unbearable. Without informing any one, he had been to Langres and consulted an officer of his acquaintance on the subject of the formalities required previous to enrolment.

At last, one morning he resolved to go over to the military division and sign his engagement. But he was not willing to consummate this sacrifice without seeing Reine Vincart for the last time. He was nursing, down in the bottom of his heart, a vague hope, which, frail and slender as the filament of a plant, was yet strong enough to keep him on his native soil. Instead of taking the path to Vivey, he made a turn in the direction of La Thuilière, and soon reached the open elevation whence the roofs of the farm-buildings and the turrets of the château could both alike be seen. There he faltered, with a piteous sinking of the heart. Only a few steps between himself and the house, yet he hesitated about entering; not that he feared a want of welcome, but because he dreaded lest the reawakening of his tenderness should cause him to lose a portion of the courage he should need to enable him to leave. He leaned against the trunk of an old pear-tree and surveyed the forest site on which the farm was built.

The landscape retained its usual placidity. In the distance, over the waste lands, the shepherd Tringuesse was following his flock of sheep, which occasionally scattered over the fields, and then, under the dog's harassing watchfulness, reformed in a compact group, previous to descending the narrow hill-slope. One thing struck Claudet: the pastures and the woods bore exactly the same aspect, presented the same play of light and shade as on that afternoon of the preceding year, when he had met Reine in the Ronces woods, a few days before the arrival of Julien. The same bright yet tender tint reddened the crab-apple and the wild-cherry; the tomtits and the robins chirped as before, among the bushes, and, as in the previous year, one heard the sound of the beechnuts and acorns dropping on the rocky paths. Autumn went through her tranquil rites and familiar operations, always with the same punctual regularity; and all this would go on just the same when Claudet was no longer there. There would only be one lad the less in the village streets, one hunter failing to answer the call when they were surrounding the woods of Charbonnière. This dim perception of how small a space man occupies on the earth, and of the ease with which he is forgotten, aided Claudet unconsciously in his effort to be resigned, and he determined to enter the house. As he opened the gate of the courtyard, he found himself face to face with Reine, who was coming out.

The young girl immediately supposed he had come to make a last assault, in the hope of inducing her to yield to his wishes. She feared a renewal of the painful scene which had closed their last interview, and her first impulse was to put herself on her guard. Her countenance darkened, and she fixed a cold, questioning gaze upon Claudet, as if to keep him at a distance. But, when she noted the sadness of her young relative's expression, she was seized with pity. Making an effort, however, to disguise her emotion, she pretended to accost him with the calm and cordial friendship of former times.

"Why, good-morning, Claudet," said she, "you come just in time. A quarter of an hour later you would not have found me. Will you come in and rest a moment?"

"Thanks, Reine," said he, "I will not hinder you in your work. But I wanted to say, I am sorry I got angry the other day; you were right, we must not leave each other with ill-feeling, and, as I am going away for a long time, I desire first to take your hand in friendship."

"You are going away?"

"Yes; I am going now to Langres to enroll myself as a soldier. And true it is, one knows when one goes away, but it is hard to know when one will come back. That is why I wanted to say good-by to you, and make

peace, so as not to go away with too great a load on
my heart."·

All Reine's coldness melted away. This young fellow, who was leaving his country on her account, was the
companion of her infancy, more than that, her nearest
relative. Her throat swelled, her eyes filled with tears.
She turned away her head, that he might not perceive
her emotion, and opened the kitchen-door.

"Come in, Claudet," said she, "we shall be more comfortable in the dining-room. We can talk there, and you
will have some refreshment before you go, will you not?"

He obeyed, and followed her into the house. She
went herself into the cellar, to seek a bottle of old wine,
brought two glasses, and filled them with a trembling
hand.

"Shall you remain long in the service?" asked she.

"I shall engage for seven years."

"It is a hard life that you are choosing."

"What am I to do?" replied he, "I could not stay
here doing nothing."

Reine went in and out of the room in a bewildered
fashion. Claudet, too much excited to perceive that the
young girl's impassiveness was only on the surface, said
to himself: "It is all over; she accepts my departure as
an event perfectly natural; she treats me as she would
Théotime, the coal-dealer, or the tax-collector Boucheseiche. A glass of wine, two or three unimportant
questions, and then, good-by—a pleasant journey, and
take care of yourself!"

Then he made a show of taking an airy, insouciant
tone.

"Oh, well!" he exclaimed, "I've always been drawn toward that kind of life. A musket will be a little heavier than a gun, that's all; then I shall see different countries, and that will change my ideas." He tried to appear facetious, poking around the kitchen, and teasing the magpie, which was following his footsteps with inquisitive anxiety. Finally, he went up to the old man Vincart, who was lying stretched out in his picture-lined niche. He took the flabby hand of the paralytic old man, pressed it gently and endeavored to get up a little conversation with him, but he had it all to himself, the invalid staring at him all the time with uneasy, wide-open eyes. Returning to Reine, he lifted his glass.

"To your health, Reine!" said he, with forced gayety, "next time we clink glasses together, I shall be an experienced soldier—you'll see!"

But, when he put the glass to his lips, several big tears fell in, and he had to swallow them with his wine.

"Well!" he sighed, turning away while he passed the back of his hand across his eyes, "it must be time to go."

She accompanied him to the threshold.

"Adieu, Reine!"

"Adieu!" she murmured, faintly.

She stretched out both hands, overcome with pity and remorse. He perceived her emotion, and thinking that she perhaps still loved him a little, and repented having rejected him, threw his arms impetuously around her. He pressed her against his bosom, and imprinted kisses, wet with tears, upon her cheek. He could not leave her, and redoubled his caresses with passionate ardor, with the ecstasy of a lover who suddenly meets with a burst of tenderness on the part of the woman he has tenderly loved, and whom he expects never to fold again in his arms. He completely lost his self-control. His embrace became so ardent that Reine, alarmed at the sudden outburst, was overcome with shame and terror, notwithstanding the thought that the man, who was clasping her in his arms with such passion, was her own brother.

She tore herself away from him and pushed him violently back.

"Adieu!" she cried, retreating to the kitchen, of which she hastily shut the door.

Claudet stood one moment, dumfounded, before the door so pitilessly shut in his face, then, falling suddenly from his happy state of illusion to the dead level of reality, departed precipitately down the road.

When he turned to give a parting glance, the farm buildings were no longer visible, and the waste lands of the forest border, gray, stony, and barren, stretched their mute expanse before him.

"No!" exclaimed he, between his set teeth, "she never loved me. She thinks only of the other man! I have nothing more to do but go away and never return!"

CHAPTER IX

N arriving at Langres, Claudet enrolled in the seventeenth battalion of light infantry. Five days later, paying no attention to the lamentations of Manette, he left Vivey, going, by way of Lyon, to the camp at Lathonay, where his battalion was stationed. Julien was thus left alone at the château to recover as best he might from the dazed feeling caused by the startling events of the last few weeks. After Claudet's departure, he felt an uneasy sensation of discomfort, and as if he himself had lessened in value. He had never before realized how little space he occupied in his own dwelling, and how much living heat Claudet had infused into the house which was now so cold and empty. He felt poor and diminished in spirit, and was ashamed of being so useless to himself and to others. He had before him a prospect of new duties, which frightened him. The management of the district, which Claudet had undertaken for him, would now fall entirely on his shoulders, and just at the time of the timber sales and the renewal of the fences. Besides all this, he had Manette on his conscience, thinking he ought to try to soften her grief at her son's unexpected departure. The ancient housekeeper was like Rachel, she refused to be comforted, and her temper was not improved by her recent trials. She filled the air with lamentations, and seemed to consider Julien responsible for her troubles. The latter treated her with wonderful patience and indulgence, and exhausted his ingenuity to make her time pass more pleasantly. This was the first real effort he had made to subdue his dislikes and his passive tendencies, and it had the good effect of preparing him, by degrees, to face more serious trials, and to take the initiative in matters of greater importance. He discovered that the energy he expended in conquering a first difficulty gave him more ability to conquer the second, and from that result he decided that the will is like a muscle, which shrivels in inaction and is developed by exercise; and he made up his mind to attack courageously the work before him, although it had formerly appeared beyond his capabilities.

He now rose always at daybreak. Gaitered like a huntsman, and escorted by Montagnard, who had taken a great liking to him, he would proceed to the forest, visit the cuttings, hire fresh workmen, familiarize himself with the woodsmen, interest himself in their labors, their joys and their sorrows; then, when evening came, he was quite astonished to find himself less weary, less isolated, and eating with considerable appetite the supper prepared for him by Manette. Since he had been traversing the forest, not as a stranger or a person of leisure, but with the predetermination to accomplish some useful work, he had learned to appreciate its beauties. The charms of nature and the living creatures around no longer inspired him with the defiant scorn which he had imbibed from his early solitary life and his priestly education; he now viewed them with pleasure and interest. In proportion, as his sympathies expanded and his mind became more virile, the exterior world presented a more attractive appearance to him.

While this work of transformation was going on within him, he was aided and sustained by the ever dear and ever present image of Reine Vincart. The trenches, filled with dead leaves, the rows of beech-trees, stripped of their foliage by the rude breath of winter, the odor peculiar to underwood during the dead season, all recalled to his mind the impressions he had received while in company with the woodland queen. Now that he could better understand the young girl's adoration of the marvellous forest world, he sought out, with loving interest, the sites where she had gone into ecstasy, the details of the landscape which she had pointed out to him the year before, and had made him admire. The beauty of the scene was associated in his thoughts with Reine's love, and he could not think of either separately. But, notwithstanding the steadfastness and force of his love, he had not yet made any effort to see Mademoiselle Vincart. At first, the increase of occupation caused by Claudet's departure, the new duties devolving upon him, together with his inexperience, had prevented Julien from entertaining the possibility of renewing relations that had been so violently sundered. Little by little, however, as he reviewed the situation of affairs, which his cousin's generous sacrifice had engendered, he began to consider how he could benefit thereby. Claudet's departure had left the field free, but Julien felt no more confidence in himself than before. The fact that Reine had so unaccountably refused to marry the *grand chasserot* did not seem to him sufficient encouragement. Her motive was a secret, and therefore, of doubtful interpretation. Besides, even if she were entirely heart-whole, was that a reason why she should give Julien a favorable reception? Could she forget the cruel insult to which he had subjected her? And immediately after that outrageous behavior of his, he had had the stupidity to make a proposal for Claudet. That was the kind of affront, thought he, that a woman does not easily forgive, and the very idea of presenting himself before her made his heart sink. He had seen her only at a distance, at the Sunday mass, and every time he had endeavored to catch her eye she had turned away her head. She also avoided, in every way, any intercourse with the château. Whenever a question arose, such as the apportionment of lands, or the allotment of cuttings, which would necessitate her having recourse to M. de Buxières, she would abstain from writing herself, and correspond only through the notary, Arbillot. Claudet's heroic departure, therefore, had really accomplished nothing; everything was exactly at the same point as the day after Julien's unlucky visit to La Thuilière, and the same futile doubts and fears agitated him now as then. It also occurred to him, that while he was thus debating and keeping silence, days, weeks, and months were slipping away; that Reine would soon reach her twenty-third year, and that she would be thinking of marriage. It was well known that she had some fortune, and suitors were not lacking. Even allowing that she had no afterthought in renouncing Claudet, she could not always live alone at the farm, and some day she would be compelled to accept a marriage of convenience, if not of love.

"And to think," he would say to himself, "that she is there, only a few steps away, that I am consumed with longing, that I have only to traverse those pastures, to throw myself at her feet, and that I positively dare not! Miserable wretch that I am, it was last spring, while we were in that hut together, that I should have spoken of my love, instead of terrifying her with my brutal caresses! Now it is too late! I have wounded and humiliated her; I have driven away Claudet, who would at any rate have made her a stalwart lover, and I have made two beings unhappy, without counting myself. So much for my miserable shufflings and evasion! Ah! if one could only begin life over again!"

While thus lamenting his fate, the march of time went steadily on, with its pitiless dropping out of seconds, minutes, and hours. The worst part of winter was over; the March gales had dried up the forests; April was tingeing the woods with its tender green; the song of the cuckoo was already heard in the tufted bowers, and the festival of St. George had passed.

Taking advantage of an unusually clear day, Julien went to visit a farm, belonging to him, in the plain of Anjeures, on the border of the forest of Maigrefontaine. After breakfasting with the farmer, he took the way home through the woods, so that he might enjoy the first varied effects of the season.

A WOODLAND QUEEN

The forest of Maigrefontaine, situated on the slope of a hill, was full of rocky, broken ground, interspersed with deep ravines, along which narrow but rapid streams ran to swell the fishpond of La Thuilière. Julien had wandered away from the road, into the thick of the forest where the budding vegetation was at its height, where the lilies multiply and the early spring flowers disclose their umbel-shaped clusters, full of tiny, white stars. The sight of these blossoms, which had such a tender meaning for him, since he had identified the name with that of Reine, brought vividly before him the beloved image of the young girl. He walked slowly and languidly on, heated by his feverish recollections and desires, tormented by useless self-reproach, and physically intoxicated by the balmy atmosphere and the odor of the flowering shrubs at his feet. Arriving at the edge of a somewhat deep pit, he tried to leap across with a single bound, but, whether he made a false start, or that he was weakened and dizzy with the conflicting emotions with which he had been battling, he missed his footing and fell, twisting his ankle, on the side of the embankment. He rose with an effort and put his foot to the ground, but a sharp pain obliged him to lean against the trunk of a neighboring ash-tree. His foot felt as heavy as lead, and every time he tried to straighten it his sufferings were intolerable. All he could do was to drag himself along from one tree to another until he reached the path.

Exhausted by this effort, he sat down on the grass, unbuttoned his gaiter, and carefully unlaced his boot. His foot had swollen considerably. He began to fear he had sprained it badly, and wondered how he could get back to Vivey. Should he have to wait on this lonely road until some woodcutter passed, who would take him home? Montagnard, his faithful companion, had seated himself in front of him, and contemplated him with moist, troubled eyes, at the same time emitting short, sharp whines, which seemed to say:

"What is the matter?" and, "How are we going to get out of this?"

Suddenly he heard footsteps approaching. He perceived a flutter of white skirts behind the copse, and just at the moment he was blessing the lucky chance that had sent some one in that direction, his eyes were gladdened with a sight of the fair visage of Reine.

She was accompanied by a little girl of the village, carrying a basket full of primroses and freshly gathered ground ivy. Reine was quite familiar with all the medicinal herbs of the country, and gathered them in their season, in order to administer them as required to the people of the farm. When she was within a few feet of Julien, she recognized him, and her brow clouded over; but almost immediately she noticed his altered features and that one of his feet was shoeless, and divined that something unusual had happened. Going straight up to him, she said:

"You seem to be suffering, Monsieur de Buxières. What is the matter?"

"A—a foolish accident," replied he, putting on a careless manner. "I fell and sprained my ankle."

The young girl knit her brows with an anxious expression; then, after a moment's hesitation, she said:

"Will you let me see your foot? My mother understood about bone-setting, and I have been told that I inherit her gift of curing sprains."

She drew from the basket an empty bottle and a handkerchief.

"Zélie," said she to the little damsel, who was standing astonished at the colloquy, "go quickly down to the stream, and fill this bottle."

While she was speaking, Julien, greatly embarrassed, obeyed her suggestions, and uncovered his foot. Reine, without any prudery or nonsense, raised the wounded limb, and felt around cautiously.

"I think," said she at last, "that the muscles are somewhat injured."

Without another word, she tore the handkerchief into narrow strips, and poured the contents of the bottle, which Zélie had filled, slowly over the injure member, holding her hand high for that purpose. Then, with a soft yet firm touch, she pressed the injured muscles into their places, while Julien bit his lips and did his very utmost to prevent her seeing how much he was suffering. After this massage treatment, the young girl bandaged the ankle tightly with the linen bands, and fastened them securely with pins.

"There," said she, "now try to put on your shoe and stocking; they will give support to the muscles. Now you, Zélie, run, fit to break your neck, to the farm, make them harness the wagon, and tell them to bring it here, as close to the path as possible."

The girl picked up her basket and started on a trot.

"Monsieur de Buxières," said Reine, "do you think

you can walk as far as the carriage road, by leaning on my arm?"

"Yes;" he replied, with a grateful glance which greatly embarrassed Mademoiselle Vincart, "you have relieved me as if by a miracle. I feel much better and as if I could go anywhere you might lead, while leaning on your arm!"

She helped him to rise, and he took a few steps with her aid.

"Why, it feels really better," sighed he.

He was so happy in feeling himself thus tenderly supported by Reine, that he altogether forgot his pain.

"Let us walk slowly," continued she, "and do not be afraid to lean on me. All you have to think of is reaching the carriage."

"How good you are," stammered he, "and how ashamed I am!"

"Ashamed of what?" returned Reine, hastily. "I have done nothing extraordinary; any one else would have acted in the same manner."

"I entreat you," replied he, earnestly, "not to spoil my happiness. I know very well that the first person who happened to pass would have rendered me some charitable assistance; but the thought that it is you—you alone—who have helped me, fills me with delight, at the same time that it increases my remorse. I so little deserve that you should interest yourself in my behalf!"

He waited, hoping perhaps that she would ask for an explanation, but, seeing that she did not appear to understand, he added:

"I have offended you. I have misunderstood you, and I have been cruelly punished for my mistake. But what avails my tardy regret in healing the injuries I have inflicted! Ah! if one could only go backward, and efface, with a single stroke, the hours in which one has been blind and headstrong!"

"Let us not speak of that!" replied she, shortly, but in a singularly softened tone.

In spite of herself, she was touched by this expression of repentance, so naïvely acknowledged in broken, disconnected sentences, vibrating with the ring of true sincerity. In proportion as he abased himself, her anger diminished, and she recognized that she loved him just the same, notwithstanding his defects, his weakness, and his want of tact and polish. She was also profoundly touched by his revealing to her, for the first time, a portion of his hidden feelings.

They had become silent again, but they felt nearer to each other than ever before; their secret thoughts seemed to be transmitted to each other; a mute understanding was established between them. She lent him the support of her arm with more freedom, and the young man seemed to experience fresh delight in her firm and sympathetic assistance.

Progressing slowly, although more quickly than they would have chosen themselves, they reached the foot of the path, and perceived the wagon waiting on the beaten road. Julien mounted therein with the aid of Reine and the driver. When he was stretched on the straw, which had been spread for him on the bottom of the wagon, he leaned forward on the side, and his eyes met those of Reine. For a few moments their gaze seemed riveted upon each other, and their mutual understanding was complete. These few, brief moments contained a whole confession of love; avowals mingled with repentance, promises of pardon, tender reconciliation!

"Thanks!" he sighed at last, "will you give me your hand?"

She gave it, and while he held it in his own, Reine turned toward the driver on the seat.

"Felix," said she, warningly, "drive slowly and avoid the ruts. Good-night, Monsieur de Buxières, send for the doctor as soon as you get in, and all will be well. I will send to inquire how you are getting along."

She turned and went pensively down the road to La Thuilière, while the carriage followed slowly the direction to Vivey.

The doctor, being sent for immediately on Julien's arrival, pronounced it a simple sprain, and declared that the preliminary treatment had been very skilfully applied, that the patient had now only to keep perfectly still. Two days later came La Guite from Reine, to inquire after M. de Buxières's health. She brought a large bunch of lilies which Mademoiselle Vincart had sent to the patient, to console him for not being able to go in the woods, which Julien kept for several days close by his side.

This accident, happening at Maigrefontaine, and providentially attended to by Reine Vincart, the return to the château in the vehicle belonging to La Thuilière, the sending of the lilies, were all a source of great mystification to Manette. She suspected some amorous mystery in all these events, commented somewhat uncharitably on every minor detail, and took care to carry her comments all over the village. Very soon the entire parish, from the most insignificant woodchopper to the Abbé Pernot himself, were made aware that there was something going on between M. de Buixères and the daughter of old M. Vincart.

In the mean time, Julien, quite unconscious that his love for Reine was providing conversation for all the gossips of the country, was cursing the untoward event that kept him stretched in his invalid-chair. At last, one day, he discovered he could put his foot down and walk a little with the assistance of his cane; a few days after, the doctor gave him permission to go out of doors. His first visit was to La Thuilière.

He went there in the afternoon and found Reine in the kitchen, seated by the side of her paralytic father, who was asleep. She was reading a newspaper, which she retained in her hand, while rising to receive her visitor. After she had congratulated him on his recovery, and he had expressed his cordial thanks for her timely aid, she showed him the paper.

"You find me in a state of disturbance," said she, with a slight degree of embarrassment, "it seems that we are going to have war and that our troops have entered Italy. Have you any news of Claudet?"

Julien started. This was the last remark he could have expected. Claudet's name had not been once mentioned in their interview at Maigrefontaine, and he had nursed the hope that Reine thought no longer about him.

All his mistrust returned in a moment on hearing this name come from the young girl's lips the moment he entered the house, and seeing the emotion which the news in the paper had caused her.

"He wrote me a few days ago," replied he.

"Where is he?"

"In Italy, with his battalion, which is a part of the first army corps. His last letter is dated from Alexandria."

Reine's eyes suddenly filled with tears, and she gazed absently at the distant wooded horizon.

"Poor Claudet!" murmured she, sighing, "what is he doing just now, I wonder?"

"Ah!" thought Julien, his visage darkening, "perhaps she loves him still!"

Poor Claudet! At the very time they are thus talking about him at the farm, he is camping with his battalion near Voghera, on the banks of one of the obscure tributaries of the river Po, in a country rich in waving corn, interspersed with bounteous orchards and hardy vines climbing up to the very tops of the mulberry-trees. His battalion forms the extreme end of the advance guard, and at the approach of night, Claudet is on duty on the banks of the stream. It is a lovely May night, irradiated by millions of stars, which, under the limpid Italian sky, appear larger and nearer to the watcher than they appeared in the vaporous atmosphere of the Haute-Marne.

Nightingales are calling to one another among the

trees of the orchard, and the entire landscape seems imbued with their amorous music. What ecstasy to listen to them! What serenity their liquid harmonies spread over the smiling landscape, faintly revealing its beauties in the mild starlight.

Who would think that preparations for deadly combat were going on through the serenity of such a night? Occasionally a sharp exchange of musketry with the advanced post of the enemy bursts upon the ear, and all the nightingales keep silence. Then, when quiet is restored in the upper air, the chorus of spring songsters begins again. Claudet leans on his gun, and remembers that at this same hour the nightingales in the park at Vivey, and in the garden of La Thuilière, are pouring forth the same melodies. He recalls the bright vision of Reine: he sees her leaning at her window, listening to the same amorous song issuing from the coppice woods of Maigrefontaine. His heart swells within him, and an overpowering homesickness takes possession of him. But the next moment he is ashamed of his weakness, he remembers his responsibility, primes his ear, and begins investigating the dark hollows and rising hillocks where an enemy might hide.

The next morning, May 20th, he is awakened by a general hubbub and noise of fighting. The battalion to which he belongs has made an attack upon Montebello, and is sending its sharpshooters among the corn-fields and vineyards. Some of the regiments invade the rice-fields, climb the walls of the vineyards, and charge the enemy's column-ranks. The sullen roar of the cannon alternates with the sharp report of guns, and whole showers of grape-shot beat the air with their piercing whistle. All through the uproar of guns and thunder of the artillery, you can distinguish the guttural hurrahs of the Austrians, and the broken oaths of the French troopers. The trenches are piled with dead bodies, the trumpets sound the attack, the survivors, obeying an irresistible impulse, spring to the front. The ridges are crested with human masses swaying to and fro, and the first red uniform is seen in the streets of Montebello, in relief against the chalky façades bristling with Austrian guns, pouring forth their ammunition on the enemy below. The soldiers burst into the houses, the court-yards, the enclosures; every instant you hear the breaking open of doors, the crashing of windows, and the scuffling of the terrified inmates. The white uniforms retire in disorder. The village belongs to the French! Not just yet, though. From the last houses on the street, to the entrance of the cemetery, is rising ground, and just behind stands a small hillock. The enemy has retrenched itself there, and, from its cannons ranged in battery, is raining a terrible shower on the village just evacuated.

The assailants hesitate, and draw back before this hailstorm of iron; suddenly a general appears from under the walls of a building already crumbling under the continuous fire, spurs his horse forward, and shouts: "Come, boys, let us carry the fort!"

Among the first to rally to this call, one rifleman in particular, a fine, broad-shouldered active fellow, with a brown moustache and olive complexion, darts forward to the point indicated. It is Claudet. Others are behind him, and soon more than a hundred men, with their bayonets, are hurling themselves along the cemetery road; the *grand chasserot* leaps across the fields, as he used formerly in pursuit of the game in the Charbonnière forest. The soldiers are falling right and left of him, but he hardly sees them; he continues pressing forward, breathless, excited, scarcely stopping to think. As he is crossing one of the meadows, however, he notices the profusion of scarlet gladiolus and also observes that the rye and barley grow somewhat sturdier here than in his country; these are the only definite ideas that detach themselves clearly from his seething brain. The wall of the cemetery is scaled; they are fighting now in the ditches, killing one another on the side of the hill; at last, the fort is taken and they begin routing the enemy. But, at this moment, Claudet stoops to pick up a cartridge, a ball strikes him in the forehead, and, without a sound, he drops to the ground, among the noisome fennels which flourish in graveyards—he drops, thinking of the clock of his native village.

.   .   .   .

"I have sad news for you," said Julien to Reine, as he entered the garden of La Thuilière, one June afternoon.

He had received official notice the evening before, through the mayor, of the decease of "Germain-Claudet Séjournant, volunteer in the seventeenth battalion of light infantry, killed in an engagement with the enemy, May 20, 1859."

Reine was standing between two hedges of large

peasant-roses. At the first words that fell from M. de Buxières's lips, she felt a presentiment of misfortune.

"Claudet?" murmured she.

"He is dead," replied Julien, almost inaudibly, "he fought bravely and was killed at Montebello."

The young girl remained motionless, and for a moment de Buxières thought she would be able to bear, with some degree of composure, this announcement of the death in a foreign country of a man whom she had refused as a husband. Suddenly she turned aside, took two or three steps, then leaning her head and folded arms on the trunk of an adjacent tree, she burst into a passion of tears. The convulsive movement of her shoulders and stifled sobs denoted the violence of her emotion. M. de Buxières, alarmed at this outbreak, which he thought exaggerated, felt a return of his old misgivings. He was jealous now of the dead man whom she was so openly lamenting. Her continued weeping annoyed him; he tried to arrest her tears by addressing some consolatory remarks to her; but, at the very first word, she turned away, mounted precipitately the kitchen-stairs, and disappeared, closing the door behind her. Some minutes after, La Guite brought a message to de Buxières that Reine wished to be alone, and begged him to excuse her.

He took his departure, disconcerted, downhearted, and ready to weep himself, over the crumbling of his hopes. As he was nearing the first outlying houses of the village, he came across the Abbé Pernot, who was striding along at a great rate, toward the château.

"Ah!" exclaimed the priest, "how are you, Monsieur de Buxières, I was just going over to see you. Is it true that you have received bad news?"

Julien nodded his head affirmatively, and informed the curé of the sad notice he had received. The Abbé's countenance lengthened, his mouth took on a saddened expression, and during the next few minutes he maintained an attitude of condolence.

"Poor fellow!" he sighed, with a slight nasal intonation, "he did not have a fair chance! To have to leave us at twenty-six years of age, and in full health, it is very hard. And such a jolly companion; such a clever shot!"

Finally, not being naturally of a melancholy turn of mind, nor able to remain long in a mournful mood, he consoled himself with one of the pious commonplaces which he was in the habit of using for the benefit of others: "The Lord is just in all His dealings, and holy in all His works; He reckons the hairs of our heads, and our destinies are in His hands. We shall celebrate a fine high mass for the repose of Claudet's soul."

He coughed, and raised his eyes toward Julien.

"I wished," continued he, "to see you for two reasons, Monsieur de Buxières: first of all, to hear about Claudet, and secondly, to speak to you on a matter—a very delicate matter—which concerns you, but which also affects the safety of another person and the dignity of the parish."

Julien was gazing at him with a bewildered air. The curé pushed open the little park gate, and passing through, added:

15 [225]

"Let us go into your place; we shall be better able to talk over the matter."

When they were underneath the trees, the Abbé resumed:

"Monsieur de Buxières, do you know that you are at this present time giving occasion for the tongues of my parishioners to wag more than is at all reasonable? Oh!" continued he, replying to a remonstrating gesture of his companion, "it is unpremeditated on your part, I am sure, but, all the same, they talk about you—and about Reine."

"About Mademoiselle Vincart?" exclaimed Julien, indignantly, "what can they say about her?"

"A great many things which are displeasing to me. They speak of your having sprained your ankle while in the company of Reine Vincart; of your return home in her wagon; of your frequent visits to La Thuilière, and I don't know what besides. And as mankind, especially the female portion, is more disposed to discover evil than good, they say you are compromising this young person. Now, Reine is living, as one may say, alone and unprotected. It behooves me, therefore, as her pastor, to defend her against her own weakness. That is the reason why I have taken upon myself to beg you to be more circumspect, and not trifle with her reputation."

"Her reputation?" repeated Julien, with irritation. "I do not understand you, Monsieur le Curé!"

"You don't, hey! Why, I explain my meaning pretty clearly. Human beings are weak; it is easy to injure a girl's reputation, when you try to make yourself agreeable, knowing you can not marry her."

"And why could I not marry her?" inquired Julien, coloring deeply.

"Because she is not in your own class, and you would not love her enough to overlook the disparity, if marriage became necessary."

"What do you know about it?" returned Julien, with violence. "I have no such foolish prejudices, and the obstacles would not come from my side. But, rest easy, Monsieur," continued he, bitterly, "the danger exists only in the imagination of your parishioners. Reine has never cared for me! It was Claudet she loved!"

"Hm, hm!" interjected the curé, dubiously.

"You would not doubt it," insisted de Buxières, provoked at the Abbé's incredulous movements of his head, "if you had seen her, as I saw her, melt into tears when I told her of Séjournant's death. She did not even wait until I had turned my back before she broke out in her lamentations. My presence was of very small account. Ah! she has but too cruelly made me feel how little she cares for me!"

"You love her very much, then?" demanded the Abbé, slyly, an almost imperceptible smile curving his lips.

"Oh, yes! I love her," exclaimed he, impetuously; then coloring and drooping his head. "But it is very foolish of me to betray myself, since Reine cares nothing at all for me!"

There was a moment of silence, during which the curé took a pinch of snuff from a tiny box of cherry wood.

"Monsieur de Buxières," said he, with a particularly

oracular air, "Claudet is dead, and the dead, like the absent, are always in the wrong. But who is to say whether you are not mistaken concerning the nature of Reine's unhappiness? I will have that cleared up this very day. Good-night; keep quiet and behave properly."

Thereupon he took his departure, but, instead of returning to the parsonage, he directed his steps hurriedly toward La Thuilière. Notwithstanding a vigorous opposition from La Guite, he made use of his pastoral authority to penetrate into Reine's apartment, where he shut himself up with her. What he said to her never was divulged outside the small chamber where the interview took place. He must, however, have found words sufficiently eloquent to soften her grief, for when he had gone away the young girl descended to the garden with a soothed although still melancholy mien. She remained a long time in meditation in the thicket of roses, but her meditations had evidently no bitterness in them, and a miraculous serenity seemed to have spread itself over her heart like a beneficent balm.

A few days afterward, during the unpleasant coolness of one of those mornings, white with dew, which are the peculiar privilege of the mountain-gorges in Langres, the bells of Vivey tolled for the dead, announcing the celebration of a mass in memory of Claudet. The *grand chasserot* having been a universal favorite with every one in the neighborhood, the church was crowded. The steep descent from the high plain overlooked the village. They came thronging in through the wooded glens of Praslay, by the Auberive road and the forests of Char-

bonnière; companions in hunting and social amusements, foresters and wearers of sabots, campers in the
woods, inmates of the farms embedded in the forests—
none failed to answer the call. The rustic, white-walled
nave was too narrow to contain them all, and the surplus
flowed into the street. Arbeltier, the village carpenter,
had erected a rudimentary catafalque, which was draped
in black and bordered with wax tapers, and placed in
front of the altar steps. On the pall, embroidered with
silver tears, were arranged large bunches of wild flowers,
sent from La Thuilière, and spreading an aromatic odor
of fresh verdure around. The Abbé Pernot, wearing
his insignia of mourning, officiated. Through the side
windows were seen portions of the blue sky; the barking
of the dogs and singing of birds were heard in the distance; and even while listening to the *Dies iræ*, the curé
could not help thinking of the robust and bright young
fellow who, only the year previous, had been so joyously
traversing the woods, escorted by Charbonneau and
Montagnard, and who was now lying in a foreign land,
in the common pit of the little cemetery of Montebello.

As each verse of the funeral service was intoned,
Manette Séjournant, prostrate on her *prie-dieu*, interrupted the monotonous chant with tumultuous sobs.
Her grief was noisy and unrestrained, but those present
sympathized more with the quiet though profound sorrow of Reine Vincart. The black dress of the young
girl contrasted painfully with the dead pallor of her
complexion. She emitted no sighs, but, now and then,
a contraction of the lips, a trembling of the hands testi-

fied to the inward struggle, and a single tear rolled slowly down her cheek.

From the corner where he had chosen to stand alone, Julien de Buxières observed, with pain, the mute eloquence of her profound grief, and became once more a prey to the fiercest jealousy. He could not help envying the fate of this deceased, who was mourned in so tender a fashion. Again the mystery of an attachment so evident and so tenacious, followed by so strange a rupture, tormented his uneasy soul. "She must have loved Claudet, since she is in mourning for him," he kept repeating to himself, "and if she loved him, why this rupture, which she herself provoked, and which drove the unhappy man to despair?"

At the close of the absolution, all the assistants defiled close beside Julien, who was now standing in front of the catafalque. When it came to Reine Vincart's turn, she reached out her hand to M. de Buxières; at the same time, she gazed at him with such friendly sadness, and infused into the clasp of her hand something so cordial and intimate that the young man's ideas were again completely upset. He seemed to feel as if it were an encouragement to speak. When the men and women had dispersed, and a surging of the crowd brought him nearer to Reine, he resolved to follow her, without regard to the question of what people would say, or the curious eyes that might be watching him.

A happy chance came in his way. Reine Vincart had gone home by the path along the outskirts of the wood and the park enclosure. Julien went hastily back to the château, crossed the gardens, and followed an interior avenue, parallel to the exterior one, from which he was separated only by a curtain of linden and nut trees. He could just distinguish, between the leafy branches, Reine's black gown, as she walked rapidly along under the ash-trees. At the end of the enclosure, he pushed open a little gate, and came abruptly out on the forest path.

On beholding him standing in advance of her, the young girl appeared more surprised than displeased. After a momentary hesitation, she walked quietly toward him.

"Mademoiselle Reine," said he then, gently, "will you allow me to accompany you as far as La Thuilière?"

"Certainly," she replied, briefly.

She felt a presentiment that something decisive was about to take place between her and Julien, and her voice trembled as she replied. Profiting by the tacit permission, de Buxières walked beside Reine; the path was so narrow that their garments rustled against each other, yet he did not seem in haste to speak, and the silence was interrupted only by the occasional flight of a bird, or the crackling of some falling branches.

"Reine," said Julien, suddenly, "you have so often and so kindly extended to me the hand of friendship, that I have decided to speak frankly, and open my heart to you. I love you, Reine, and have loved you for a long time. But I have been so accustomed to hide what I think, I know so little how to conduct myself in the varying circumstances of life, and I have so much mistrust of myself, that I never have dared to tell you before now. This will explain to you my stupid behavior. I am suffering the penalty to-day, for while I was hesitating, another took my place; although he is dead, his shadow stands between us, and I know that you love him still."

She listened to him with bent head and half-closed eyes, and her heart began to beat violently.

"I never have loved him in the way you suppose," she replied, simply.

A gleam of light shot through Julien's melancholy blue eyes. Both remained silent. The green pasture-lands, bathed in the full noonday sun, were lying before them. The grasshoppers were chirping in the bushes, and the skylarks were soaring aloft with their joyous songs. Julien was endeavoring to extract the exact meaning from the reply he had just heard. He was partly reassured, but some points had still to be cleared up.

"But still," said he, "you are lamenting his loss."

A melancholy smile flitted for an instant over Reine's pure, rosy lips.

"Are you jealous of my tears?" said she, softly.

"Oh, yes!" he exclaimed, with sudden exultation, "I love you so entirely that I can not help envying Claudet his share in your affections! If his death causes you such poignant regret, he must have been nearer and dearer to you than those that survive."

"You might reasonably suppose otherwise," replied she, almost in a whisper, "since I refused to marry him."

He shook his head, seemingly unable to accept that positive statement.

A WOODLAND QUEEN

Then Reine began to reflect that a man of his distrustful and despondent temperament would, unless the whole truth were revealed to him, be forevermore tormented by morbid and injurious misgivings. She knew he loved her, and she wished him to love her in entire faith and security. She recalled the last injunctions she had received from the Abbé Pernot, and, leaning toward Julien, with tearful eyes and cheeks burning with shame, she whispered in his ear the secret of her close relationship to Claudet.

This painful and agitating confidence was made in so low a voice as to be scarcely distinguished from the soft humming of the insects, or the gentle twittering of the birds.

The sun was shining everywhere; the woods were as full of verdure and blossoms as on the day when the young man had manifested his passion with such savage violence. Hardly had the last words of her avowal expired on Reine's lips, when Julien de Buxières threw his arms around her and fondly kissed away the tears from her eyes.

This time he was not repelled.

MLLE. DESROCHES

MLLE. DESROCHES

CHAPTER I

LITTLE THÉRÈSE

O N that day—the last day of July, 1850 —the little town of St. Clement was bathed in a flood of glorious sunlight, and long, golden rays stretched down the main street.

Among all these sleepy houses of the town, there was one that looked especially shut up and forsaken.

The main room of the second story contained nothing but old oak shelves, almost bending under the weight of countless books.

The straw-bottomed chairs had, strangely enough, well carved wooden backs, and the one leather chair in the room was filled by the owner of the house, Dr. Jacques Desroches.

He was only fifty-five years old, but looked older; tall, lean, and stiff in his carriage, his face was deeply lined; he was almost bald. His almost painfully rigid features relaxed only for a moment now and then, when a noise from the window brought to his bitter lips a grimace of annoyance.

The noise was not continuous, nor was it more than

a confused murmur of words which were hardly articulated. At last the old man could endure it no longer; he gave his chair a half turn, then rose all of a sudden, and raising one of the window-shades said, in a stern voice, "Thérèse!"

A flood of light inundated the room, and revealed the guilty couple to be a young girl of sixteen and a dog!

The girl was sitting on a low chair in the deep embrasure of the window, and with one arm raised high in the air she was waving an old glove which the dog—a beautiful Royal Dane with a tawny skin—crouching on his hind legs with his head resting on his forefeet, was coveting with his keen eyes, while uttering a low, half-smothered barking.

"Can you not remain quiet for a moment?" Dr. Desroches asked her, very angrily; "your talking annoys me terribly!"

At this sudden appearance, both the guilty parties had paused penitently. The young girl dropped her glove and came out of her concealment.

"I beg your pardon, papa!" she said, "I did not know I was making any noise. It is hard to keep still so long! We were trying to find some amusement, Dacho and I, till the time for our walk should come."

"Time is never long when we know how to use it properly," replied the doctor; "take a book and keep quiet! I have a horror of idle people!"

The young girl went to one of the shelves of the library, chose a quarto volume and sat down in a corner.

Dr. Desroches did really suffer from an old wound

in his heart, which had been so badly cured that it bled anew at the slightest provocation. He had married, when thirty-seven, a wife who was much younger than he, and she had deceived him. To avoid scandal he had at first borne it all in silence, trying to save appearances, but one fine day—it was now seven years ago—Madame Desroches had run away with a country neighbor. The doctor might have looked upon the whole thing as a mere bad dream, if she had not left behind her a child, who recalled to the poor injured man all the bitterness and all the griefs of the past. During the first years the sight of this child had been so unbearable to him that he had sent her down into Lorraine, the province from which her nurse had come. The father and the mother of this woman were simple farmers, but excellent people; they had a great fondness for little Thérèse, and were delighted to keep her with them. Here the young maiden had lived just as other simple country people live, and it was with sincere regret that she left her friends to go for three years to a convent, where her education was to be completed. It was only when she was sixteen years old that her father thought it best to call her back to him at St. Clement.

These thoughts filled the doctor's mind, while Thérèse turned the leaves of her book, unconscious of the tempest that was brewing in his head.

While the poor girl was absorbed in mournful thoughts, everything around her had relapsed into absolute silence. An hour went by; then suddenly in this deep silence a feeble tinkling of small bells, the rumbling of heavy wheels formed an echo in the house from afar off, on the high road. Thérèse raised her head and listened.

"Ah!" she murmured, "it is the mail!"

She was not mistaken; the stage with its four horses made a tremendous ado on the rough pavement of St. Clement, and seemed to rouse the whole little sleepy town. Suddenly shutters were heard to open, people ran out and questions were interchanged.

"Here is the stage!" exclaimed the young girl, throwing down the book she had been reading. Then rising impetuously, without minding what her father might think of it, she drew the curtain, opened the window, and looked out full of curiosity.

Dr. Desroches, yielding less to curiosity than to that mechanical old habit which had for so many years made the coming of the stage the great event of the twenty-four hours, rose also and followed his daughter to the window.

By the side of the conductor, a young man, apparently about twenty-two years old, flushed from his efforts to blow the long horn, seemed to attract the attention of the citizens looking out of the windows. He was pointed out to others, he was welcomed with a nod of the head, and gayly returned the compliment by raising his hat. Without being handsome, he looked winsome with his large bright eyes and his curly, blond moustache. Thérèse, who did not know what to make of these familiar greetings, turned round with an air of inquiry to Dr. Desroches.

The young traveller on the roof of the stage had not

escaped the physician's observant eye; he slightly shrugged his shoulders, smiled sarcastically, and said, in his most biting tones:

"Ha! ha! Here is young Maupin coming home to the dove-cot! if dove-cot is right name for the roost of a bird of prey such as his estimable father is."

"Oh, yes!" said Thérèse. "I see Monsieur and Madame Maupin standing before the door of the Hôtel de France. They evidently came to meet him!"

There was really a couple standing at the end of the street, near the hotel stables; they were busy sending signals to the stage. The lady was waving her handkerchief, while the husband held his cane as high as he could and shook it in the air.

The heavy, lumbering machine had at last reached its resting-place at the gates of the stable-yard, and the young man, descending leisurely from the elevation on which he was perched, had embraced his mother and then received his father's warm welcome, who seemed to be happy to see his son and heir return. He seized his two hands and then examined him from top to bottom.

"Upon my word!" said Dr. Desroches, "how Papa Maupin pulls about his progeny! He looks at his young man's hands to see if the claws have grown finely. Be content, sparrow-hawk! Blood will tell! He'll have your beak and your talons!"

"These Maupins," said Thérèse, turning to her father, "are very rich and very polite to every one, yet nobody likes them. Why? Are they not honorable in their business transactions?"

Dr. Desroches shrugged his shoulders.

"Honorable? What do you mean?" he cried, full of sarcasm. "A man is always honorable who does the work for which he is fit. In this world we must either cheat or be cheated, eat or be eaten. The Maupins belong to the race of men who eat, that is all! Let us go back! The sight of these people unnerves me!"

CHAPTER II

COME, my dear, you have talked enough for to-day! Don't you see that your son can hardly keep awake?"

The dinner at the Maupins' had lasted long. The newcomer, Stephen Maupin, looked a little dazed, partly by the long journey in the uncomfortable diligence, and partly, no doubt, by the copious dinner, accompanied by capital Bordeaux wines. He only replied in monosyllables to his father's questions, and smiled, while he looked with an air of ineffable self-content at the faces of his parents aglow with admiration, and at the familiar furniture of the room.

"He has hardly slept since he left Paris," said the anxious mother. "He needs rest, and you will have plenty of time to talk to-morrow!"

M. Maupin shrugged his shoulders.

"Worn out by one sleepless night and seven hours' travel! At his age I walked my twenty miles a day and after my return I worked still till midnight! The present generation is far inferior to ours! Come, Monsieur Attorney, go to bed! Good-night! While your mamma will tuck you in your bed, I'll go down to

see that all the doors are locked and the clerks have
left nothing lying about!"

He lighted a candle, and going down to the first story
he entered the office and opened the windows to see if
the shutters were fastened; and closed operations by
reading over the correspondence of the day. All this
took him a full hour, and when he returned to his own
room, he found that Madame Maupin had gone to bed,
but was not yet asleep. Her delicate, fair-haired little
head, framed in the rich laces of her coquettish night-
cap, contrasted charmingly with the white pillows.

"Well," asked M. Maupin, as he blew out his
candle, after emptying his pockets on the night-table,
"is the boy sleeping soundly?"

"Yes. The journey has tired him!"

"Pshaw! to-morrow there will be no trace left!
He has made no bad debts and he has come back in
good health. That is the most important thing. I
think he looks well."

"Yes," replied Madame Maupin, with much satisfaction, "he has developed well in Paris, and is almost
a handsome young man."

"A man is always handsome when he has money
in his pockets," sententiously exclaimed the husband,
"and I have enough to make him as handsome as an
angel! Without counting what I mean to make in
the future," he continued, cheerfully, cracking his
short, stubby fingers with their hairy joints. "I have
not played all my cards yet, and have a few trumps
left in my hand."

He had begun life as a contractor, building houses;

then, his success encouraging him, he had enlarged the circle of his operations, and now he was considered one of the most skilful dealers in money in the whole province. He owned much real estate, and was looked upon as one of the leading men of St. Clement.

"Yes," he continued, "I am not at the end yet. Your son, Laura, shall have enough to buy himself a pair of yellow kid gloves every day of his life, and some other things besides!"

"Fie!" exclaimed Madame Maupin, knowing full well what her husband's sarcastic smile and laughing tone meant to suggest. She added:

"Did you have him admitted to the bar in order to lead such a life?"

"There is a time for all things," replied Simon, "and I see no harm in his enjoying life a little before he goes to work in earnest."

"You had much better initiate him at once into business; he might assist you in managing the bank till he will take it altogether in hand."

M. Maupin, started up, and cried, angrily:

"My business concerns me alone; I do not mean yet awhile to fold my arms and give up the ship! Upon my word, I should think so far I have not managed so very badly! Your son would comprehend very little of my operations; his thoughts are too immature yet! First let him learn at his own cost what life is, and then we'll see——"

"And if he kicks over the traces in the mean time?"

"So much the better! It will teach him caution; I have known people as stiff as bars of iron, veritable

Don Quixotes as far as their principles were concerned: after they had once passed through the hands of pretty women and the constable, they came to me as supple as old gloves! When Stephen shall have sown his wild oats, I will put his nose down upon the ledger—not before!"

Madame Maupin shook her little head.

"You need not try to persuade me, Simon. All that is not moral!"

M. Maupin paced to and fro, with his hands in his trousers' pockets; he turned round, faced his wife on her pillow, and said, in a peremptory tone: "It is practical!"

But the lady did not give up the battle. She would have preferred to see Stephen well married, so as to gain some prestige, some consideration for the firm "Simon Maupin."

"Why could he not marry one of the girls of the neighboring nobility?"

"Girls without money?"

"There are some who belong to old families—that is always something!"

M. Maupin whistled contemptuously. "'Too lean! For a young man in our boy's condition to exchange his hard dollars for a name, would be folly. I do not mean that for you, Laura," he added quickly, seeing in her eyes a flash of indignation, "when I took you in your father's house, the position was not the same, and for a master-mason, as I was then, your old name was a good enough match—besides, you were clever; you had a regular talent for business, and you have helped me essentially."

"If my advice has now and then proved useful to you," resumed Madame Maupin, much put out, "I wish you would be kind enough to listen to me to-night!"

Then she repeated to him, in her bland and insinuating voice, that what their house needed most at this time was respectability. She did not indulge in any illusions on that subject. She knew very well that in St. Clement M. Maupin was not highly respected. "They would not speak of us so lightly," she concluded, "if we were connected with one of these pious and highly respected families."

"Would I have to become pious, too?" the old mason asked, sarcastically.

"Great Heavens! would that be very bad, do you think?" asked his wife.

"Thank you, ho! I do not care to hear mass."

"That is your weak side. You are not religious, and there you are wrong. Believe me, infidelity is no longer the fashion, and the day is not very far off when an irreligious man and a disorderly man will be considered the same thing!"

"You might just as well call me at once a Socialist!" cried the banker, laughing outright.

"You laugh, but I know better than you, and I foresee many things!"

"Ha! ha! There is some truth in that!" he said.

"Don't you see now, Simon!" said his wife, triumphantly. "Great Heavens! I do not advise you all of a sudden to break off your old habits and to go to mass to-morrow morning——"

"No, that would be rather strong!"

"But I advise you to change your mode of life, step by step, to be considerate with the noble families and with the clergy, and gradually to get rid of all friends and acquaintances that might be embarrassing. Look here!" she suddenly cried, "will you give me *carte blanche?* If you do, I promise in less than two years you shall be Mayor of the town and hold the county in the hollow of your hand!"

Simon Maupin looked at her in amazement. "Upon my word, Laura, I accept it as a good omen. You are a real diplomat in your lace cap! It is certain that the Conservatives will remain in power, and we must build upon that foundation. Come," he added, getting up, "we must lay aside the Old Adam!"

He slipped gently into the conjugal bed. "You are a little bit of a woman," he murmured, "but I was a lucky man the day I carried you away from your dovecot at Saviot!"

At break of day Stephen was waked by the song of a young boy who was taking his horses to water. The bells, ringing merrily with many chimes, reminded him that this was Sunday, and that he had promised his mother to go to mass with her. He dressed himself for church, and punctually at ten he offered his arm to Madame Maupin. She also had dressed for the occasion, and felt proud of having preserved so youthful an appearance, thanks to her blond hair and slender waist, that she looked like her son's elder sister. The women, on their knees, whispered behind their books as Stephen passed by, and pointed him out to each other with their eyes as he took a seat in the family pew.

Stephen tried to recognize the young girls he saw around him, or to put the right name to the right face. In the midst of this inquisitive examination his eyes fell upon a face that was entirely new to him. Not far from the railing of the choir, a young girl was kneeling upon a low straw-chair, her head a little bent, and thus showing the delicate outline of her neck, the supple sweep of her waist, the swelling of the puffed-out petticoat and the tiny brown boot.

From time to time the devout girl raised her head, and then Stephen caught a glimpse of a pale complexion, a lively eye, and a charming mouth with full red lips. This unknown face troubled him.

After the last "Let us pray!" when one of the lower priests turned to the congregation and intoned the welcome *Ite, missa est*, the young girl remained for a few moments longer on her knees; then she rose while the organ was pouring forth its gentlest roar to accompany the *exit*. Stephen, who had risen at the same time and was following his mother, did not lose sight of the stranger, and managed gradually to diminish the distance between them. When they reached the holy-water font, he looked around stealthily and saw her close behind them. He dipped his fingers into the shell, touched those of his mother, and then, turning round and bowing, he offered the holy water to the young girl who was standing close behind him.

To his great amazement the unknown person drew

back, her eyebrows almost met in indignation, her lips
curved with disdain, and without noticing the cour-
teous offer of the young man, she passed him, dipped
her fingers into the font, made the sign of the cross,
and rapidly went down the steps in the porch.

This incident had not escaped Madame Maupin's
wide-awake eyes; she blushed slightly and bit her lips.
When they were outside, Stephen, greatly mortified,
asked his mother, glancing at the unknown lady:

"Who is this young stranger who refuses to take
holy water from my hands?"

"A foolish girl!" replied Madame Maupin. "She
is Doctor Desroches's daughter. This Desroches, who
is one of the high and mighty in town, has taken it
amiss that we did not choose him as our physician, and
his daughter has taken up her father's quarrel."

"That is a pity, for she is pretty!"

"Pshaw!" said the mother, contemptuously, "a
country beauty. Her father had banished her to the
country after her mother's deplorable adventure, and
she has, no doubt, acquired the bad manners of the
people with whom she lived."

They had turned the corner of the market when
they were accosted by a tall young man, who bowed
to Madame Maupin and to Stephen.

"Ah!" exclaimed the latter, recognizing one of his
father's upper clerks, "you are Célestin Tiffin! How
are you, my friend?"

"So, so! Monsieur Stephen, so, so!" repeated the
young man, not daring to put on his hat in the presence
of his master's only son. Stephen shook hands with

him and made him cover his head. The clerk obeyed, though reluctantly, for he was a great formalist and almost worshiped the family.

"I am happy, Monsieur Stephen," he began again, walking respectfully about two steps behind Stephen, "I am happy to see you restored to us and in good health. Madame Maupin knows how impatiently I have been waiting for you!"

"And why were you so impatient, my good friend?"

"Why? Has not your father told you?"

Stephen shook his head.

"He probably thought it more proper that I should announce it to you myself—I am going to be married, Monsieur Stephen," he added with a smile, which showed every one of his teeth—"I am going to marry Mademoiselle Bardin, the daughter of the man who farms your beautiful estate of Brenil. The contract has been drawn up these three months and we have waited only for your return to fix the day—and speaking of this, permit me to submit to you a request——"

"Tell me what it is, and be sure, Célestin, that it is granted at once."

"I had already mentioned my request to Monsieur and Madame Maupin—you would overwhelm me with kindness, Monsieur Stephen, if you would honor me on this occasion by being my best man—I know it is asking of you a great favor, but we should all of us be so happy—my betrothed and her family would be so proud, that I think you can hardly refuse me!"

"How can I? I shall be delighted, my dear Célestin! When is the wedding?"

"They are going to marry us day after to-morrow, Tuesday, and if you could make it convenient to reach Brenil toward ten o'clock, I would come to meet you on the road!"

Stephen promised to be punctual. Célestin was overwhelming in compliments and thanks, bowed, and left them, greatly delighted.

"What a good creature!" said Stephen.

"Yes—rather weak, but devoted to us, and that is the main point!"

CHAPTER III

N Tuesday morning, before eight o'clock, Stephen was gayly walking down the turnpike to Brenil.

The sight of the lonely landscape, so calm and green and picturesque, awakened in the young man all his artistic instincts, and he began to wish he might have sufficient talent one of these days to reproduce its charms successfully. Absorbed in such thoughts, he had nearly reached the bridge, when he heard himself hailed and, upon turning his head, he saw the sharp outline of lean M. Tiffin on the green background.

"Am I behind time?" asked Stephen.

"Oh, no! no! There is no time lost, Monsieur Stephen! The bride is still dressing and the musicians have but just come. You see I could not sit still any longer, and so I came out to meet you. Besides, I had another reason! I have prepared a great surprise for the wedding-guests. A great surprise, I assure you! No one knows as yet that you are going to do us the honor of being present. They do not expect you in the least, and you can imagine what a jubilee there will be when they find out that Monsieur Maupin is to be my best man. Won't that make a sensation!"

ANDRÉ THEURIET

Stephen was not particularly enchanted at being thus produced like a sort of official personage; he would have preferred a little less mystery and less ceremony, but the bridegroom was so perfectly enchanted that he had not the courage to spoil the fun.

Célestin suddenly stopped, and taking the young Parisian by the button of his coat, said to him with his pleasant, frank laugh: "And as for you, Monsieur Stephen, I have also my little surprise for you!"

"What? Another surprise?" said Stephen.

"Yes, and a very good one, I hope!" said Célestin; "you shall have a Valentine, as we here call the best man's lady, who is at the same time the first bridesmaid. She is not one of us, but a charming young lady who has been at boarding-school, and will not be at a loss how to talk to you, I am sure. Ha! ha! I tell you! Ha! ha! you will see!"

"Tell me what is the name of this young lady?"

"No! no! You are not to know it. She does not know your name, either! I have managed it all myself and kept my secret. But you will see—you will thank me for what I have done."

"I am afraid you have given yourself much trouble for my sake, my dear Célestin!"

"Trouble? You are not in earnest! It is an honor for us to have at our wedding the son of the man to whom I owe everything, the representative of the great firm of Simon Maupin. If I were to live a hundred years, Monsieur Stephen, I would never forget the day when your father first took me into his office. What would I have been without him? A little clerk

[254]

in a little corner shop. Oh! what a man—what a masterly man your father is, Monsieur Stephen!"

"Yes," replied the latter, "my father is a man of rare intelligence!"

"Eminent! Monsieur Stephen, eminent! And what a will! What capacity for work! It is true, he is hard upon idlers and those who do not pay their debts, but in his very hardness there is a sentiment of justice which I can not but admire. Think of it! Only the other day the cashier's wife had a sick child: this tormented the poor man's mind and he had the ill luck to make a mistake of fifty dollars against the house. He was trembling, the poor man, and felt sure he would be dismissed. But—what does your father do?"

"He put it down to profit and loss," guessed Stephen.

"No, not exactly! But instead of dismissing poor Père Martin, as everybody expected, he only made him refund the amount in weekly payments of ten dollars out of his wages! Now I call that justice tempered by humanity."

"Hm!" said Stephen, not particularly edified by this example of paternal clemency.

They were approaching the farmhouse. Célestin made his way through the crowd of young men, all adorned with bright ribbons, to introduce his guest in the principal room.

The mother of the bride, in her striking costume, with a quaint, tall cap and enormous skirts, was moving about with plates and dishes. At the upper end of the room the bride—a pretty girl with rosy cheeks and blue eyes—was standing stiff and straight among a group of five or six young men who were trying to fasten the crown of orange-blossoms to her lace cap.

"Come, Célestin," said the old farmer, "we are only waiting for you to go to the Mayor's office!"

"One moment," cried the young man, with an air of radiant joy, "I bring you my best man. Monsieur Bardin, you were asking me who would be my witness to the ceremony? Here he is, Monsieur Stephen Maupin, the son of my master and patron!"

Célestin then chose a favor of blue and red ribbon and fastened it to the buttonhole of his new friend; and, taking him by the hand and leading him into the courtyard, he said:

"Now I wish to present you to your Valentine. Mademoiselle Thérèse, where are you?" he cried, looking in all directions for the missing damsel—"you shall see, Monsieur Stephen, ah! you shall see!"

"Here I am!" replied at last a melodious voice.

Stephen looked at the direction from which the voice came, and, to his distress, recognized at once the daughter of Dr. Desroches!

She also had recognized him; her face darkened, and she seized the arm of a young man in velveteen, who was standing near her.

"You are mistaken, Mademoiselle!" exclaimed the bridegroom. "That is not your escort to church—here is your gentleman, Monsieur Stephen Maupin!"

This announcement did not produce the effect which Tiffin had expected. The young girl whispered a few words into her neighbor's ear and did not let him go.

MLLE. DESROCHES

"Thank you, Monsieur Tiffin," she said, in a very decided voice, "I have my escort and I keep him!"

"There is a mistake here!—a misunderstanding," Célestin wailed piteously, turning to Stephen, who bit his moustache with vexation. The procession formed, and Célestin had to obey his father-in-law's orders and take his place. They wound their way down the street, mostly between tall hedges of privet and honeysuckle. Stephen had been left behind among the old men, and watched with mixed feelings the elegant leghorn hat of Mademoiselle Desroches, as it now and then appeared in some break of the hedges, amid the tall white caps and the broad-brimmed black felt hats of the natives.

Young Maupin could not help feeling vexed; the doctor's daughter had a second time shown her aversion for him, and his presence among the peasants, so far from pleasing and flattering them, seemed only to embarrass the good people.

When the double ceremony—the civil and the church marriage—was accomplished, the firing of guns began once more, and, still with music at the head, the procession returned to Brenil, where the wedding-feast was awaiting the people. When they met again at the long table, the bridegroom began once more to make his excuses for the conduct of Mademoiselle Desroches, whom lucky Monsieur Jonset had brought home in triumph.

"Take your seat there, by my wife," said the new husband, with contrite heart, "and pardon this morning's mishaps. It was all my fault. You see, Mademoiselle Desroches was not aware of my intentions,

17 [257]

and she had already chosen her 'Valentine,' whom she could not well dismiss on the spot. But we will set that all right this evening at the ball."

At the very end of the crowd, through a slight mist, Stephen could distinguish Thérèse's graceful head. Stephen thought her charming, and this increased the mortification which the young lady's marked aversion was causing him.

"And now let us enjoy the dance!" cried Célestin, when the feast was ended. He dragged Stephen along with him to the barn, where the musicians had taken their stand upon some casks.

One of the most indefatigable dancers was Thérèse Desroches. She never rested for a moment, and fully compensated herself for her long, quiet solitude in her father's old house. Not a dance nor a cotillon did she omit. Supple, airy, and full of elasticity, she seemed barely to touch the floor; the pure, fresh air intoxicated her; her eyes smiled as her lips smiled. There was a remnant of childish petulance surviving yet in the rather wild energy with which she danced. She seemed to avoid only one of the guests, and that was Stephen. He tried repeatedly to join her, but instantly she would escape, or she would summon that inevitable Jonset, like a body-guard.

Once only chance brought him near to Thérèse. The evening was already far advanced, and the day had grown weary of looking at all these mad dancers, but the bagpipes were indefatigable, and the young people jumped merrily in the court where the moon had taken the place of the sun. Mademoiselle Desroches had paused a moment to get her breath, and fanned herself with a bunch of fig-leaves.

"I have not yet had the pleasure of dancing with you," suddenly said Stephen, coming forth from the shade of the barn.

She turned her bright black eyes, which shone in the moonlight, straight upon him, and her eyebrows threatened to unite. "Really, Monsieur!" she said, curtly, with affected indifference.

"The musicians are going to play a valse; will you dance it with me?"

"Thank you! I am engaged to Monsieur Jonset!"

"For all time to come?" he asked, ironically.

"For all time!" she replied, in the same tone.

"Monsieur Jonset is lucky!"

"Well, Monsieur Maupin, we can not all of us have all things!"

"I should be willing to exchange my lot for his!"

The young girl said, disdainfully: "Perhaps he would not like the exchange!"

"And you would not advise him to do it, would you?" he continued, amused by the play.

She looked him boldly in the face with her clear, limpid eyes, and said: "I? Certainly not, Monsieur Maupin!" and she left him.

This time the purpose to offend was too patent to give Stephen any room for doubt. "What a disagreeable, ill-bred child!" he said, as he left the place.

This last defeat had seriously annoyed him, and he no longer took any pleasure in the ball. He went to the room where he was to sleep and retired.

He awoke very early, and although he had promised Célestin vaguely to spend the day with him, he determined to return to town at once.

He had already passed the suburbs and was entering Main Street, when he suddenly found himself face to face with his father.

"Why!" said, the elder Maupin, "back already? To judge from your long face, you have had a bad night."

"No, I went to bed at eleven, and only got up a little while ago."

"Dear me! How prudent! Were there no pretty girls, then, at the wedding? Well, as you have slept well, you may as well come with me! I want to show you an acquisition I have made during your absence!" They went across the fields in the direction of the table-land that overlooks St. Clement.

"Yes, I have bought the 'Elms.' I had coveted the place for a long time, and as the present owner is embarrassed in his finances, J have taken advantage of the chance and bought it cheap!"

By this time they had entered a beautiful avenue of old elm-trees, with their noble, wide-spreading branches, and saw at the other end of it the porch of the dwelling.

"You see," he said to Stephen, pointing out to him with his cane the four cardinal points, "there is something here of everything; meadows and fields, even heather are here, thanks to our wretched system of farming! But I mean to change all that! I shall send away, as soon as I can, the four tenants that now hold the lands, and engage, in their places, a first-rate Belgian farmer, who will manage the whole with one hand and not leave an inch of soil lying fallow. In my bank every dollar must bring its interest; in agriculture, every yard of soil ought in like manner to produce its profit." At this moment, on this radiant summer morning, in face of this luxuriant nature, Stephen was almost proud of his father. He forgot the mortifications of the evening, and became expansive in his turn.

"What a charming place!" he said to his father. "I am delighted with your purchase! I shall come and paint it soon."

The banker shrugged his broad, square shoulders. "You are still a child for your age," he replied. "What enthusiasm for a bit of wheat-field and a ruin of a house! The only attraction you find in the 'Elms' is that you can come here and daub at your pleasure! You are not practical!"

"No! I am a painter, and I look at your property with an artist's eyes."

"Artist!" repeated M. Maupin, making a face. "You have not given up that old fancy? Well, I am rich enough to give you a few years during which you can amuse yourself as you like. After that, I hope you will look at life seriously."

"But, dear father, in Paris there are many men who look upon painting as a very serious profession."

"That may be so in Paris," said the banker, dryly, "but here, that is about the last profession in life, with the exception of that of a rope-dancer."

They had reached one of the wheatfields, where two peasants were busy unloading sheaves and beginning a stack. The younger of the two men was throwing down the sheaves from the cart on which he was standing, and the old peasant arranged them carefully in a circle.

"Look!" said M. Maupin, "here is Father Jacques, making a stack of wheat! I must ask him how his wife is; she has been very ill."

To Stephen's great surprise, the two peasants hardly raised their heads to greet the "Master," and did not for a moment stop their work.

"Neither better nor worse!" was the laconic answer, and the old man went on arranging his sheaves.

M. Maupin, a little disconcerted by this reception, walked on, but as he reached the gate he turned and said: "Let us hope that your good woman will soon be all right again. I'll send you my doctor, Jacques!"

"You are very civil, Monsieur Maupin, but perhaps it would be better were you a little less polite in words, and more just in your business!"

At first M. Maupin pretended not to hear, but Stephen stopped and looked at Jacques in surprise.

"What is that you are saying?" the banker asked, turning round, "I do not understand you!"

"I understand myself very well," replied Father Jacques, wiping the perspiration from his brow with his shirt-sleeve, "and you would understand me very well, too, Monsieur Maupin, if you chose. You must surely know that we have had an execution yesterday in the house, and you also know who sent it!"

"You are mistaken, my good man," M. Maupin said, curtly. "I am not concerned in it."

"I see very clearly," continued the peasant, getting heated, "you want to turn me out of my little bit of a farm, and you put forward that man Berloc, as if everybody did not know that he is merely your tool."

"You are a fool and an insolent fellow!" cried M. Maupin, whose anger rose beyond his control.

"Pshaw! You need not roll your eyes," said the old peasant, drawing himself up with a great effort. "You won't keep me from seeing what your game is. You caress people and your man Berloc flays them alive! Great God! How many people are lying on straw now whose beds you have taken from them! Why, sir, they count by hundreds! I am not the first and I shall not be the last! I say it is mean and that is all!"

M. Maupin had quickly left the grounds and hastened his steps, but Stephen heard it all and lost no word spoken by Father Jacques. "What does he mean?" he asked in a voice that betrayed his painful excitement. "Is it true that this Berloc——?"

"Will you subject me now to an examination? You?" asked M. Maupin in very bad humor. "If you listen to all the stories that these people tell, you will soon cease to wonder. It is a perfect race of beggars, ever complaining—they are all so, but I'll find a way to shut their mouths!"

The young man looked pale; he felt his heart beat within him. It was to him as if the imposing form of his father had suddenly been torn from the pedestal on which he had raised it but just now, with such great admiration.

CHAPTER IV

A BETTER UNDERSTANDING

FTER breakfast, Stephen pleaded his bad night and long morning walk to retire to his room. He threw himself, fully dressed, on his bed, feeling an indescribable relief as he gradually saw things less sharply defined before his eyes, and at last fell pleasantly asleep. For an hour he was unconscious. But his mind had been too painfully affected to allow his sleep to continue long and peacefully. His memory of a sudden awoke, and he saw once more the whole scene, with the two peasants before his mind's eye. Instantly also the one terrible question that had possessed him during the whole morning, arose again. "Can it be that my father is not an honest man?"

From early childhood Stephen had been brought up in respect and admiration for his father.

To Stephen, his father was always the impeccable man, the rich and keen-sighted banker whom he had learned to respect and admire from his tenderest age. The insinuations of the old peasant were thus the first blow inflicted upon his father's prestige. Could they be true? Was it possible that the ease and comfort by which he had been surrounded from infancy were purchased with money unjustly taken from poor helpless folk?

As he was thus meditating, there returned to his memory a number of unpleasant incidents that had struck him at the wedding. He remembered the mistrustful looks of his neighbors, the conversation suddenly interrupted at his approach, and above all the downright hostile position assumed by Mademoiselle Desroches. He asked himself if the young girl could be aware of the reports concerning his father, and had, on that account, refused to know him?

These reminiscences naturally brought back to him also the picture of his old friend Célestin, and he instantly resolved to question him. He got up and looked at the clock. It was three. The wedding festivities were to be continued that evening, and he had abundant time to reach Brenil. He thrust his head into a basin of water, arranged his clothes, and after telling his mother that he thought himself bound to play his part as best man to the end, he started once more for the wedding. The large room, but yesterday the scene of incessant laughter and loud cries and songs, was deserted, but the table was there still, and Madame Bardin and some of the servants were busy putting things in their places again.

"Good gracious!" she exclaimed, as she saw her visitor. "Here you are and quite alone! Célestin was hardly hoping for you any longer. He is gone with our child, and the young folks, fishing for crawfish near our second meadow on the river, and he told us to send you there if you should come. I'll show you the way!"

ANDRÉ THEURIET

Pointing out to him a path that led down the slope, she said:

"Only follow this path, and it will lead you straight to the river. There you'll find all our people!"

Stephen went down the path, which to his inexperienced ideas looked little better than a way for goats, and soon he became aware of the presence of the fishing party.

In the very centre of the round dance he saw Mademoiselle Desroches; her white muslin dress shone brightly on the green background, and looked strangely simple amid all the bright colored gowns of the others. He was afraid now of accosting Célestin and subjecting him to an interrogation which might possibly change his doubts into certainty. A vague presentiment warned him to wait a little longer.

He was aroused from his dreams by a sudden outbreak of laughter; the couples had separated, they were running to and fro in search of their wraps, and evidently preparing for the return home. It was time to find Célestin! Stephen, with beating heart, jumped over the fence and cut across the meadow. When he reached at last the wedding-party, the couples had once more united and were slowly filing past him, the bridal couple at their head. At the sight of his master's son, Célestin uttered a cry of delight. "Bravo, Monsieur Stephen! It is good of you to come back to us this evening! You are just in time for supper, and we are bringing home the finest crawfish you ever saw. Wait till mother makes them jump in boiling water!" Then he turned toward the procession, crying out: "Well, are we all there? Are the couples complete again?"

MLLE. DESROCHES

"There is one missing!" replied a young fellow, in whom Stephen recognized the inevitable Jonset. "Mademoiselle Desroches has gone in search of a pair of scales, that have been mislaid. But she knows the way—still, I have a mind to run——"

"Stay here, Jonset!" said the bridegroom, with an air of authority. "You look to me much too fond of fluttering around Mademoiselle Desroches! People will begin to notice it, and that might become unpleasant. I'll go myself—or rather, Monsieur Stephen, would you be kind enough to take my place? Show her that you have not taken it amiss, how she has treated you—I have given her a lecture this morning—and she expressed her regret at having behaved so. Come on, children! Monsieur Maupin and Mademoiselle Desroches will overtake us before we get home."

Searching carefully all the alder bushes, Stephen was at last lucky enough to see the young girl's white dress.

"Mademoiselle!" he cried.

"Monsieur!" she replied, in a voice full of vexation and impatience.

"I beg your pardon if I annoy you!" Stephen said, and his voice had become slightly sarcastic—"but Célestin has asked me to help you look for the lost scales and to bring you back to the house—with the scales!"

"Do not trouble yourself," she replied. "I remember now where I put them down. They are on that little island, and I'll go and get them."

"On the island? Have you a boat?"

"No, but there is a bridge. Do not trouble yourself!"

Stephen went forward and saw that there was indeed a fallen tree lying so as to cross to the opposite bank. "You are not going to venture out there, I am sure!" he said. "Pray take care, you will slip and fall into the water!"

In the mean time she had gathered the folds of her skirt, and walked across the dangerous bridge.

Mademoiselle Desroches was almost at the end of her rash undertaking, when all of a sudden there came a "plump!" and he heard a plunge into the water. In the twinkling of an eye Stephen was at the end of the tree where Mademoiselle Desroches was sitting, holding on with her hands to the withe that served as a railing, but her body, from her waist down, was in the river. She broke out into loud laughter, but it was a short, nervous laugh; the young man seized her by the arms, helped her to raise herself, and deposited her, well soaked, on the edge of the little island.

"Have you hurt yourself?" he asked her.

"No! It is nothing. I have sprained my foot, I think, that is all."

"I told you so!"

"It is your fault, too!" she cried, angrily. "If you had not been there, I would not have slipped. I have often and often crossed here; I have been across ten times at least this very day, and never missed it."

"I make you ten thousand excuses!" he said, ironically, "but after all I am here, and now I have to take you back to the farm. You can not stay all night here like Robinson Crusoe on his island. Do you feel strong enough to go back this way, resting on my arm?"

"I'll try," she replied, with an air divided between anger and contrition.

When they were once more on firm land, they walked for a while in perfect silence. Thérèse was too much mortified to complain, but a slight tremor of her chin and a corresponding motion of the lips warned her that soon her teeth would begin to chatter. She could hardly drag herself any farther. At last she stopped.

"It would be dangerous for you, soaked as you are, to attempt reaching the farmhouse. We must look for some house where you can dry yourself."

She thought for a moment, and then, in a soft and almost timid voice, she said:

"Yes, that would be better. Not far from here there is a house, where the people—nice people—know my father. They will be ready to make me a fire. Will you take me there?"

Stephen inclined his head in token of assent, and then offered her his arm. Ten minutes later they reached a humble cottage. Stephen knocked at the door. An elderly woman opened it, and Stephen told her of the accident.

"Oh!" she said at once, "you are the doctor's daughter, are you? Why, my little darling, you are wet to your bones. Come in quick. I'll make a blaze with some dry branches."

They entered the kitchen, feebly lighted by a piece of resinous bark, stuck in the cleft of a piece of wood; the woman threw a handful of vine-branches on the coals and while she was looking for some garments that she might lend Thérèse, till her own should get dry, Stephen escaped stealthily, to give the girl an opportunity to change her costume.

He was thinking of her aversion with intense bitterness, when suddenly, between the tall green stalks of the corn, he saw two black eyes shine brightly, and as slender form came forth out of the shadow, he recognized Thérèse Desroches. The young girl had donned a blue gown of some flannel-like material, which she had borrowed from the wardrobe of her hostess.

"It is I," she said, smiling; "do not start. The good woman is drying my clothes and in the mean time I have put on her daughter's dress."

"This costume is very becoming to you," he said, "you only lack the tall white cap and you would be a perfect peasant."

"Peasant? Why for four years I have been that and nothing else—of course I must show that very clearly."

"You were brought up in a village?"

"Not even in a village! On an isolated farm surrounded by vast fields. My nurse lived there and I remained with her and her people till I was thirteen." She sighed. "I was very happy with them, and I liked it much better than I like town. I love peasants!"

"Is that the reason why you preferred Monsieur Jonset's arm to mine at the wedding?"

"No!" she cried, excitedly.

"Ah! then there was another reason for it?" cried Stephen.

"No! that is to say, I had accepted him at first, and, of course I would not mortify him by giving him up for a newcomer!"

MLLE. DESROCHES

Stephen suddenly raised his eyes to her face and said, very gravely: "Mademoiselle Desroches, I think you are candid. Would you swear to me that this was the only reason why you refused last night to take my arm and to dance with me?"

She made no answer, and the darkness prevented his seeing how deeply she blushed. "You had another reason," he continued, sadly, "a reason that touches me personally."

"You are right!" she murmured at last.

"What was it?"

"What use is it to tell you?"

"You fear to mortify me as you did with Jonset!" he cried, bitterly. "Never mind! I am able to hear the truth, even unpleasant truth. Confess you disliked me, and you meant to make me aware of it!"

"You are mistaken, Monsieur, I have nothing against you. I do not know you!"

"You look to me too sensible to treat a man like me as a child would do; twice, Sunday at church, and last night at the wedding, you treated me as you would a man whom you hate and whom you wish to know of it. And yet, you acknowledge yourself, you did not know me!"

"That is true!"

"If your dislike did not arise with me, the newcomer, you meant to show it against my family? What do you object to in us?"

She shook her head. "It is not for me to speak of such things—especially not with you!"

"Oh, speak!" he resumed, vehemently, "I want it!

You must do it! I pray you! Since yesterday I feel that all around me I brush against people who hate us, and this hatred terrifies me, because it is a mystery to me. I can not endure this anguish any longer—I must see my way clear before me. Is it my father whom they charge——?"

She cast down her eyes, but said nothing.

"They say he is hard, even cruel, that he does not shrink from the harshest measures to recover money which is due to him. That is a defect in a man's character, but because he is hard and exacting, he is not dishonorable in any way, and my father is a man of honor who has amassed a large fortune by means of hard work and loyal means!"

Her eyes still downcast; she made no reply.

"You doubt that?" exclaimed Stephen. "You doubt that he is honorable in all his dealings? But where is your proof? Who among your acquaintances has the right to bring that charge against him?"

"My father! He has been ruined by your father! and not very honorably—that I can assure you!"

"That is slander!" cried the young man, furious.

"My father never tells a falsehood," Thérèse said, firmly. "You ask me to tell you the truth, and this I was told on the very evening of your return to Saint Clement. I know very well that these are things not to be spoken of, but why do you force me?"

"My father has ruined your father! How and when?" murmured Stephen, in a low, subdued voice.

"Thus: Five years ago my father stood in need of money; and he wanted it all at once. It was a big

sum; thirty thousand francs I believe. He went
to Monsieur Maupin first, who refused to lend him
money, but offered to purchase for cash, for the same
amount, a property which was worth eighty thousand
francs, and which had been in our family more than
a hundred years. That was not very honest, to begin
with, was it? To take advantage of a man's embarrassment to propose such a bargain. My father tried
elsewhere, but time was pressing, and at last he went to
a kind of money-lender by profession. This was a man
called Jean Berloc, who furnished the money, but
asked outrageous interest, and lent only for a very short
time. When the note became due, my father did not
have the money to meet it. Then he was made to renew the notes on still harder conditions, and finally,
when my father was unable to pay, Berloc took the
matter into court. The estate was sold at public auction, and do you know who bought it? Monsieur
Maupin, whose tool and agent Berloc had been, as all
Saint Clement now knows perfectly well. This is the
bare truth, Monsieur, and everybody here knows all
about it—except you!"

Stephen was crushed; he had sunk down upon the
edge of the basin, and there he sat, his head in his
hands, utterly overcome by these revelations.

"I have caused you pain," said Thérèse, in a gentle
voice, "pardon me, I am more sorry than I can tell you.
How deeply I now regret my conduct last night! If I
had not been so hard with you, all this of to-night would
not have happened."

At the same moment the owner of the house appeared

in the garden. "Your clothes are all dry, little one," she cried, "and you can put them on again whenever you wish." As she was saying this, some noise was heard at a distance. Then loud and repeated halloos reëchoed from the direction of the bridge. "That is Monsieur Célestin's voice," said Thérèse, "he is no doubt in search of us!"

She ran to the front door of the house and answered the cries. She was not mistaken. A moment later the bridegroom and Jonset appeared, and heard, with much astonishment, the story of Thérèse's adventure.

"Well!" said Jonset, "you can boast of having caused us all a great fright and much anxiety. We feared for some time you might have fallen into a big hole."

At the arrival of the young man, Stephen had gathered himself up, and, forcing himself to appear calm, had joined Célestin. "Since you are here," he said to him, "I can entrust Mademoiselle Desroches to you, and wish you good-night!"

"What!" cried Tiffin, "you will not stay and sup with us? Ah! I am certainly unlucky with my wedding!"

"Excuse me!" Stephen said, briefly, "I must be back at Saint Clement to-night."

He was already at some distance, when somebody came running after him, and in the darkness a little hand shook his cordially. "Good-night, Monsieur Stephen," murmured Thérèse, "good-night and forgive me!"

CHAPTER V

THE SON MAKES AMENDS

THE bank had hardly opened yet, but M. Maupin had already been at work more than two hours in his private office.

The clock was striking eight, when some one knocked at the door.

"May I come in?" asked Stephen Maupin.

And as the answer did not come at once, the young man entered at the very moment when a visitor slipped out and disappeared through the small door leading to the offices. Stephen barely had time to recognize the bent figure and shuffling walk of Jean Berloc.

When this client was gone, the banker turned round, and said: "Well, what do you want?"

The young man looked pale, but there was in his eye something that showed he was firm and resolved.

"Good-morning, father! I should like to have a talk with you. Can you give me a few minutes?"

The banker looked at his watch. "I can give you half an hour," he said, "but not a moment more, for I have an appointment at half past nine."

When Stephen had risen in the morning, he had felt himself strong in his purposes and had vowed to himself that he would be brave and ask his father for a full explanation. But he loved his father, who had always been just and kind to him. And now—was he to subject him to a painful interrogatory? Was he to judge, perhaps to condemn him?

"Well, I am waiting!" cried M. Maupin, who had been scribbling something on his blotter. "Of what are you dreaming? Are you going to stand there like a stick? I thought you had something to ask me?"

"Yes!" replied Stephen at last. "Ever since yesterday I have been thinking of that little farmer of whom we were speaking. I came to ask you to give orders that he be left alone!"

M. Maupin continued his scribbling with an air of perfect indifference. "I thought," he replied without raising his eyes from his book, "I had explained to you that this peasant is mistaken. I am not his creditor, and it does not depend on me to stop the prosecution."

"Is not the man who has just left you, perhaps the real creditor?"

"Which man?"

"Jean Berloc."

"That may be. Berloc has a great many such skulking debtors, and I would not be surprised to find that our friend of yesterday is one of the number."

"Well—and then?" asked the young man, looking his father in the face.

"Well, then?"

"At a word from you, Berloc would stop the suit."

"You are jesting. What right could I possibly have to interfere with his business?"

MLLE. DESROCHES

"The right of the principal, who directs his agent," said Stephen, with a firm voice. "It is well known everywhere that this man Berloc is your tool, and only does what you order him to do."

"What nonsense!" M. Maupin gave a push to his chair and turned round so as to face him. "What on earth have you to do with this? What the devil do you mean by putting your nose into matters that do not concern you, and of which you know nothing?"

"If I touch this matter it is because your name and my name can only suffer by being associated with Berloc's name!"

The banker's irritation rose. "By God!" he cried in his native jargon, "have you not dragooned me enough with your foolish questions, and your absurd scruples? Do I trouble myself about your pictures? Everybody to his taste! Leave it to me to take care of my name—I can do it without assistance from others. Make money—and that is enough!"

"Money is not everything!" remarked Stephen.

"Do you think so?" asked the old man, ironically. "It seems to me that money is the one main spring, and that he who is rich is strong, and in order to be rich we have to make use of men and their foibles, eh? There are throats that are thirsty—and there is water that flows below ground—and the wise man is he who discovers that water and leads it to the thirsty throats! Do you understand?"

"I understand that wealth is power—but is that a reason why we must value it above all considerations of honor and of humanity?"

"Words! Empty words!" exclaimed M. Maupin, once more shrugging his shoulders. "True honor consists in doing what your hands find to do, conscientiously. The world bows low to those who know how to make money, and the world is right."

"Yes, they take off their hats before their faces—and behind their backs they send them to the gallows! That is not respect—that is fear!"

"Well—what then?" exclaimed M. Maupin, "if the timid are in the majority, the strong and fearless must discount 'their foibles. I know them, for I have been poor myself and have lived with the poor! They have the same vices as the rich—only with envy and jealousy added—that is all!"

Stephen heard his father, and was stupefied.

"You wonder!" said M. Maupin, resuming his seat, and looking around with his cruelly hard eyes at the disturbed face of his son. "You will find out the truth of my words when you go to work yourself." And when Stephen shrank back, he added, not unkindly: "Oh! be not afraid! I do not mean to-day, or to-morrow. You are not ripe yet for business. Amuse yourself! A young man must sow his wild oats! Go and enjoy your young days, my boy; that is all I ask of you—just now!"

Stephen did not believe his own ears, and his sadness was only increased. "Thank you," he said, "I take no pleasure in such things!"

"Why! You are fastidious! I only wish I had had such an offer made me when I was young! I was always hungry and thirsty! I thought all the girls were pretty, and wanted to kiss every one of them. And you! You turn up your nose and play the virtuous youth. I ask you only one thing: Do not contract debts. I can not bear them. When your pocket is empty, come to me directly. By the way," he added, pulling open a drawer, "I think you must be dry now——"

He broke open a roll, and counted out on the table fifty bright gold pieces in two lines. "Here!" he said, "is something for your petty expenses. But do not come again and meddle with what is my business, and mine alone! It is bad to be between hammer and anvil!"

The clock struck half, and the banker looked at his watch. "Take them quickly!" he said, "and be gone. I am in a hurry!"

The young man collected the gold pieces and put them into his pocket. "Thank you!" he murmured, but in a way that showed how little the heart had to do with his thanks.

And this man was his father! Stephen had loved him, and even now his heart felt great tenderness for him, like a dying man who resists death to the uttermost. Soon, however, he fixed upon a plan: he would conscientiously continue his studies in art, spend a few months in Paris at the School of Fine Arts, and thus enable himself in as short a time as might be possible, to earn his daily bread.

He soon reached Jacques's farm, but the house looked deserted, and the doors were closed. Stephen knocked at the door and a feeble voice answered, calling upon him to enter. After a while he distinguished an old woman lying in a huge bedstead and looking at him with feverish eyes, full of anxiety. He told her he wished to see Father Jacques.

"Ah!" replied the sick person plaintively, "he is not in; he is gone to Saint Clement about the wretchedness they have brought upon us. Do you know, Monsieur, they want to sell my furniture Sunday, after Mass? And where shall we go? And I, sick as I am, I can not lie in the open air, like a wild beast. And to think that it is a man who is rolling in gold who brings all this misery upon us! Can you imagine anything more cruel, Monsieur, I ask you?"

"What is the amount Father Jacques owes this man who is selling him out?" asked Stephen at last.

"A mere trifle, Monsieur, thirty gold pieces, which we owe this devil of a Berloc—but that is not all; then there are the interests and the costs. Great God! it amounts in all to nearly eight hundred francs! And everything, everything we have in this world, is to go on Sunday! They might as well cut us in quarters—we could not raise eight hundred francs!"

"Look here!" said Stephen, putting on a little table the gold his father had given him. "Here are a thousand francs—tell Father Jacques to pay everything he owes by to-morrow morning!"

The gold pieces fell with a ringing sound upon the table, and Jacques's mother, utterly dumfounded, had raised herself in her bed and looked alternately at the money and at the young man.

"And this is no lie, Monsieur! Great God! Real

gold pieces! and a whole handful! By all the saints! I have not seen so many since I have been in this world. You are sure you are not fooling an old woman, Monsieur? You are really in earnest, are you?"

"Take it," said Stephen. "It is yours!"

"And what may be your name, my beautiful young master? I want to put your name in my prayers every day of my life, morning and evening."

"This money is not my money," said Stephen, and then suddenly seized with a feeling of pity and of affection for his father, he added: "This money comes to you from Monsieur Maupin, who sends it to you, but under the condition that you will mention it to no one!"

He escaped while the plaintive voice of the old woman pursued him with a long string of thanks and blessings. "At all events there will be that many people less who curse us!" he thought as he went away.

CHAPTER VI

EANING against the rock which here rose quite steeply, Stephen was sketching the fountain. Gradually, his attention became distracted, his brush less certain, and he felt that uncomfortable sensation that overcomes us when we are conscious that we are watched. After struggling for some time against this mysterious influence, he put down his brush, stretched his arm, and then looked behind him and beheld Thérèse Desroches.

"Pardon me!" she replied to M. Maupin's air of astonishment when he perceived her. "I fear I am indiscreet. I did not expect to find any one at the spring and came to get some cress——"

The young man had risen; she came up to his canvas.

"Oh, how pretty this is!" she continued. "Everything is here, the water, the trees, the sky, even this water-lily that is just opening amid its round leaves!"

Stephen sat down again, and in order not to embarrass the young girl, he began cleaning his palette and arranging his brushes. As he was about to remove his sketch, Thérèse stopped him rather brusquely. "Let me look at it once more!" she said, very gently.

He put it back upon its little easel, and she bent over the better to examine it. "You have forgotten nothing," she continued, "even that washerwoman in the distance, what a good likeness! Is it more difficult to paint people or trees?"

"The difficulty is the same," he replied. "A tree has a physiognomy which is as hard to catch as a man's."

"Then you could paint the likeness of a person as faithfully as that of a willow."

"I think I could," he said, watching the firm and regular outlines of Thérèse's profile, and then, looking straight in her face, he added: "Will you let me try to paint yours?"

"Really?" she asked, with a bright sparkle of delight in her eyes. "Would you consent to paint my portrait?"

"I should be delighted, if it were possible."

"It is very possible," she assured him, eagerly, "we can begin whenever you like."

"Where and when?" Stephen asked, a little puzzled.

"Here, every day, as long as the weather is fine!"

"But," objected the young man, "will they let you come, and won't it appear out of the way."

"Oh, I often take long walks over the country. I had gotten used to these solitary promenades during the time when I lived with peasants, and no one has interfered since."

The sad tones of these last words touched Stephen and made him sympathetic. With a look of great tenderness he said to her: "Very well, Mademoiselle, when will it please you to begin? To-morrow?"

"With the greatest pleasure!" she exclaimed.

"To-morrow, then—in the afternoon—you will find me near the spring!"

The [next 'day, at one o'clock, she appeared at the turn of the rocky wall, in the same costume that she had worn the day before.

At the sight of the canvas standing all ready on the easel, her black eyes were radiant with delight.

"Am I behind time?" she asked.

"No," was his reply. "We have three whole hours before us, and in that time we can do a good deal!"

The meetings continued throughout the whole month of August, which was exceptionally fine. As both were communicative by nature, a close intimacy sprang up between the young people. They loved to tell each other of their youth, but two subjects were carefully left out of the conversation and never touched upon: Stephen was silent on the subject of M. Maupin, and Thérèse never spoke of her mother!

This would have been perfect, ideal happiness had they lived on a deserted island; but they were actually living in a little town where everybody had lynx eyes to spy out their neighbors' doings. Before the month of August had come to an end, there was not a man, woman, or child in St. Clement who did not know that they met every day at the Angels' Mill. Soon the whole town spoke of the meetings of Dr. Desroches's daughter with young Maupin, and the charitable pitied the doctor. As to Stephen, nobody spared him, and the mothers of marriageable daughters, especially, thought his conduct unpardonable. Madame Maupin was one of the first to hear what scandal her son was causing.

"Well," she said, coming home one evening, "I hear strange stories in town! It seems that our Stephen has fallen in love with the little Desroches girl!"

She told her husband what stories were circulating.

The old banker only smiled. He was not sorry to find that Stephen had become less puritanic, and applauded himself for the advice he had given his son.

"Well, what next?" he replied, cheerily. "He amuses himself—that is natural; he is of the right age for such diversions. Surely, you did not think he would all his life long hide himself behind your petticoats?"

"But he makes people talk of the girl!"

"So much the worse for her and her father. Instead of troubling himself with politics, the old man ought to watch over his child. Stephen is a young man, and, like all young men, he is running after the girls."

"That is immoral, my dear, and, what is worse, it is dangerous! Suppose Stephen should take matters in earnest and one of these days come and ask for your consent to marry the girl?"

The banker whistled ironically. "I should like to see that! However," and here the scar across his mouth changed color, and gave him a savagely cruel expression, "I have the means to get rid of the girl should she ever become troublesome. Don't talk of it with your son. I am awake, and you can go to sleep in safety."

But Madame Maupin was not entirely reassured. She trembled lest these reports should reach the old doctor's ears, and he should hold Stephen to account.

ANDRÉ THEURIET

October had come, and the days were getting both shorter and less trustworthy so far as the weather was concerned. One afternoon, when Stephen was approaching the end of his task, and the portrait was nearly finished, they were surprised by a sudden shower, and had to run to seek refuge in one of the nearest cottages. The farmer's wife took them both into a dark room, which was at once her kitchen and her bedroom, and here she left them alone. Everything betrayed the wretched poverty of the owners. The two young people looked at each other, and although they had spent so many hours and days alone with each other in the open air, they now for the first time felt embarrassed.

"What a wretched place!" said Stephen. "It feels like a cave!"

"Yes," replied Thérèse, "and yet these people live here and are used to it."

Stephen saw how the young girl's eyes began to shine brightly and a smile played on her lips.

"Of what are you thinking?" he asked her.

"I am thinking," she replied, "how you would look if you were condemned to spend your life here!"

"I?" he exclaimed. "The place, to be sure, is poor enough and wretched—and yet, I should be happy if I could lead a simple life here—with you!"

"Oh, fie!" she said, smiling, but shaking her head.

"I swear it, Thérèse!"

Their eyes met once more and both felt a sudden accession of melting tenderness. Stephen had seized Thérèse's hands.

The farmer's wife was shaking her wooden shoes at

the door before coming in. The young people let go their hands and she entered.

"You left home in a very bad state of the weather, my little one," she said, dropping a little curtsey, "and so have you done, Monsieur Maupin; but you need only have a little patience. The sky is clearing up toward Saint Clement—it was only a heavy shower."

In fact, already the kitchen had become a little lighter and a milky whiteness appeared on the sky. A quarter of an hour later the rain ceased altogether and the young people could leave the house. But the roads were deep in mud, and Stephen would not let Thérèse go home alone.

Thérèse left her friend at the first bridge, and when she at last reached her home, she found the Doctor standing in the vestibule of his house; he seized her rudely by the arm and thrust her into the library. Then he locked the door and asked her:

"Where have you been?"

Thérèse looked at him, surprised at the question and at the tone in which it was asked.

"I went to the Angels' Mill and was caught in the rain!"

"You were walking, and alone?"

Thérèse blushed slightly. "No!" she answered. "Why?"

"Because I should like to know the companion with whom you were running about over the country."

She raised her head and replied, in a firm voice: "It was Monsieur Stephen Maupin!"

"Really? And you do not die for shame when you

confess it? It is not enough that you forget the reserve
which an honest girl must show; to be pointed at with
scorn you must needs go and choose the son of the
man who has robbed me!"

"I have done nothing to be pointed at with scorn!"
Thérèse said; "as to Monsieur Stephen Maupin, if his
father has done wrong, he is the very first man to regret it, and he is an honest man, I am sure!"

"And I must accept your certificate of honesty?"
asked the father, with a laughter full of sarcasm.

"Yes, for I have never told a falsehood in my life,
and when I tell you on what occasion I made Monsieur
Maupin's acquaintance, you will be less surprised that
we should have become friends."

"To be sure," he replied, ironically, "I am all anxiety to know this edifying story in all its details."

She told him very frankly and briefly what had
occurred at the famous wedding, then of her meeting
with Stephen at the Angels' Spring, and the sittings for
the portrait, as if it were the simplest and most natural
matter in the world.

"Thus this clandestine intercourse has gone on two
months already?"

"There was nothing stealthy about it—why should
we hide? We were doing nothing wrong."

"What? Nothing wrong?" he laughed, scornfully,
"you will next try to persuade me that you spent your
time in reciting Paternosters?"

"I do not understand you," said Thérèse, "but I
feel that you are cruel, unutterably cruel, to your child.
It may be, since you assert it, that my conduct has been

thoughtless, incautious, and it may also be that I have done, without knowing it, things which the world considers wrong, but let me tell you in my turn, that if I had been loved more and guided better, I would have acted with more discernment; I should have been a well educated and prudent girl, like others, if my father——"

"Your father!" broke in Dr. Desroches, furiously, "do not speak of your father! You bear my name, to be sure, but let me tell you once for all time—you can hear it now—I have always doubted that you are my daughter—and now I believe it less than ever!"

Thérèse sank upon the floor, and, her brow leaning on the edge of the table, her face hid in her hands, remained thus, crushed with shame and humiliation.

Dr. Desroches, in spite of his anger and the tempest of furious passions which this scene had let loose, felt that he had gone too far and was ashamed of his own severity. In his dried-up heart arose an instinct of pity; his lips opened and he was about to speak a word of compassion to his child. But he was too wise not to know that there are wounds which never heal. He knew that certain words, once pronounced, can not, by any power on earth, be made unsaid. He suddenly turned on his heel, opened the door on the staircase-landing, slammed it violently, and left Thérèse alone.

CHAPTER VII

COMPLICATIONS

AT the house of President Lourdeval they were celebrating the natal day of his wife, Léonarde. Every year on the sixth of November, the husband availed himself of this occasion to invite the members of his Courts, the principal functionaries of St. Clement, and a few intimate friends, to come and spend the evening at his house.

This year the day had been rainy. The poor ladies who possessed no carriages, and had no kind friends more favored by fortune to offer them seats in their vehicles, did not hesitate to put heavy wooden shoes over their delicate silk *bottines* to defy the muddy roads, for the house stood at a long distance from the last town-house.

The President, remarkable for his great height and his habit of complimenting all and every one, went forward to meet the ladies as they were announced, and in his fine old fashion kissed their hands. Madame Lourdeval allowed him to play the butterfly around the ladies, as she sat enthroned majestically in her chair.

She was aided in doing the honors of the house by her three nieces, the Mesdemoiselles Boisse. Their

family was old; it went back as far as the days of Fair
Melusine, but unfortunately it was as poor as it was
old, and the three Graces had no dower!

Among the last comers were Madame Maupin and
her son. The banker had sent his excuses, but his wife,
full of ambitious desires, took care not to miss such an
opportunity of getting into society. Stephen had accompanied her for another reason. He knew that Dr.
Desroches and the President were old friends from
childhood up, and he had come in the hope of meeting
Thérèse. For nearly a month—ever since the day of
the storm—he had not seen her again. Stephen had
haunted the street where she lived, but in vain; he had
not missed a mass—all in vain! Since he had entered
the President's house, he had forgotten nearly all his
social duties; searching every room, looking into every
corner, he presently saw Dr. Desroches and his daughter enter the room.

Madame Lourdeval received the Doctor ceremoniously, and dryly welcomed his daughter, whom the
President, with many compliments and fine speeches,
led to an empty chair near the embrasure of a window.
Thérèse felt that she was received with curiosity and an
attention not overkind. She divined that at this moment her face, her dress, her smallest gestures, were
observed and commented upon by all the women and
the majority of the men in the room. This embarrassed
her to such a degree that she hardly dared move.
Stephen, after a time, profited by the general movement
to slip into the window embrasure near which Thérèse
was sitting. He tried to meet Thérèse's eyes but she

seemed, on the contrary, determined to avoid his. Presently he heard her voice appealing to him, and saying: "I pray you, do not remain near me!"

She spoke in short, nervous accents.

"Why?" asked young Maupin. "What has happened?"

"I can not tell you, but I beseech you, for God's sake, leave me!"

Astonished and distressed, Stephen dared not insist. He obeyed and left the window.

In the mean time, tables for the games had been arranged in the large drawing-room. Stephen seated himself between his mother and one of the nieces; opposite him sat Thérèse. The game they were playing fortunately required but little attention; the players could give free course to their tongues while they picked up or laid down their cards. Hence the conversation was very lively, touching now upon this and now upon that new subject, interrupted only by the bursts of laughter, the questions of the banker, or the wails of the losers.

"I want a card!—Do you hear the wind? How it blows! What weather!"

"Yes! Winter begins early.—A card!—No more walks in the country!"

Glances fell upon Thérèse, but she seemed not to notice the allusion.

"Do you know, ladies," said the banker, in a moment of leisure, "that we have an artist at Saint Clement?"

All eyes fell upon Stephen. "Really?" asked some one. Madame Maupin sat upon thorns.

"Yes," continued the speaker, innocently, "we have a photographer here, who came a week ago, and is staying at the Green Oak. His portraits are excellent."

"We have seen them," said the oldest niece. "Mamma thinks of having us photographed."

"What, Mademoiselle Césarine, shall you risk it? They say the instruments make you look very ugly!"

"Oh!" she replied, looking fixedly at Thérèse, "we poor girls do not have the good fortune of finding an artist to paint our portrait."

Madame Maupin, who felt ill at ease, changed the subject of conversation and spoke of a young lady who had taken the black veil in a convent of the Benedictine nuns.

"I understand how one can take the veil," said Mademoiselle Césarine again, "but if I were to leave the world, I should choose the strictest of all orders. I should become a Carmelite—and you, Mademoiselle Desroches?"

"I?—I have no opinion on the subject. I am not fond of convents."

At this reply the ladies looked at each other, shocked.

"Mademoiselle Desroches is very right!" exclaimed Stephen.

Césarine replied with bitter irony: "Mademoiselle Thérèse does not like convents, she prefers the open air and long walks in the country!"

"What would you have, Mademoiselle Césarine. We can not all have a vocation for celibacy!"

This reply came cruelly home to Mademoiselle **Boisse,** who had two or three times been on the point of being married. She turned as red as a poppy. It was her turn next to keep bank. She got together with trembling hands the two packs of cards, shuffled them furiously, and abandoning the game they had been playing so far, she dealt two cards to each player with the sacramental question: Sympathy or Antipathy? The player won or lost according as his answer was in harmony with the card that was turned up. When Césarine reached Thérèse, she looked at her in the most impertinent manner and asked, imperiously: "Sympathy or Antipathy?" Thérèse bravely met her adversary's eye and with a vibrating voice she said: "Antipathy!"

Her expression of face and her accent left no doubt on any one's mind as to the meaning she meant to give to her answer. Some of the young people could not conceal their ironical smiles. Césarine caught them, and feeling beaten, the tears flowed from her eyes. She threw the cards upon the floor and rose, crying: "When people insult me I give way!"

"What is the matter?" asked the President's wife.

"Mademoiselle Desroches has insulted me!" replied the niece, breaking out in sobs.

"What, Thérèse, can this be?"

"Your niece is mistaken, Madame," replied Thérèse, "I only answered her question."

"Oh! what a story!" exclaimed the insulted lady. "It is the tone that makes the insult, and your tone of voice was an insult—I take all these gentlemen to be my witnesses!"

"I maintain," cried Stephen, excitedly, "that the

only person here who has a right to complain is Mademoiselle Thérèse!"

"Oh," replied Mademoiselle Césarine, with a convulsive laugh, "Monsieur Maupin defends Mademoiselle Desroches! Of course, that is quite natural!"

At the same moment, however, a hand was laid upon the young man's shoulder, rudely pressing it. "By what right, young man," said the Doctor, in his icy voice, "do you appear here as the defender of my daughter? There is only one man here who has that right, and that man is her father. I forbid you to meddle with my affairs! Come, Thérèse, let us go!"

He took the young girl by the arm and they left the room, while Stephen remained distressed. Madame Maupin bit her lips, and the bystanders, shocked and delighted at once, began to whisper.

Toward midnight Madame Maupin entered her conjugal chamber, roused her husband from his slumbers and told him the unpleasant occurrences of the evening. "I had foreseen it all," she said, "but you would not listen; now this little absurdity will give us trouble."

"You are right," replied the banker, frowning, "these Desroches are becoming dangerous, but never mind, I have an idea that they will not trouble us much longer."

CHAPTER VIII

T was the third day of December and a bitter cold morning. Célestin Tiffin, his overcoat drawn over his ears and walking very carefully, was crossing the square on his way to the bank. At the corner of the café he saw a very unusual scene; a small crowd of curious people had assembled around some placards. The young man went up to the three notices.

The first of these papers decreed the dissolution of the National Assembly; the second was the well known effort Napoleon made to justify the *coup d'état;* and the third admonished all good citizens to rejoice and to keep calm. "Now more than ever," this paper concluded, "the wicked ought to tremble and the good to be reassured."

Célestin had just finished reading the last paper, when he heard a voice growling near him: "Infamous!" He turned round and saw it was Dr. Desroches in his long black overcoat, buttoned up to the throat, brandishing his cane in a threatening manner at the placards. "This is a crime," he cried; "the man who has done that is a traitor—is outside of the law, and those who have stuck up these proclamations have committed an illegal act. That is what good citizens ought to say of it."

Eight o'clock was striking, and Célestin hastened to reach the office in time; as he walked along with rapid strides, he thought of the Doctor's words. He was greatly excited when he reached the bank, and here he found others similarly irritated and eagerly discussing the legality of the President's acts.

"After all," said the old cashier, "if it is true that they were going to turn him out, he is right, this man, to be ahead of them, and to sweep them all out."

"No!" cried Célestin, "no, a man is never right if he breaks his word, and this man had sworn to observe the Constitution!"

"What!" cried one of the younger clerks, "is Célestin becoming a politician?"

"This is not a question of politics," the young man said, bravely, "but of honesty. What would you think of a man, who had sworn fidelity to his master, and in the night would go and break open his bank? I am only a poor little clerk, but this *coup d'état* goes against my conscience."

"Hear! hear! Now Célestin has become an orator!"

"Yes," cried the young man, losing control over himself, "I shall protest against it as an illegal act, and I shall not be alone; there will be other people——"

At this moment a heavy step was heard outside, and one of the clerks, more curious than the others, looked out: "A gendarme! and he is coming here!" he exclaimed.

Tiffin was thunderstruck. The steps approached, the door opened, and the gendarme appeared in the opening in the full splendor of his three-cornered hat, his old-fashioned uniform buttoned back, and his broad, yellow shoulder-belt.

"Monsieur Maupin!" said the man of war, saluting, military fashion.

He was told that the banker was in his office.

"Inform him, if you please, that they want him instantly at the Sub-prefect's office. Matter of urgency!" he added.

And turning stiffly round, he saluted and left, relieving Célestin, whose heart had been beating furiously.

For a month or so, M. Maupin had been frequently sent for in the same way, so that the message did not surprise any one. While the cashier was going upstairs to deliver it, one of the clerks murmured audibly: "Anyhow, Tiffin has had a nice shock!"

Five minutes later the banker came down, putting on his gloves and buttoning his overcoat.

He did not return till late in the afternoon, and the first thing he did was to send for the unlucky clerk, who went up, shaking and trembling all over, and timidly knocked at the door. "Come in!" cried a rough voice, and he went in.

The banker, bent over his table, was writing a letter; he did not even turn to look at his clerk. At last he condescended to turn his chair half way round and to, cast a furious look at the poor young man.

"So," he said, "you meddle with politics now? You dare criticise the acts of Government? And you are not afraid to disseminate such rebellious views in my house? You bite the hand of your benefactor! You are a monster of ingratitude!"

"Pardon me, Monsieur Maupin!" Célestin stammered, "I have done wrong; I am in despair if I have spoken without weighing the effect my words might possibly have on others; I humbly ask pardon."

"Idiot!" continued the banker, playing now on the chord of terror, after making the chord of feeling vibrate its best, "you dare raise your voice against your monarch, who has saved society once more? But, you worm, you, don't you know that a word from him would suffice to send you to the uttermost parts of the earth?"

"Oh! master, I am lost!" cried the clerk. "Have mercy on me, and if not on me, have mercy on my poor wife!"

"Well!" growled M. Maupin, "be it so! I will overlook it this time, but on one condition: You must fully and frankly act with us! To begin: You were this morning present when Doctor Desroches was making a great fool of himself and tearing down the proclamations—were you not? Well, then, tell me the whole story with all the details!"

The poor clerk saw the trap in which he was caught, and blushed. Dr. Desroches was to be ruined, and he was to be the instrument that was to bring about his ruin! What could he do? He told the story as it had happened.

"Now, come with me," said Maupin, "and tell the same story to the Sub-prefect and to the Attorney-General!"

"But," said poor Célestin, blushing again, "that would be a regular denunciation!"

"Ah!" said M. Maupin, "what big words you use!" He rose, faced his terrified clerk, and said:

"Very well! You can do it or not do it, as you like! If you refuse to repeat to these gentlemen what you have just confessed to me, I turn you out this morning. I do not wish to keep in my house a man who delivers revolutionary speeches, and associates with men openly defying the will of our sovereign! I give you five minutes for reflection!"

He then turned his back upon him, resumed his chair and went on writing again. The wretched clerk saw in the air the dark figures of the judges, the cells of the public prison, even the "Black Maria" that was to take him to the ship. Perhaps he should never see his wife again! A sob escaped and the banker looked at him.

"I'll go with you," he said, almost inaudibly.

"Very well! Go down, get your hat and come back here! But before this is settled, mind this: If you breathe to a living being a word of what has happened or of what you hear, you are to-morrow in jail!"

Five minutes later the banker drove to the residence of the Sub-prefect, with the unhappy clerk.

He did not return home till six o'clock, and went directly upstairs to his wife's room.

"Laura," he said, "the old mayor is dismissed and I have the appointment in my pocket. To-morrow I think we shall be rid of those Desroches! All is going on well. Only, keep your son from going out to-night, and let him put a lock on his mouth!"

MLLE. DESROCHES

Somewhat later, about eight o'clock, a man of tall stature, wrapped up in a cloak, turned the corner of Main Street, keeping close to the houses. The man stopped at Dr. Desroches's house, opened the gate in the railing of the court and made his way into the vestibule and then went upstairs. He quickly entered the room and found the Doctor, as usual, sitting in his armchair. At the noise of the opening door he turned round and saw the President, who was taking off his cloak.

"Lourdeval!" he exclaimed as he recognized his visitor.

"Hush!" replied the latter in a mysterious whisper. "Nobody has seen me come in, and I do not care to be seen. You know, of course, unhappy man, why I am here. You are in great danger!"

"What is the matter?"

"You have been informed against by Maupin, who can not endure the sight of you. One of his clerks witnessed your destruction of the proclamations. The banker took him to headquarters, made him repeat all he saw and heard, and——"

"Well?"

"You are about to be arrested!"

The Doctor smiled ironically. "Ah! Maupin has become a spy! A good recruit for the new cause!"

"I have arranged it so," continued the President, "that the order to arrest you shall not be executed to-night, but to-morrow morning the gendarmes will be here. You must get away to-night and flee across the frontier. Do not trouble yourself about your daughter; we will take care of her."

"Very well!" said the Doctor, calmly, getting up. "I thank you, Lourdeval! I shall leave to-night!"

They shook hands. The President concealed himself again in his cloak. "Good luck, poor old man! " he said. "Try to keep your servant out of my way! Adieu!"

As soon as he was gone, Desroches sought his daughter's chamber. She was sewing near an almost dying fire, Dacho, the great Dane, at her feet. "Ah! you are still up! Do not go to bed till you have seen me again! I have to talk to you!"

Then he returned to the library, and emptied drawer after drawer, throwing the contents into the fire. When all was burned, he took a razor and cut off his big beard; no one would easily have recognized him. Then he dressed himself as he always did for his visits to the country, put money into his pockets, and went once more to Thérèse's room.

When she saw her father's shaved face and his costume, she started. "Thérèse," said the father, "I am threatened with an arrest to-morrow morning! The Maupins have informed against me. I endanger the safety of the father and I interfere with the pleasures of the son. You have given your heart to a nice man! I must leave this very night!"

Thérèse threw herself upon his arm, and cried:

"Take me with you!"

"Do not speak so loud," said the Doctor, taking her hands off his arm. "What you ask is impossible. Here is a little money; keep it carefully. Now," he added, with a slight tremor in his voice, "we are going to part

MLLE. DESROCHES

—Heaven knows for how long. After what has happened, and what I have told you of your mother, we can not well have scenes of great tenderness—I only regret leaving you here alone and without means, but the President has promised me he will take care of you——"

"That is useless. I do not want to be under obligations to any one here."

"And what will you do?"

"I shall leave to-morrow for Poitiers and go out to the farm of my nurse; there are people there who love me and who will watch over me."

"Very well. I prefer that, I believe." He took his cane and went to the glass door that opened upon the garden. "I shall get out by the garden-gate and take to the country at once. Do not come with me—it is more prudent. Good-by!"

He opened the door, and plunged into the tempestuous night.

CHAPTER IX

FAMILY QUARRELS

THE news of the *coup d'état* had excited Stephen Maupin much more than was generally supposed. On that fatal night of the third of December his mother had succeeded in keeping him at home, but early the next morning he went down into the town. The first person he met was Célestin, who looked as if he had not slept for a year.

"You look badly," he said to him. "I hope Madame Tiffin is not unwell."

"Oh, no! But have you not heard the sad news? You know Mademoiselle Thérèse Desroches, who was at my wedding——"

"What has happened to her?" Stephen asked, turning deadly pale.

"Her father was to have been arrested this morning!"

"Is it possible? Are you sure?"

Poor Célestin was but too sure.

"Just think of the poor young lady!" he said, after telling what he knew. "What is to become of her—alone, and at her age? The poor lady!"

Stephen listened no longer, but hastening to the

house of Dr. Desroches he rushed in and found the servant in the kitchen lamenting their fate.

"Where is Doctor Desroches?" asked the young man. The girl simply shrugged her shoulders.

"Has he been arrested?"

"They came to take him, but they did not find him—oh, the poor man!"

"And Mademoiselle Thérèse?"

"She is upstairs!"

He rapidly ran up the stairs and entered the library.

Thérèse was sitting in her father's chair, her head in her hands, and her eyes fixed upon space. At the sound of steps she slowly turned, but when she perceived young Maupin, she rose, and, with an indignant air, said to him:

"How dare you intrude here? Do you also come in search of him? He has escaped in time, God be thanked, and his enemies will not find him!"

"I was afraid he might have been arrested," replied Stephen, "and I took the liberty of coming in to offer you——"

He stammered and stopped, disconcerted by the strange look of contempt which he read in Thérèse's face.

"Offer what?" she asked with bitter irony, "your kind advice? Yesterday it would have been acceptable!"

"Yesterday!" he said, amazed. "But I knew nothing. I have only heard of it this morning."

"Why will you tell a falsehood?" she said, angrily. "You knew it all, just as well as Célestin Tiffin. Both of you knew very well that your father had betrayed him."

"My father! Mademoiselle Desroches, your anger blinds you! How could you ever think my father capable of such villainy?"

"I believe Monsieur Maupin to be capable of anything. He disliked my father, we annoyed him—he simply has gotten rid of us! We have proofs enough!"

"Proofs!" he said. "What proofs have you against us?"

"Yesterday your father went to see the Sub-prefect and informed against my father. He took Monsieur Tiffin with him to support the accusation, and upon their testimony my father has been arrested. Question Célestin, and if he is not entirely lost to honor, he will confess the truth!"

"But that would be infamous."

"It is so. However," she added, sadly, "what is the use of explanations? Leave me. I am tired. I am going to leave here, and in going away I have but one wish: that I may be able to forget the name of Maupin and all who bear it."

"Mademoiselle Desroches," said Stephen, trembling with excitement, "if what you say is true, I have no right to reproach you; however, I venture to doubt yet. But if it is really so, if my father really has the fatal power which you attribute to him, I swear by all that is sacred that before the evening has set in he shall have made ample amends for all he has done, or all is over between him and me——"

He tried once more to catch Thérèse's eye, but she

had turned her face away from him. Then he left the room hastily, and soon he was in the vestibule of his own house, and without knocking, entered the banker's office.

M. Maupin, all in black, was opening his letters at his table, where his hat and his gloves, lying ready, showed that he was about to go out. When he saw his son come in so abruptly, he frowned and said:

"Since when is this room as public as a mill? And could you not have asked first whether I was ready to see you just now? I do not like such ways, you know!"

"Father," began Stephen, losing no time in excuses, "the gendarmes have been at Doctor Desroches's house to arrest him!"

The banker looked impassively at his son. "Well?"

"They say he has been informed against by you and Célestin Tiffin!"

M. Maupin could not repress his anger. "Ah! that fool Tiffin could not keep his tongue! Thunder of God! I'll make him swallow it!"

"It was true, then!" said the son, in a heartrending voice. Then he continued, in a calmer tone: "Tiffin has not talked. I have heard it from Mademoiselle Desroches, from whom I have just come."

"Ah! Then the young lady has told you only half the truth: Doctor Desroches had denounced himself by his seditious speeches in public. He was considered a danger to the public safety and it became my official duty to order his arrest."

"A sad business, surely. It would have been better to let Justice act!"

"My duty," said M. Maupin, drawing himself up, and buttoning his overcoat, "is to secure the success of the saving act of December second, and to free the country of all who would destroy it by fire and sword!"

"This is not a question of politics, but of humanity," Stephen replied. "Think, if you do not interfere, this man will be thrown into prison or forced to live in exile; in either case he is ruined, and his daughter, a child of seventeen, left alone, without means, exposed to a thousand dangers——"

"Ah!" said the banker, almost contemptuously, "what fine words! That girl is very near to your heart, is she?"

"Yes!" Stephen confessed, imprudently, "I love her, and the blow you are aiming at her strikes me down!"

M. Maupin smiled ironically, and, crossing his arms, he said:

"And you expect that for the sake of a foolish sentiment, for a miserable little love-affair, I am to stop the proceedings of justice, to imperil my own position, and to destroy plans carefully prepared? My boy, you know little yet of Simon Maupin! They expect me at the Mayor's office. I am in a hurry."

"Father," Stephen began once more and placed himself between M. Maupin and the door. "Father, do not let this be your last word! Show yourself generous, just, and humane, as I have always thought you were! I beseech you, dear father, be kind and good as you always have been to me, since I was a child! I beseech you in the name of the old happiness of our family, of the peace and repose of your house—in the name of my mother!"

"You are talking nonsense!" said the banker, seizing his hat, "and I have no time to listen!" He pushed his son aside and slipped out of the small side-door.

When she found herself alone, Thérèse ordered the maid to carry her trunk to the stage-office. The stage for Poitiers had left in the morning, and Thérèse was too poor to hire a private carriage. She had determined, therefore, to walk the two long miles to the White House rather than spend another day in this hateful place. She put a shawl around her, and, carrying in her hand a small bag and followed by Dacho, whom she did not like to leave among strangers, she left the house forever.

She took some by-streets, and thus reached the turnpike unnoticed. A fine rain was falling, and soon St. Clement disappeared behind her in the mist. Profoundly saddened, her eyes in tears, her heart swelling, Thérèse walked bravely along the highroad to meet the stage-coach.

CHAPTER X

T was the time when painters in Paris are always in a state of unusual excitement. On the twenty-third of July, the works of the young aspirants for fame who had been admitted to compete for the famous "Prix de Rome," were to be exhibited in public.

Eleven o'clock struck. At that moment the great doors opened, and the whole band, with loud cries, rushed into the vestibule and thence into the Hall of First Prizes.

In the background of the hall appeared a placard with the subject prescribed by the authorities: "Ruth and Boaz" with these verses from the Bible: *And behold, Boaz came from Bethlehem, and said unto the reapers, The Lord be with you. And they answered him, The Lord bless thee. Then said Boaz unto his servant that was set over the reapers: Whose damsel is this? And the servant that was set over the reapers answered and said, It is the Moabitish damsel that came back with Naomi out of the country of Moab.*

Two pictures seemed from the first to attract the curious: one with the number three, the other numbered

[310]

seven. The latter especially drew the crowd; they formed a circle around the easel on which it was placed, and there was a moment when the crowd there became so dense that the circulation was stopped.

Number Seven had conceived and executed his painting with entire disregard of classic conventionality. Had it not been for the turban which Boaz wore, the scene would have recalled an ordinary French village. The reapers, bronzed and half naked, had entirely modern faces. Ruth, half kneeling in the rows of wheat, with her frock turned up, a piece of linen on her black hair, looked exactly like a fair peasant woman of Touraine.

"Eh! That is Nature!" said one painter to another. "You feel you are there!"

"And how well it's done! No trick! No artifice! Look at those hands! Are they not amazing? Here is a man who can draw, and who does not tell the old story over again!"

"He'll get the prize!"

Some curious people went behind the easel to discover the signature of the canvas, and they read the name out aloud: Stephen Maupin.

During this time Stephen Maupin was walking impatiently up and down on the quay of the Seine. Every time he passed Bonaparte Street, he looked with feverish anxiety at the clear spot made by the School of Arts amid the other black buildings. At last, when he came down for the fifth time, a comrade joined him. Stephen looked him anxiously in the eye, without daring to ask him.

"My compliments, my dear fellow," he cried, pressing his hand, "there is a regular crush around your picture. You may be proud—such a success!"

"No bad jokes, I pray you!" said Stephen, blushing all over. "Is it true?"

"I tell you people walk over each other's toes to see it. There is but one cry: Yours is the best, and you will get the prize most assuredly!"

"You think so?" murmured Stephen, breathing at last more freely.

"Well, come and see for yourself."

He drew him to the building, and went with him into the room. Stephen hid in the embrasure of a window, and watched with intense delight how the people crowded each other to get at his work. The connoisseurs would bend their heads and examine long and carefully, then they would raise their heads again, and their faces betrayed perfect satisfaction. A very well known art-critic stood a long time before the picture. His face, usually rather sleepy-looking, brightened up; he dropped a few words of praise, which his disciples treasured up with looks of admiration. Suddenly an attendant cried: "Gentlemen! the doors are closed!"

It was four o'clock. The hall was cleared gradually; Stephen was pushed out and found himself in Bonaparte Street. He felt a need of quiet under the trees and a desire to take violent exercise to recover his equanimity. The anxiety had been too much for him. One thing was certain; his work was good, and he had drawn the attention of the public. Now, whether he got the prize or not, they could not deny that he had real talent. The five years of hard work and painful privations which he had voluntarily undergone were not lost. His name would be famous. And looking triumphantly into the past, he saw the winter morning on which he left St. Clement.

How proud he was now, this evening, with this first certain evidence of success! He went into an open-air restaurant at Bellevue.

During the next two days the papers were full of accounts of the exhibition. The majority of critics praised No. 7, and assigned the first rank to it. At last the day of judgment came. Stephen had not slept, and, in spite of the July heat, was shivering all over. "Surely," he told himself, "they will give me the prize; they can not keep it from me. And yet, if they did!"

Toward two o'clock one of the secretaries came down to the courtyard and was instantly surrounded.

"Well?" asked a friend of his among the students.

"Well, it goes on slowly; they vote and vote and Maupin is losing every time!"

At last, at three o'clock, some noise was heard upstairs, the session was over, and the academicians still continued their conversation as they descended the steps. One of them came down smoking his cigar and looking half asleep. A student approached him and asked what the result was. "They have given the great prize to Lagune," he said. Stephen, leaning against the wall of the wharf, facing the opening of the street, suddenly saw the students scatter from the building and run in all directions. He knew then that the decision had been made, and rapidly crossed the street. He had not taken ten steps when Lagune's name met him full in the face. He stopped, turned pale and supported himself against the show window of a dealer in pictures.

"Yes, old man!" said a friend coming upon him. "These idiots have given you only the second prize. And do you know what decided them?—'Gentlemen.' said one of the academicians, 'Lagune is poor, and he is too old to compete again next year. Maupin is young, his father is enormously rich, he has time and the means; he can wait.' And thus these donkeys have made you lose the prize!"

He turned his back upon his friends and went back again toward the river. He had reached the corner, when he heard his name called by somebody, who had hastened his steps to overtake him.

"Is not this Monsieur Stephen Maupin whom I have the honor of meeting?"

"Yes," replied Stephen, impatiently.

"Sir," began the unknown, "I have seen your canvas. I compliment you. It is a very fine piece of painting, but the Academy has done right in not sending you to Italy; Rome would have ruined you. Italy is not for you. If I tell you this so bluntly, it is because I understand it. I am Schwartz!"

Stephen opened his eyes and ears. Schwartz was a Jew, well known at great auction sales and in the art world, half amateur, half dealer, whose specialty it was to buy up the works of artists as yet unknown but giving great hopes.

"If I take the liberty of stopping you," he continued, while Stephen, not yet himself again, stammered something, "it is because I wish to buy your painting for two thousand francs, and at the same time to order a second. You understand peasants; I see that. We must work that vein. Go into the provinces, pick out some landscape that suits you, paint me a picture of the open air, very personal. I'll pay you five thousand francs for it. Do not hurry—I give you till next year."

"Pardon me," said Stephen, who at last began to breathe more freely, "such a painting as you ask of me will take a great deal of time, and time is money for me, for I have nothing but my brush, whatever the Institute may say of it."

"On that account I mean to pay you half the amount in advance. You see that I have great confidence in you. Is it a bargain?"

Stephen did not take long to reflect. Paris was hateful to him just now, and this journey in search of a landscape had its charms for him.

"I thank you, sir," he said, "and I accept."

"Very well. Here is my card; come and see me tomorrow at ten o'clock; I'll show you my little gallery, and I'll pay you the money. Good-evening!"

CHAPTER XI

THE PEASANT MAID

IT was the evening of the Assembly at Lesin. Stephen Maupin, tired and hungry, after three hours spent in the open air, watching the dancers and sketching peasants' heads, had come back to the tavern. He was exhausted, and wanted nothing but a chair and a place at the table where he might eat his dinner. But here began the difficulty. The inn was full.

"Could you not give me my dinner in some corner of the house?" inquired Stephen of the hostess.

"You see, Monsieur, everything is full. I have a room upstairs, it is true, but Monsieur Brossard, the tax-collector, has engaged it for his supper."

"That gentleman might be so very kind as to share it with me?"

"I'll ask him!" said the landlady.

While she went upstairs, Stephen had seated himself on the edge of the well. After his interview with Monsieur Schwartz, he had left Paris with the intention of returning to his home, and there to look for a village in which he might make the studies necessary for the execution of the picture he had promised to paint.

But so far, chance had been unkind to him, and

aside from a few rough sketches of characteristic peasants' heads, he had gained nothing by his tramp down here, save the somewhat doubtful privilege of supping in company with the collector of taxes. For the landlady had come back promptly with the message that M. Brossard would be delighted, and begged him to come up at once, as the soup was on the table.

Stephen, ran up the staircase, and entered a rather tidy-looking, square chamber. On the table a tureen was smoking, and M. Brossard himself was putting down an additional cover opposite his own.

"Upon my word you are welcome," he said in a jovial tone. "I detest solitude, and I am delighted to have you keep me company. Madame Jacob, send us up two bottles of your best wine, and tell your cook not to burn our chicken."

At dessert M. Brossard, leaning his elbows on the table and showing clearly the exhilarating effect of the old wine, asked Stephen in which village he thought of settling down for a time, to pursue his studies.

"I really have no idea," was the reply, "I shall float hither and thither, looking for heads that may furnish interesting typical characters, and for models who will consent to sit for me."

"If that is all," cried the collector, "you must come with me to Pressy; life is easy there and pleasant. I know a lodging that will suit you exactly, and, upon my word, if you are in want of models, I'll make you acquainted with all the pretty girls."

"I accept!" said Stephen, in whose memory the name of Pressy awakened pleasant reminiscences.

"Done! I'll carry you off to-night and hope you will stay with me till the lodging I spoke of is ready. Have you any traps here?"

"No; I left my luggage at the White House!"

"Well, you can send for them to-morrow; we can walk there together, it is only two miles, and smoke our pipes. Let us say good-by to Madame Jacob and be gone, for the weather looks threatening, and it would be annoying to be caught in the rain."

They had not gone half way across when rain began to fall, and Brossard said:

"It will not amount to much. Are you a good walker?"

"Yes!"

"Well, in that case we'll put on our seven-league boots, and perhaps we can escape the worst."

They lost some more time by the directions which Stephen had to give at the White House about his traps, and when they left the wood, the wind rose, and soon the rain came, whipping their faces with considerable severity.

"*Laperlipopette!*" cried the collector, turning up his collar. "It is raining pitchforks now, and at the same time it is as black as night." He stopped, uncertain where he was; he tried to pierce the darkness, and of a sudden he uttered a sigh of satisfaction. Raising his right arm, he pointed at a faint little star that was shining afar off through the rainy night, and said:

"If I do not see double, that light must be at the Joubards!"

MLLE. DESROCHES

He had hardly pronounced that name than Stephen exclaimed in his turn: "The Joubards!"

"Yes, it is a farm where we can wait for the rain to cease, and where they will give us a good fire to dry our clothes."

"The Joubards," said Stephen, "was that it?"

"Yes. The name is quite common here. I myself know at least three or four farms which all bear the same name of owners. These are good people, and will treat us well."

Stephen followed him, feeling his heart beat in a long-forgotten way. The collector went up the steps and opened the door, which was closed only with a latch.

The room was a vast kitchen with an enormous fireplace; before it a small lamp was hanging, the light of which hardly went beyond the middle of the apartment. Seated on a low chair, her back turned to the door, a young peasant woman was shelling beans, the pods and leaves of which lay in a heap of verdure by her side.

She turned her head slowly round, and suddenly seeing strangers in the room, she started up, frightened.

"Do not fear, Mademoiselle," said Brossard, shaking his soft hat, "it is I who come to seek shelter at your house on account of this abominable rain that has overtaken us on the road."

"Ah! the collector!" she said in a clear, ringing voice, which made Stephen tremble to the tips of his fingers, "you must pardon me, Monsieur, I thought for a moment it was father and mother who were returning."

"Are they both out in this weather that is fit for ducks only?"

"They went to the Assembly at Lesin, in the hope of meeting there a new shepherd. Ours has drawn the lot, you know, and is a conscript. But they will not be long. Take a seat. I will light some wood and dry your clothes."

She put two chairs before the fire, and threw a handful of dry branches on it, which soon made a pleasant blaze. Now the newcomers could see the young person, brilliantly illumined from head to foot. They saw the large folds of her black gown on the hips, the brown cotton of the apron and bib, pinned on the shoulders and tight at the waist, while a white fichu was crossed over her bosom. The light delicately gilded her sunburned cheeks, reddening her full lips and making her black eyes sparkle. Stephen was overcome with emotion; he recognized Thérèse, the peasant girl Thérèse, such as he had seen her on the first evening—the eventful evening of Célestin's wedding.

The sudden shock, together with the sorrowful impression which the sight of Thérèse, reduced to this more than modest condition, made on him, kept him nailed to the spot where he stood.

The collector was already sitting astride on his chair and drying his jacket.

"Are you not also wet, Monsieur, and in need of drying your clothes?" Thérèse asked the young painter, who did not stir. "Come, make yourself comfortable!"

He obeyed, came forth out of the darkness, and entered, greatly embarrassed, into the circle of light.

MLLE. DESROCHES

Presently he turned to the young girl, and asked:

"Am I really so changed, Mademoiselle Thérèse, that you no longer know who I am?"

"I beg your pardon, Monsieur Maupin," she replied, after some hesitation, as if to make sure that her voice would be firm; "I recognized you very well."

"And yet you treated me like a stranger."

"Because I did not know whether you would like to renew our acquaintance. You yourself, it seemed to me, were not very eager to let your friend here know that we had known each other long ago."

"You are mistaken," he said, turning his chair halfway round. "It was the first shock only which kept me from speaking, and then I was afraid——"

"Afraid of what?"

"I feared your anger against me might still continue——"

She shook her head. "Oh!" she sighed, "since then so many things have happened. Besides, I know now that you could not help what was done!"

There was a pause. She drew the basket with the beans to her and quietly continued her work, filling her apron rapidly.

"What has become of Monsieur Desroches?" Stephen asked, timidly.

"He was arrested, banished to Africa, and there died!"

"Pardon me, Thérèse!"

"Why do you ask me to pardon you?" she demanded, looking at him with her frank and limpid eyes.

21   [321]

"For all the harm my family has done you!"

"He whom your father has harmed has died far off in Africa, and he alone has the right to forgive. As for myself, I do not blame you—neither you nor any one, for I have never been happier in my life than I am now!"

"But you were not born for the life you are leading!"

"On the contrary—I think I was good for nothing but a peasant girl! And this time I have become one in good earnest. Look at my hands! Believe me," she continued, "I like this life and would not exchange it for any other. But you—what has become of you? Do you live in our province?"

He told her in a few words what he had done and what he proposed to do. "I think," he said in conclusion, "I shall settle down for some time at Pressy—will you permit me to come and see you occasionally?"

She frowned for a moment.

"Does my purpose or my request displease you?" he asked.

"Neither! But in the life that I lead, there are not many moments of leisure, and I do not see that we shall have many occasions to meet each other. However, if you at times pass by here and will come in, you will always be welcome," she added, offering him her hand, "provided——"

"Provided what?" he replied. He had taken her hand and was pressing it cordially.

"Provided the thing pleases my old nurse and her husband. Here they come!"

MLLE. DESROCHES

In truth the dogs had commenced barking once more, and a little vehicle stopped at the door. Thérèse opened the door and hastened to meet her friends. All this noise had roused the collector, who had fallen asleep, but who now sat up and rubbed his eyes.

"Eh?" he asked. "You were saying—Why! The fire is out and here are the people of the farm coming home! I verily believe—the devil take it—I have had a doze! Upon my word, Monsieur Maupin, if it does not rain any more I should like to go and finish it in my bed!"

CHAPTER XII

T Pressy, Stephen arose every morning with the sun. During the two first weeks of his stay there, he went only once as far as the farm of Thérèse, but his ill luck pursued him; the people were all out at work and the house was empty.

One evening the collector himself came early to Stephen's studio.

"My dear artist," he said, after having carefully closed the door, "I come to ask you a service, and only fear you will refuse me."

"Nevertheless, ask," replied Stephen. "I'll do it most cheerfully."

"Permit me to present you to the notary and his wife!"

Stephen cried out against it.

Stephen protested, but the collector was persevering, and finally the painter, moved partly by curiosity and partly tired of saying No! had to give way. Thus he was introduced in the notary's household.

The two sisters received the painter as a distraction that heaven sent them for their benefit. Madame Athenaïs was well content to have M. Brossard now entirely to herself, while Mademoiselle Marcelle had made up her mind from the beginning that she would make poor Stephen Maupin fall in love with her. Unfortunately the young painter soon tired of hearing incessantly the same senseless babbling, the same impertinent questions, and heartily repented ever having yielded to M. Brossard's request. Then he would dream of Thérèse, of the peasant girl who worked in the fields with the other girls; he compared her maidenly dignity, her exquisite grace, her almost harsh reserve, with the impure mind of Marcelle and her blank and frivolous existence.

CHAPTER XIII

"HAVE you ever seen a harvest feast, Monsieur Maupin?"

"No, Mademoiselle Marcelle; in my little town people have become too city-like and have forgotten such good old customs."

"I congratulate you. Here the peasants lose no opportunity to amuse themselves and always at the expense of the landowner. The end of every kind of harvest furnishes an occasion for an entertainment. There is the harvest feast of the hay crop, of the wheat crop, of the vintage—what do I know?"

"Their life is hard; it is but natural that after so much hard work they should look for a little fun."

"You seem to like peasants?"

"Yes, I do—much!"

"You will soon get tired of them, when you see them near by," said Marcelle, contemptuously, whirling her sunshade over her fair head. "You are too warm in the sun," she continued; "give me your arm, and you will at least have the benefit of my parasol!"

Stephen obeyed. They followed a foot-path barely wide enough to let two persons pass. Before them walked the collector with the notary's wife, and far beyond them was visible the straw hat of the notary, who was showing them the way to the meadow, where the celebration of the bringing in of the last sheaf was to be held.

As the procession passed the group of friends, Stephen could not restrain a gesture of surprise, when he noticed Thérèse among the binders.

Marcelle looked sarcastically at the young man.

"Why," she asked, "do you know that girl?"

"Yes!" replied Stephen.

"You need not blush," she cried, laughing aloud and facing Stephen, who really had blushed very red, "she is no doubt one of your models! You know there is quite a romantic story connected with that girl; she is an outcast; her father died in exile, and the farmer who rents our other place has taken her in."

"I know it," said Stephen, curtly, "she is a very brave girl and bears her misfortunes nobly!"

"Pshaw!" cried his companion, "she is like all the rest, and her misfortunes will not keep her from dancing the whole evening with her lover!"

Stephen was put out. This girl spoiled his pleasure.

Mademoiselle Marcelle slipped her arm into the painter's arm and asked: "Well, where shall we go? Do you wish to invite one of these reapers for the first waltz?"

He shook his head.

"Well, then! Besides, I ought to warn you; you would lose your reward. Each has her lover with whom she dances all night long, and who escorts her home.

Come, let us go down to the river and look out a cool place where we can wait till the dancing begins."

Stephen tried to protest, but she insisted, adding:

"Come, if you will obey I will give you something!"

They went, and Thérèse, still immovable near the musician, her eyes fixed, her eyebrows contracted, followed, with a strange expression in her eyes, half angry and half contemptuous, the management of Mademoiselle Marcelle.

The two promenaders, after having wandered a while under the chestnut-trees, hung with hops, reached a place where five or six linden-trees formed a group, and here Marcelle, closing her sunshade, sank down into the tall grass.

"I don't believe you knew of this place, Monsieur Maupin!" she said. "Come and sit down. Is not this charming?"

"There," she continued, making herself comfortable in her nest, as she called the place, "now tell me a story, Monsieur Maupin. You are romantic—hence, the place ought to inspire you——"

"Romantic? You are mistaken, Mademoiselle Marcelle!" he replied, beginning to feel very embarrassed.

"Why, yes! You live in the clouds—you are in pursuit of the ideal! You are not like Monsieur Brossard —flesh and blood seem to have no charms for you— you are good and serious, like a book that mamma allows her child to read with safety."

Stephen was shocked and rose.

MLLE. DESROCHES

"What is the matter?" cried Marcelle, surprised.

She held him by the arm and forced him to sit down again.

"Do you hear the hurdy-gurdy?" she asked, in her ironical voice. "At this moment your little peasant girl perhaps opens the ball with her lover!"

"What is that to you?" he asked, frowning and stammering.

"I am interested in the girl. Her story is like a fairy-tale. What did you call her?"

"I pray you," he cried, imperatively, "let us not talk of Mademoiselle Desroches!"

"Ah! You know her family name, too! You know perhaps a great deal more, eh?" Thereupon she rose, shook out her skirt, put on her hat, and pushed aside the branches that obstructed her passage.

She took a few steps, and then, turning round again, she said:

"If I meet Mademoiselle Desroches, I'll send her to you!"

He walked slowly down the dark highroad, his head hanging low. Suddenly his meditations were broken by the sound of a light, quick step behind him, and as he turned instinctively he saw Thérèse. When she recognized Stephen, she looked at first rather shocked; while he, at the sight of Thérèse, felt joy coming back to his heart and his face brightened up. "Good-evening, Mademoiselle Thérèse!" he said, and offered her his hand.

"Good-evening, Monsieur Maupin!" she said, without stopping.

"You are coming back alone?" he asked, walking by her side.

"I left father at the feast and am going home to supper."

"Let me accompany you a little," he said, "I am so happy to have met you! I blamed myself for not speaking to you in the meadow there, and you must have thought it strange in me!"

"I thought you probably had nothing special to say to me, or rather—I thought you did not wish to displease the person with whom you were."

Stephen shrugged his shoulders. "That person is perfectly indifferent to me. I care little whether I please or displease her."

"That is not what people say!"

"What do people say?"

"That you are going to marry her!"

"People are mistaken!" he exaclimed, angrily. "I never dreamed of such nonsense! There was a time when I dreamed of a home of my own, a cottage, and in it a beloved wife, perhaps a child—my father has upset all that. What have I to offer a wife? A doubtful future, a discredited name, execrated by all around him whose daughter she would have to become——"

"You never see your father?" she asked.

"I have not seen him since my mother's death."

"Look!" said Thérèse, describing a circle with her arm; "up there the Courtils forest, down there the valley of stables; here for five long years my life has been spent, and I have but one wish: that it may continue here—till the end!"

Stephen remained silent. With the clear insight of woman, Thérèse, who was watching him by the starlight, divined his thoughts, which darkened his face.

"Monsieur Stephen," she said, "will you come in and share our supper?"

Stephen's eyes brightened. "Ah!" he said, "I would accept with great pleasure, if I were not afraid to be troublesome."

"Oh, no! You will have a poor supper, that is all! Come in!"

By the light of the lamp, the old lady was spinning industriously.

"Mamma!" Thérèse said to the good old woman, who opened her eyes wide, "this is Monsieur Stephen Maupin, of whom, you know, I have often spoken. He has brought me home, and will take supper with us!"

CHAPTER XIV

THE TRIAL

ONSIEUR STEPHEN, your breakfast is ready!"

As soon as Thérèse's early summons rose from the courtyard and reached the upstairs room through the open window, which the broad leaves of a tall fig-tree nearly concealed, Stephen Maupin went down to the kitchen, where a bright fire was blazing and dancing.

Since the day of the Harvest Feast he had become a frequent guest at the farm. He saw that Thérèse was evidently the very soul of the place, she had an eye for everything, and nothing was done in which she did not take a part. The old farmer and his wife, who had lost their children when quite young, had transferred all their affection to her. One evening, when the men were reaping the aftermath, Stephen, who had spent a whole week at the farm, had gone down to the meadow to say good-by to the young girl before returning to his lodgings in the village. Thérèse was binding a last handful of hay.

"How I admire you!" cried Stephen, "always active, always the first at the work, and the last at the end."

"What can I do? Father is getting old and mother

is quite busy enough. Besides, I can not bear being inactive: motion, work, exercise in the open air—all that I must have, or I perish.

"You are going away to-night?" she asked, suddenly.

"Yes, I must go down and see if anything has happened, but I shall be back very soon—in fact as soon as I possibly can—provided always you are not tired of me here at the farm."

"What an idea! Father and mother both love you, and everybody at the farm sings your praise."

"And you, Thérese?"

"I," she answered, laughing heartily. "Of course I chime in with the chorus!"

He also had risen and secured her hand. "Thérèse," he began, "I—" Then he paused, raised her hand to his lips and said: "To-morrow!"

The next day in the afternoon, he was leisurely busy in his studio, trying to put some little order among the studies that were mostly leaning against the wall, when somebody knocked cautiously, and a moment later M. Brossard appeared.

"At last," cried the newcomer in a somewhat arrogant tone, "at last one can find you at home, Monsieur. I have knocked my nose to pieces against your door this week, but the bird had flown! What in the world has become of you?"

"I have spent a week or so at the farm, you know, and I have been hard at work."

"From Nature?" asked the man with a still more unpleasant tone.

"Yes," replied Stephen. "Why do you laugh? I have made a number of studies of open-air views—and, what is more, I am not dissatisfied with them!"

"I dare say—with such a model!"

"Eh! What do you mean?"

"Oh, nothing! nothing! I understand. You want to play the discreet lover with me, but you ought to know that I am not a chicken!" Then he came up to Stephen, seized his hand and shaking it with comic seriousness, he added: "My compliments, you scamp!" he whispered into his ears. "She is pretty—delightful, that little girl at the farm!"

"Stop there, Monsieur Brossard! Mademoiselle Desroches is a lady whom I highly respect and you will be pleased to say that to all who slander her!"

"I will do it, if you wish it," said the collector, gradually losing his self-command. "I will proclaim it in the market-places," he added, imperceptibly shrugging his shoulders, "but you know, they will not believe it—not a word of it—well? Now you frown at me and look as if you meant to cut me into small pieces! Is it really forbidden in this house to laugh and be merry? —Yes? Well, then, I am gone. Good-night."

Stephen had remained immovable in the centre of his studio, biting his lips and crushing a piece of stiff drawing-paper. He saw it clearly; the collector was right in what he said.

He started for the farm, choosing the high road, without thinking how he might avoid the curious eyes of the village people and M. Brossard's ironical glances. When he reached the farmhouse he was told that

MLLE. DESROCHES

Thérèse had gone to help father to dig potatoes in a field that lay close to the edge of the forest.

Almost at the very edge of the woods, Thérèse was busy pouring a basketful of potatoes into a sack that stood before her.

"What? Is that you?" she said. "They did not expect you to-day!"

"I came back," replied Stephen, standing still to recover his breath; "I came back for the single purpose of speaking to you about a matter which I did not venture to mention yesterday, and which yet I must bring to your notice. Have you time to listen to me?"

"Speak!" she replied in a low whisper, while she threw the last potatoes into the sack and then rested her elbows on the full sack. "What is it?"

"Thérèse!" he began, almost solemnly and with deep feeling, "do you remember that rainy day on which we took refuge at the Angels' farm?"

She bowed her head. "Yes," she breathed, "it ended too sadly for me ever to be forgotten!"

"And do you remember our conversation while we were waiting until the shower should be over? We thought the house a very poor one, and yet I told you that I should be perfectly happy if I could lead a peasant's life in such a house—with you!"

"I remember!" she whispered under her breath.

"Thérèse! I have never changed my mind—and I, who am now quite as poor as the man of the Angels' farm, ask you if you will marry me, and lead, with me, a simple and pure peasant's life?"

[335]

Thérèse, deeply moved at his words, looked him in the face and said: "You can not think of it. I have changed my position in life, while you are the same yet that you were then. Our daily habits are no longer the same, nor our ways of thinking and of talking. There would certainly come a day when you would blush for me. No! no! never!"

"And why should I ever blush for you? Because you cultivate the soil? Idleness alone is a coming down. Thérèse! you are a girl of high thoughts and of a high mind! Those are the qualities we demand first of all in a woman whom we wish to choose!"

"Yes," she murmured, lowering her head again; "but at the very least that woman ought to bring her husband a spotless name and one that truly and certainly belongs to her. And I—painful as it is to me— I am bound to tell you, that—you know—I have my mother—but, you know her history, do you not?"

"And I? Have I not my father?" replied Stephen, with an accent of profound grief; "believe me, Thérèse, you and I are not responsible for our parents! You will never be out of place anywhere, Thérèse, and my profession has this advantage, that it permits me to live where I choose—in the country or in town. Besides, I do not ask you to marry me on the spot. Only promise you will be my wife! In the space of a year I shall be able to see my way clear before me, and then I shall come and remind you of your promise. Say yes and I will ask no more. You do not answer me? Are you possibly no longer free? Do you love another man?"

"I?" she exclaimed, with startling vehemence. "Oh! Great God! No!"

"Well then, Thérèse, I love you, and I beg you to let me love you!"

Suddenly a high, sharp voice was heard from the other end of the field.

They turned round. On the red evening sky both saw the long and lean outlines of Célestin Tiffin, sharply defined. He came running up to where the two were standing.

"Oh!" he exclaimed, utterly out of breath. "Ah! Monsieur Stephen! But you are hard to find! Pardon me, my child, I have to speak to Monsieur Maupin in private!" He suddenly recognized Thérèse and raised his long arms to heaven. "Mademoiselle Desroches! What accidents will happen! I surely did not think I should meet you here this evening!"

"Célestin!" young Maupin broke in anxiously, "what is the matter? What brings you here?"

Célestin wiped his brow. "This is the matter," he said at last, "you are wanted at Saint Clement! To make matters more certain, your father sends me instead of a messenger, and I have been running after you ever since yesterday—an hour ago I reached Pressy at last, and thanks to a gentleman who was looking out of a window and who had seen you pass by, I was lucky enough to find you here."

"Is my father ill?" Stephen asked.

"Ill? no! At least not physically! But it is the Maupin Bank that is ailing! For the last two months many people have come without intermission and drawn their money out—for so many depositors to come at once, you see, that looks badly. Yesterday at last Monsieur Maupin sent for me to come to his private office. He was walking up and down there like a caged lion. 'Go and bring me my son!' he said, giving me a paper with your address on it. 'Go and tell him the matter is urgent, he must come instantly—he must lose no time!"

"Yes!" replied the young man in a changed voice. "In a moment!"

He went back to Thérèse, who had not stirred.

"Thérèse!" he said, "I am compelled to leave instantly for Saint Clement. I am needed down there. Who knows under what circumstances I may return? But I shall return! Let me clasp your hand! That will give me strength."

She gave him her hand. "Courage!" she said. "We shall surely meet again!"

His hands behind his back, his eye restless, and his lips drawn in bitterly, Simon Maupin was walking up and down in his private office.

Suddenly Stephen and Célestin, covered with grayish-white dust, entered in great haste. "At last you are here!" exclaimed the banker in a hoarse voice."

"You sent for me," said Stephen, "and here I am! What do you want of me?"

The banker hesitated a moment; then, getting the better of his pride, he seized Stephen by the arm, and drew him into the embrasure of the nearest window. He felt in his heart the necessity of moving his son in some way and by some means—was he not his only support now, his only hope?—and to ascertain to some extent what his means were, and how far he was ready to stand by him. "Come this way!" he whispered. "Are you not hungry? Would you have anything?"

Stephen replied that Célestin and he had breakfasted on their way, and M. Maupin said:

"Well, then, we can go to work at once! Célestin, you can leave us!"

Tiffin bowed and left the room. Stephen had taken a chair, and the banker threw himself back in his large armchair, trying to find a beginning, while he was mechanically arranging the papers on his desk.

"Do you want me?" at last asked the young man.

"Yes! I thought it best to inform you verbally of the —of my situation. Did Célestin tell you——"

"He told me the Bank was not doing well, and you were sadly in want of money——"

"Oh! That is only for the moment," the banker cried aloud. "But, after all, I am in want of money just now! I have speculated unluckily. You know that may happen to the wisest. The Emperor was all the time saying: The Empire means Peace! I believed in what he said, I believed in both, the Empire and Peace! I built a number of houses—a whole quarter of the city—I expected trade would flourish and the shops would come and crowd around the railway station! I thought I would sell my houses for their weight in gold! And behold, here comes this accursed Crimean War, breaking me legs and arms and everything!"

He brought down his fist upon the table and got up, swearing fiercely. "When I think that if I had only had six months more I should have been at the pinnacle! I was sure of it—as sure as I touch this wall. I was going to be a candidate for the assembly, supported by government. And to think that all this splendid edifice is to tumble down like a badly built scaffolding! However, I am not at the end yet! I can set everything right yet, if you will lend me a hand!"

Stephen had listened to his father at first with a certain want of confidence, then with more and more emotion.

"You were right to count upon me, father," he said, in an almost affectionate voice. "When you speak of the honor of our name, I can refuse you nothing. The firm Simon Maupin must not suspend payment. I have left you the entire management of my inheritance from my mother; sell the lands and the bonds, I give you *carte blanche*—when they see you pay as usual, confidence will return and you will be saved!"

"Is that all you can find to remedy the evil? Thank you! If I counted upon you, it was for far more efficient assistance!"

"I do not understand you!"

"Really?" asked the father, fixing his sharp eyes upon Stephen's face, "in that case I will enlighten you. We have here a very influential family, the Leguins; they have not a large fortune, but they are nearly related to the President and to the Bishop of the diocese. There are three daughters in the house, and the youngest, Christine, is only twenty-one; she is pretty, intelligent, and eager to marry. It seems, moreover, that artists are special favorites with her, and that she likes you. They are quite ready to give her to you, and you have only to say so; on the day of your marriage our bank is saved!"

The banker had continued to study his son's face, while making these explanations, but his features had remained impassable and impenetrable.

"But this family of Leguins must know our situation, and it seems to me improbable that they could conclude an alliance under such very hazardous conditions!"

"Pshaw! They know that you possess in your own right a fortune which my creditors can not touch. I have attended to that! Besides, father and mother are devout—I have the clergy on my side, who have a number of thousands placed for security in my bank, and who are, therefore, interested to prevent a mishap. These gentlemen, some high in dignity, will use a mild pressure upon the family——"

"To deceive them?" broke in Stephen.

"Eh? what are you saying?"

"To deceive them," repeated the young man, coolly. This marriage is not feasible, and will not take place!"

"You would rather see me ruined, dishonored?"

"There is no disgrace in being poor; and your honor will suffer less if I refuse than if I were to consent."

"Yes, for I have not told you all yet," replied M. Maupin, lowering his voice.

At this moment there came a knock at his door. He rose with a gesture of impatience, went and opened the door, but started back as he perceived on the threshold the person and the ruddy, smoothly shaven face of M. Landor, sheriff of the town of St. Clement.

ANDRÉ THEURIET

"Beg your pardon, Monsieur Maupin," sputtered the official, "beg your pardon, if I trouble—I come with a summons of appearance *in re* Berloc."

He drew from his pocket a paper folded twice, and handed it to the banker.

"Very well!" growled M. Maupin in his haughtiest tone. "Thank you! You can go!"

The officer disappeared and the door closed gently behind him. Then Maupin turned to his son, throwing him the paper, and repeating, in a breathless, low voice: "I did not tell you all. Read that!"

Stephen thereupon read the mandate which summoned Simon Maupin, banker, to appear before the justice of the town of St. Clement, as charged with habitual usury, committed in complicity with John Berloc —a crime punishable by the law of September 3, 1807, etc.

The young man put the paper down and asked "Is that true?"

Maupin shrugged his shoulders:

"Now you will understand what must be done. The judge is the uncle of Monsieur de Leguin, and if you marry the little one, it is clear that he will not sentence the father-in-law of his niece! But to do that, you must to-night ask for the hand of Christine de Leguin through the kind mediation of the priest of Saint Nicholas. All now depends on you. You can save me— you can ruin me!"

His voice was trembling slightly, and his eyes sought to meet Stephen's eyes, but the son had turned his head aside.

"You do not answer?" asked the banker.

"What you ask is impossible!"

"Impossible!" repeated the banker very angrily. "After all you know? After all I have told you?"

"Especially after what you have told me!"

"Then," he cried, with exasperation, "you prefer my ruin? You mean to ruin me, do you? I may be sent to prison, and if you do not marry his niece, the judge will not spare me. But is it nothing to you to see your father ruined, dishonored, sent to prison?"

"Understand me rightly, father! I am willing to do for you all that can be done fairly and openly. My fortune and my work are yours. Use them as you choose! Announce at once the sale of your property, of all you possess, and surrender the proceeds to your creditors. This will predispose the judges in your favor, and strengthen your defense."

"And am I to die on the straw?"

"Is it not better to strip yourself than to be stripped by the Courts?"

"But I mean neither to be stripped nor to be condemned. Nothing of that kind will happen if you consent to the marriage I propose!"

"Never! Do not let us speak of it any more!

"I do not know what kind of a man you are," replied the banker, in a low, almost furious voice. "One thing is sure: You are not my son! A boy for whom I have done everything! For you ought to know it, if I have been a slave, if I have been hard against myself and hard against others, if I have consented to certain operations for which I am now reproached, if I have done that which threatens to land me in prison, it was for you!"

"I think so little of forsaking you that I offer you all I possess. Sell everything, leave Saint Clement, come with me. I shall work so hard that you shall never know what it is to be poor, even after having given up all your property."

"Why, that is ridiculous! You might just as well open my veins at once and bleed me to death! No! no! I shall not let go one penny, not one foot of land! I mean to meet my enemies to their face! They shall see that old Simon Maupin has still his beak and his talons!"

He raged like a wild beast up and down in the narrow room. Stephen stood in silence by the writing-table. The banker took both of Stephen's hands in his own, and spoke in an imploring voice. "Be a good son! I beseech you by all that is most holy to you! In your mother's name! Shall I go down on my knees? Come, you have not a heart of stone, I am sure! If you were to ask me such a favor, I would certainly listen. I would not be inflexible!"

"I did address you, one day," replied Stephen, "just such a prayer, and you would not listen! I remember it! And yet, if you were now to ask me a possible sacrifice, I should be ready to make it—but what you ask of me is disloyal, and in spite of my desire to save you, in spite of what I suffer, I am bound to say no!"

"Ah! You are harder than I have ever been in my life! I am sorry now I ever called you! Go back where you came from!"

"No!" replied the son, firmly. "No, I shall not

leave your side, however ill you may think of me! I shall remain here. I shall stand by you before the judge. I shall be here when sentence is given, and help you to face your misfortune!"

"But I do not want you! I can defy the world and the devil alone and unaided!" cried the banker in his exasperation. "I shall show you all what is in me, and point you out to all who want to see a good-for-nothing son, who forsakes his father in the hour of need. Go— or I shall——"

M. Maupin opened the door and put his son out with a final imprecation; then once more alone, he threw himself into his armchair, uttering a cry of rage which sounded like a wild beast's roar.

It was all over; that last plank on which he had counted for safety, had broken under him.

At the beginning of November, the great cause of Berloc and Maupin had been fully prepared and was announced to be tried at one of the first meetings of the police tribunal. A compact crowd filled from early morning the square that extends before the modest court-house of St. Clement. It happened to be market-day, and all the peasants who had had cause, more or less, to complain of the firm of Simon Maupin, had come to town to enjoy revenge.

Eleven o'clock struck. The usher of the court ceremoniously opened the double door. Suddenly was heard the official summons of the court-usher who cried out: "The Court! gentlemen, take off your hats!" The tumult subsided. Almost at the same moment, another usher, admitted through another door Simon Maupin, accompanied by Célestin and Stephen, John Berloc and their two lawyers.

All heads were raised to catch a glimpse of the principal actors in the drama. The banker, in his frock-coat buttoned up to the throat, with the red ribbon of the Legion of Honor in the buttonhole, remained standing for a moment, as arrogant and haughty as ever, and indifferent to the looks that converged from all sides on him. Stephen, on the contrary, looked pale and terribly worn: strangers might well have thought that he was the accused and not his father. As to Berloc, he had never in his life appeared as small, as humble, and as supple, as now; he had slipped into the room like a lizard, and kept very quiet, casting every now and then a sneaking, contrite look at the judges.

The proceedings were at first very dull and uninteresting. At last the usher was heard with his stentorian voice to announce: "The Public Prosecutor against Berloc and Maupin!"

"Simon Maupin! Rise and come forward!" said the President of the court in a dry tone which was not usual to him. The banker came out of his bench, holding his head high, and answered all questions in a clear, precise voice. The Court came at once to the loan which Dr. Desroches had obtained through the agency of Berloc, and accused Maupin of having managed the loan in such a way as to obtain possession of the Doctor's valuable estate for a ridiculously small sum of money.

"Where is the evidence?" Maupin asked, boldly.

This reply created in the audience so strong a feeling

of indignation that the ushers had to command silence —otherwise the President would order the room to be cleared. Simon Maupin sat down and Berloc's examination began.

He was as humble as his patron the banker had been haughty and insolent. Alleging his extreme poverty and his great ignorance, he appealed in a piteous manner to the Court. He was only a kind of very humble go-between, often totally ignorant of what was going on between his principal, M. Maupin, and other parties. If he had ever imagined in his wildest dreams that such abominations were committed by his aid and assistance, he would have cut off his right hand rather than to sign the smallest little bit of paper! But everything was settled at the bank, and when they sent for him, all that he had to do was to say, "Amen!"

"Do you hear?" asked the President, turning to Maupin. "What do you say to it?"

"Nothing!" the banker replied, coolly.

Then the witnesses appeared. Their story was nearly the same in all cases: notes given to Berloc first, then discounted and renewed by Maupin at enormous commissions which increased the originally trifling debt to fabulous proportions; next execution and public sale of the same piece of land at enormous prices.

At last all preparatory steps had been taken, and the Imperial Procurator rose to deliver his charge against Simon Maupin. This young lawyer, with his stiff and stern ways, and a clear but gentle tone of voice, was comparatively mild in his attack upon the accused. As he knew that the banker was sustained by the clergy, he thought it prudent to spare him as much as possible.

Simon Maupin breathed freely, and felt the weight that had oppressed him considerably lessened. The judges were taken by surprise, and the President did not know what to make of it.

But the most surprised of all was the great lawyer whom Simon Maupin had engaged to come down and defend him. Pompous, loquacious, and aggressive, he was unwise enough to exalt Maupin as the champion of the party of order in St. Clement. He made of the banker a kind of providential hero, ostentatiously numbered his public services, his devotion to the Emperor, and the grand enterprises which he had conceived, and which could not but redound to the welfare and the honor of the whole department. To hear him, all the charges brought against Maupin were manifestations of the Liberals, who, not daring to oppose the great man at the helm, were satisfied with attacking, in a cowardly manner, the man who was in his confidence.

He finished at last his unfortunate speech and sat down, exhausted and out of breath, wiping his forehead and looking for gratitude and admiration in the faces of Maupin and his son.

The faces of the judges now looked sinister and almost grotesque in the fading light, and enlarged the strongly marked features of the Imperial Procurator, who rose to reply.

At the very first words he uttered it became clear that the plea of the Parisian lawyer had irritated his nerves, and that he would show no mercy. He admitted that at a certain time the banker had appeared as the champion of the constituted authorities, but he proved that this great speculator had become the friend of the party of order only to gratify his private rancor.

"Ah!" he exclaimed, becoming excited, "Justice sees clearly in spite of the bandage before her eyes; she discerns the mean tricks of the money dealer disguised as a politician! As there are hypocrites in religion, so there are hypocritical lovers of the public welfare, and Simon Maupin is one of them!" Then he showed how the banker had abused the prestige of authority, crushing poor people whose shipwreck he had premeditated—and then, with all this money, indulging in scandalous speculations.

The voice of the Procurator had become as sharp as a razor; it fell like the blows of a whip upon M. Maupin's reputation.

Without paying any attention to the torture suffered by his victim, the Imperial Prosecutor continued: "And this man has received favor after favor from the head of the State! He bears on his breast the cross of the Legion of Honor! But the government, which is the offspring of popular votes, is too great a friend of the laboring classes to let itself be duped any longer by a cheat who has lived and fattened upon the life's blood of the humblest of peasants. He shall be deprived of all the honors he has so unworthily known to obtain; he shall be publicly degraded! And we shall see what marvellous ignominy, what corruption and outrageous scandals are hidden under that villainous institution called the Maupin Bank!"

The speaker sat down, and M. Maupin rose as if moved by a spring, indicating that he wished to speak. "Mr. President," he began, in a hoarse voice, "I protest, gentlemen——"

He suddenly fell back upon his bench like an inert, lifeless mass.

"A physician! Quick! A physician!" cried Célestin Tiffin.

Fortunately there was a physician in the house and he hurried to the passage, where Célestin and Stephen had laid Maupin down, while the former opened his waistcoat and unfastened his cravat. The doctor declared that his patient must be instantly carried home a litter was hastily contrived, and the banker was carried into his house.

Across silent back streets, through the dark night, two men, accompanied by Stephen and Célestin, carried him to the bank. The private office was on a level with the vestibule, and there he was put down by the orders of the physician, who was utterly bewildered by the amazingly rapid progress of the disease, and scrawled one prescription after the other. But, fast as his pencil ran across the paper, death was faster still. The clock on the mantelpiece had not had time to strike seven o'clock with its cracked voice, when Stephen uttered a sudden cry. M. Maupin moved on his mattress; suddenly his eyes met his son's eyes, he raised himself on his hands, his eyeballs assumed a strange fire: "Fallen! Fallen!" he repeated. And indeed he fell never to rise again.

"The stroke has fallen like a flash of lightning," murmured the doctor, impassively. "It is over!"

CHAPTER XV

T was night. In his studio, lighted up modestly by a fire of pine-cones, Stephen, after his return to Pressy, two days before, was walking up and down mechanically like a man who had lost his reckoning. From time to time he stopped, pressed his brow against the window-panes, and with melancholy eyes contemplated the sleeping landscape in the cold light of the full November moon. The furious wind blew apparently from all sides upon M. Minique's house; it threatened to blow in the windows, to creep in under the ill-fitting doors, and played with the creaking vanes and slammed with growing rage the ill-secured shutters.

Stephen was watching this disturbance with great avidity. He longed to have more of it. He wished those distant voices were a great deal louder, that this roaring of the tempest would never cease for a moment, so great was his horror at finding himself once more alone in the stillness of the night.

For every moment of his life is just now filled with hallucinations of judges in their black robes, of the Imperial Procurator crushing the banker under the

[351]

violence of his speech, of the malignant crowd that filled the whole Court-House. He sees Simon Maupin again stretched out on his litter, and carried away through the dark streets. He sees him again, lying dead, in his coffin, buried in haste and without ceremony like a criminal that had been executed. The punishment was fearful, and the disaster even greater than had been anticipated. At this hour the great firm of Simon Maupin, banker, is in liquidation, and Célestin Tiffin has the matter in charge!

"There must be an end of dreams!" he said to himself. "I must go and face the questions of life, must fight the battle, earn my daily bread and fulfil the engagements I have made!" The painting which Schwartz has ordered was not begun yet, and Stephen was ashamed to live on money which had not been earned. It was high time to pass from vague dreams to hard work—to the execution. "Come, I must be bold and have courage! I must try to work in earnest!" And at once he lights his lamp, chooses from his supply a large sheet of drawing-paper, and remains in meditation before the blank sheet!

The white page is soon covered with zebra-lines; at first all is in confusion, after awhile it becomes more precise. Five or six times the young man wipes them out and begins once more. The hours pass, but he remains bent over his paper, hearing nothing, not even the wind that roars and the vane that squeaks. In the fireplace the fire has gone out and even the lamp is giving out. At last Stephen throws away his blunt pencil and raises himself, his head on fire, his feet like lumps of ice. But he has finished the sketch of his painting—a village funeral.

The next morning he puts on his painter's costume, buckles his gaiters, throws his bag over his shoulder, and accompanied by the boy who carries his traps, he reaches the point he has chosen for the execution of his work, in the open air.

Stephen has sought the acquaintance of the priest. This good man, tempted by the promise of a picture for his church, has handed over his sexton to the young painter, with his deputy and his little choristers, to serve as models. The short winter days pass but too quickly; his painting absorbs him and puts him in a fever.

At the farm where Thérèse lives, on the contrary, the days seem too long. The work in the fields is all finished, and from early morning Thérèse sits in her room, close by the window, and sews and sews, barely allowing herself, now and then, a glance at the distant hills and the fleeting clouds.

She thinks of Stephen. She asks herself what sad events keep him so long at St. Clement; she begins to wonder at his long absence. Since the young man has left her, she has gone down to church but once, to be present at the High Mass said on All Saints' Day. She reads in the looks and smiles of the people assembled at church, that half curious, half sarcastic expression of which she has once before suffered so much. She never doubts Stephen, but still she is troubled.

One evening, at last, she determines to write to Célestin Tiffin; she knows his discretion, his devotion to the firm he serves, and she feels certain that he at least, with all his discretion, will tell her the truth. This letter, being written and entrusted to the messenger employed in such cases, she returns to her work in her upper chamber.

In the meantime Stephen's painting is nearly finished. The picture has come out well, and the whole gives forcibly the impression at which the painter had aimed. It is the funeral of a young girl. The coffin, hid under a white cloth, is carried by four peasants. At the head of the procession three young girls of the Rosary-Guild, in white dresses, accompany the banner of the Virgin, worked in silver. They are followed by the priest and the singers in their surplices. You can not help feeling deeply touched by this sympathetic harmony between this landscape covered with white frost and this white mourning for a young girl. You tell yourself that the painter who has succeeded in reproducing these secret affinities must needs have felt them strongly and been deeply moved by them himself.

At one moment his courage forsakes him, and the young painter is tempted to flee from M. Minique's house, to ascend the slopes, to run to the farm, to see Thérèse for the last time, and to explain to her the reason why he must leave her. But there comes to him an overwhelming thought. If he should go to the farm now, he would appear to be invoking her pity and trying to influence her will so as to obtain from her kind heart a Yes, which she would not grant him, perhaps, if she were left to herself. No! He will not do that!

MLLE. DESROCHES

He will go away in silence, and then, when he is gone, he will write to her and give her a final explanation. To-morrow night he will be in Paris, eighty miles from the farm.

He sat down once more before the canvas; his eyes rested upon the young girl who was carrying the cross; he had painted the head from a study of Mademoiselle Desroches's head, which he had made at the farm. It was indeed Thérèse, with her fair complexion and the two bands of brown hair coming out beyond the sides of her tall provincial cap. There are the same fresh and frank lips, the same eyes with those brilliant black pupils, resembling black cherries, the same charming, though shy face he has loved so dearly.

Suddenly it seems to him that somebody has slightly pushed the door of the studio, although the painting is between him and the entrance. He raises his eyelids and suddenly starts up. It is no longer the figure painted on canvas; it is Thérèse in flesh and blood who stands before him.

"Thérèse!"

Those fresh and frank lips part to let a kind smile pass out; those jet-black eyes look into his eyes, and while she lays her cape aside, she says:

"How long have you been back here?"

Stephen is embarrassed. All his heroism has forsaken him, he stammers and replies, evasively: "Only since yesterday!"

"Story-teller!" says Thérèse, threatening him with her finger.

He hangs his head and does not know what to say.

[355]

"You have been here six weeks," she continues, "why have you not come to see us at the farm?"

"I have not been here all the time. I have been over at Châtel, painting—this," and he shows her his "Village Funeral."

"This is beautiful, although the subject is so sad. I can understand that this work has kept you busy—but you are nevertheless very unkind, that you have never let me hear from you! That was not what you promised me when we parted!"

"Thérèse!" exclaimed Stephen, "I did not come back to you, because I had to tell you things that were too painful, and I preferred writing them. If you knew all that has happened at Saint Clement!"

"I know it. Célestin has written."

"You know everything?" he asked again, blushing and casting down his eyes.

"I know that now you are unhappy, as I was before, but I do not see how your unhappiness prevented you from coming for a reply to the proposition which you made me the last time we met? Have you forgotten that? A simple, pleasant country life for both of us?"

"Ah!" he cried, confused and overcome, so that he could only utter unconnected words, "that offer—I can not now—I must not repeat it. I am too wretched already—I mean to suffer alone!"

"You are too proud! Well, then, I, I am not so proud, and since you could not prevail on yourself to come up to us, I have come to tell you that I accept—because I know you love me, and because——"

MLLE. DESROCHES

"Thérèse!" He has drawn near to her and taken both her hands.

"Because I love you!" she continued, sinking into his arms.

They remained thus for some time, holding each other closely, before that great silent painting. The house is still buried in silence; at a distance only the vesper bells continue to ring out their slow and lulling music.

www.ingramcontent.com/pod-product-compliance
Lightning Source LLC
Chambersburg PA
CBHW021214090426
42740CB00006B/220